THE MUSLIM SPEAKS

About the Author

Khurram Hussain is an Associate Professor of Religion Studies at Lehigh University where he teaches modern Islamic thought, philosophy of religion and religious ethics. He received his PhD in 2012 from Yale University. Before joining the faculty, Hussain was the recipient of a pre-doctoral fellowship funded by the Mellon Foundation through the Center of Global Islamic Studies at Lehigh University.

THE MUSLIM SPEAKS

KHURRAM HUSSAIN

ZED

The Muslim Speaks was first published in 2020 by Zed Books Ltd, The Foundry, 17 Oval Way, London SE11 5RR, UK.

www.zedbooks.net

Copyright © Khurram Hussain 2020

The right of Khurram Hussain to be identified as the author of this work has been asserted by him in accordance with the Copyright, Designs and Patents Act, 1988

Typeset in Galliard by Swales and Willis Ltd, Exeter, Devon
Index by John Barker

All rights reserved. No part of this publication may be reproduced, stored in a retrieval system or transmitted in any form or by any means, electronic, mechanical, photocopying or otherwise, without the prior permission of Zed Books Ltd.

A catalogue record for this book is available from the British Library

ISBN 978-1-78699-887-3 hb
ISBN 978-1-78699-888-0 pb
ISBN 978-1-78699-886-6 pdf
ISBN 978-1-78699-971-9 epub
ISBN 978-1-78699-885-9 mobi

For my mother

Contents

Preface ix

Introduction: Can the Muslim Speak? 1

1 The Slanted Abyss 47
2 Mirror, Mirror ... 89
3 Freedom Talk 141
4 Reason Talk 187
5 Culture Talk 237

Conclusion: *Amor Mundi* 283

Notes 299
Bibliography 331
Index 355

Preface

This book began many years ago as a series of conversations I had mostly with myself following the events of September 2001. It was a strange and awkward time. These conversations were back-and-forth self-reflections on what was happening around me at a time when speaking to others was fraught with anxiety. I had been cocooned in one college town or another for the duration of my time in America. But now America itself was invading these places. The ubiquitous flags, the constant droning of the national anthem, the elegiac hymns that sounded so ominous to my ears were like so many signs of innocence lost. I had been somewhere and then suddenly I was someplace else. In this new environment, not talking too loudly or too much seemed the appropriate response. There was, in any case, an instantly formulaic quality to the conversations taking place around me that belied the novelty of the situation. My more left-leaning friends spoke in hushed tones of imperial comeuppance, of how *America had it coming*. The liberal crowd was naturally inclined toward both confusion and a heavy dose of righteous indignation. The patriotic types were already talking revenge and the use of hard military power to teach Muslims a lesson (although I myself was generally exempt from suspicion on account of being a whiskey drinker). Elsewhere, the ruling establishment had wasted little time in framing the attacks as directed against the American values of freedom, democracy and toleration. Many Christian leaders, on the other hand, proclaimed them more broadly as confirmation of Islam's infernal character. Among the general public, though, there was disgust and disbelief mixed with disorientation: *What to make of this madness? Why do they hate us?*

Aggravating an already tense situation were sporadic reports circulating in the media that as the towers came down, one after another, Muslims everywhere had become possessed by a strange jubilation. That as information about events transpiring in the skies over America percolated through the Muslim world, it produced wave upon wave of euphoria. Hijab-clad women rocked immodestly to the beat of the unfolding news. Children danced in the streets and bearded men distributed sweets. There was little credible evidence for any of this, but these reports had what Stephen Colbert calls an air of 'truthiness' about them. The meme of Muslim crowds cheering the towers' destruction has had great staying power in the American imagination for precisely this reason. There was some public disagreement in those early days about whether Islam had been hijacked by radical Muslims for their own evil

Preface

ends, or whether Muslims were themselves in the grip of an evil ideology. But in response to the viral meme of cheering crowds, there was an immediate consensus on one crucial point: there is something profoundly depraved about the kind of society that not only produces hateful murderers but also openly approves of their heinous acts. This was reminiscent of Winston Churchill's description of Germans as "carnivorous sheep" who "combine in the most deadly manner the qualities of the warrior and the slave ... They do not value freedom themselves and the spectacle of it in others is hateful to them."[1] Muslims were the Germans of our times. They may not be fascists themselves, but they approve of fascist acts. They do not grieve. They feel no shame. They celebrate. Such a reaction clearly signifies a defect in their national character. A visceral hatred of Western people, of Western values, of life itself. The enlightened among them need to make a heroic effort at social re-engineering and theological reform. They are to make themselves saints or be content with being treated as scoundrels. After 9/11, the American conscience would not allow Muslims any middle ground.

* * *

The conversations happening on the other side were equally formulaic. Among many Muslims around the world, conspiracy theories were the immediate, and predictable, first response to 9/11. *The American government did it themselves to justify invading Muslim lands.* The more historically minded referenced the Crusades. There was the obligatory mention of oil, or Israel, even colonialism. *This is all smoke and mirrors. Do you not recall how these Westerners colonized us, through intrigue and machination? How they turned us against one another. Divided us and ruled us. This is all a grand conspiracy. They are at it again.* Opinion polls taken in the near aftermath of the events also showed that most Muslims thought of Americans as "ruthless, aggressive, conceited, arrogant, and easily provoked," and that perhaps they did have it coming.[2] There were obviously those who, being cut from a different cloth, felt deep horror and grief; who felt shame at the possibility that this was done in their name, and on their behalf. But such good souls were badly outnumbered.

And from the beginning, there was also something else. A kind of perverse enjoyment did indeed creep into some reactions among Muslims, a grim satisfaction of sorts at the pain and suffering of Americans. If you ask them now, most such Muslims would flatly deny feeling these kinds of sentiments. The 'shock and awe' of the American response, and the enormous violence visited upon the Muslim world during the War on Terror by their co-religionists and Westerners alike, has dulled their senses and memories. Or perhaps they are just tired of being collectively blamed in the West for a crime they did not commit only because they may have remotely enjoyed its commitment. Few Muslims have ever seriously countenanced living in bin Laden's dystopia, or had any love whatsoever for his ideology and his

Preface

methods. To be lumped in with him and his ilk is difficult to reconcile with their everyday lives and values. This being the case, what could their enjoyment of 9/11 signify?

In his wonderful little novel *The Reluctant Fundamentalist*, Mohsin Hamid takes a stab at an explanation. The protagonist is a Pakistani named Changez, a graduate of Princeton University, and a former New Yorker who used to work on Wall Street. Incidentally, this also almost perfectly describes Hamid himself. The book is structured as one long and continuous monologue by Changez directed at an unnamed American who may or may not be a CIA agent. The following excerpt from this monologue requires no setup:

> I was in my room, packing my things. I turned on the television and saw what at first I took to be a film. But as I continued to watch, I realized that it was not fiction but news. I stared as one – and then the other – of the twin towers of New York's World Trade Center collapsed. And then I smiled. Yes, despicable as it may sound, my initial reaction was to be remarkably pleased.
>
> Your disgust is evident; indeed, your large hand has, perhaps without your noticing, clenched into a fist. But believe me when I tell you that I am no sociopath; I am not indifferent to the suffering of others. When I hear of an acquaintance who has been diagnosed with a serious illness, I feel – almost

without fail – a sympathetic pain, a twinge in my kidneys strong enough to elicit a wince. When I am approached for a donation to charity, I tend to be forthcoming, at least insofar as my modest means will permit. So when I tell you I was pleased at the slaughter of thousands of innocents, I do so with a profound sense of perplexity.

But at that moment, my thoughts were not with the victims of the attack – death on television moves me most when it is fictional and happens to characters with whom I have built up relationships over multiple episodes – no, I was caught in the symbolism of it all, the fact that someone had so visibly brought America to her knees.[3]

Changez is self-consciously Western in every way except that he is also a Muslim. And being a Muslim, he is unable (unwilling?) to integrate into the American body politic without a *remainder*, a part of himself left over, sticking out like an extra digit. What is the significance of this remainder? It leaves Changez hooked (involuntarily?) into a world of alien experiences, feelings and emotions that confound the Western psyche. They perplex even him. This extra digit, then, is also akin to a special sensory organ, an antenna or perhaps a repository of esoteric knowledge and subaltern histories. Changez senses (though he cannot explain) that his pleasure has nothing whatsoever to do with the victims, nor even with the identity of the perpetrators. He is not thinking about either. He is not thinking at all. His suspension of shame has a carnivalesque quality to it. He is "caught," as he says, "in the symbolism of it all."

What Changez's reaction to the collapsing towers makes transparent is the symbolic, and perhaps *iconic*, meaning of 9/11 for many Muslims. It is the sense in which 9/11 is *the* pivotal event in modern Islamic history. It is neither a beginning nor an end. It is the *pivot*, the second act, the beginning of an end. It is that moment in which the inertia of the past has been exhausted in the present, but the future is as yet uncertain. This idea, that the meaning of 9/11 is critical to understanding the contemporary Muslim imaginaire is so obvious as to be controversial – scholars detest the obvious. And even as some academics complain that an excessive focus on 9/11 obfuscates the complexity of Islamic societies, many Muslims also bridle at being defined by the actions of charlatans. They are not wrong in their concerns. But grasping unreservedly at 9/11 as a historical event, as a 'happening', they are distracted from a true reckoning with its iconic character, its symbolic meaning: there is a fundamental defect in the relationship between 'Islam' and 'the West'. And this defect presents itself in history as so many signs of Muslim futility and of their liminal, abridged humanity. Muslims do not set terms for debates, not even those debates that directly concern them. Their languages of moral discourse are moribund. Their technologies of social engineering are archaic. Their capacities for political participation in the affairs of the world are trivial. History is not animated by their concerns, nor is it particularly receptive to them. Theses and antitheses circulate in a swelling whirlpool of recrimination and frustration, with nary a synthesis in sight. Splattered on the axes of history and discourse, asymptotic arcs meander meaninglessly in all directions around ground zero, forever denied a destination, a resolution, recognition. *Ressentiment* weighs down the air they breathe like the oppressive humidity of a perpetually deferred monsoon.

With this as context, what did the collapsing towers symbolize to Muslims such as Changez? *Reversal.* They had a ritual signification. Woven into the very fabric of power is the cathartic possibility of its fiery destruction. But reversal is more than mere destruction. For Muslims, the West is no abstract master, but the Master to their Slave. For all the misery visited on them by the West on pain of death for centuries, at least, and at last, a sign of things to come, perhaps ... *Look, how the mighty have fallen! The Last shall be made First* ... And what slave would not find pleasure in that.

* * *

These things are hard to write out loud, but one advantage of silent self-reflection is that they are easier to acknowledge when the conversation first goes on inside your own head. The title of this book is partly a provocation. But it is also a reflection of its origins in a series of jumbled and confusing questions that I was asking myself about the meaning of

Preface

9/11 and of the various reactions to it. Of course, these questions did not remain inside my head for long, mostly because I realized that the life of the mind is impoverished if left to rot on the inside. The venue of graduate school also helped loosen my tongue and open my mind to answers that would not have arisen solely from my own reveries. One of the very first insights to emerge from conversation with others on these matters was that the retributive pleasure of slaves is hardly a salutary model for justice in this world. Neither, incidentally, is the punitive rage of masters. If 9/11 was to have a prescriptive meaning for me, it had to be something other than this. Another insight that has remained redolent throughout comes from a different much misunderstood world-historical event from another time and place. When the French revolutionary armies rolled into the German countryside loudly proclaiming *liberté, égalité, fraternité*, they were startled by the intense resistance of poor peasantry to their military advances. *Are these not the very people who have the most to gain from being freed of oppression at the hands of their aristocratic masters?* Those in the West now confused by the general disdain with which so many Muslims regard Western attempts to help them should always keep this example in mind whenever they become particularly frustrated by the intransigence of their would-be clients. For it demonstrates, in the particular, a general insight about the human condition. The German peasants were not resisting *liberté, égalité, fraternité*; they were resisting the French.

Introduction
Can the Muslim Speak?

Is there such a thing as a Muslim way of speaking about the world? The short answer is no. After all, there are nearly 2 billion Muslims in this world, and they come in all varieties of nationality, ethnicity, class and disposition. How can one be expected to reasonably aggregate such bewildering diversity into a single, coherent point of view about the world. But perhaps there is another way of asking this question: Do the various Muslim experiences of the modern world together constitute a set of descriptions, expectations and evaluations of this world that are distinctively Muslim in important ways? I believe the answer to this second question is yes. There are debates about the nature and meaning of the modern world, and of its pasts, presents and futures, that rely on a shared library of experiences and often also a common vocabulary that is peculiarly Muslim. Theological disputes are only a small (but important) subset of these debates. The vast majority of these discussions among Muslims, and between Muslims and non-Muslims, are animated by concerns rooted more generally in the fact of being Muslim in this world. It is Muslims self-consciously bringing their understandings of Islam and of their own experiences to bear on various aspects of a modernity in which they rarely find themselves at home. While these debates seldom lead to conclusive agreements, they are nonetheless a vast and evolving repository of Islam as a rich corpus of critique.

To imagine Islam as a rich corpus of critique – let's call this Critical Islam – is to center the experience of being Muslim, and those descriptions and evaluations of the world that issue from such experience. To get a sense of what I mean by Critical Islam, consider, for example, feminism as critique centered on women's experience. Now women are at least as diverse a group as Muslims, more so in fact. But the label 'feminism' is still a viable way to isolate a particular set of debates and conversations that describe and evaluate the status quo and to challenge its dominant paradigms. Feminism is not just critique narrowly concerned with 'women's issues', but rather with the world itself that men and women all inhabit. Feminists rightly contend that their critical interventions allow us to see a more complete picture of this world, and therefore to augur better futures for it. Similarly, the moniker 'black' can refer to people scattered across the globe in a wide variety of contexts. As an identity, blackness is more amorphous than womanness or even Muslimness. Yet this abstraction has a lived reality

Introduction

in the modern world that manifests itself in recognizable critiques of this world's racial architecture and in social movements against white supremacy. Again, critical race scholars would argue that their work is not about blackness as such, but rather more generally about the human condition. To look from the vantage point of blackness merely provides access to aspects of this condition otherwise invisible. It is in this sense that feminists and those who fight for racial justice open up new vistas for all of us to re-evaluate our views of the world. And in their critiques of patriarchy and white supremacy, they even speak new worlds into existence.

These new worlds are better worlds. They are better not for having been spoken into existence by feminists and black critics, but rather in that they more completely reflect the general experience of being human. The work that these critics do is humanizing work because they challenge descriptions of the world that render vast portions of humanity either insufficiently or incompletely human. The idea that black folks and women are inferior specimens of humanity, either less evolved or lacking masculine vigor, virtue and reason, is baked into white supremacy and patriarchy. And until recently, such an idea would have gone largely uncontested in the global public square. Even now, it is not uncommon to hear the perspectives of women and blacks deemed unworthy of general consideration and described pejoratively as 'woman talk' or 'identity politics'. But political and intellectual mobilizations by women and black activists over the last few decades in various parts of the world have given greater credence to the notion that no general account of the world is adequate without their critical participation in describing it and no politics is viable without due attention to their concerns.

The idea of Critical Islam points to the possibility of a similar political and intellectual mobilization of the Muslim identity. It is the idea that centering Muslim experience makes available accounts and descriptions of the modern world that would be otherwise unavailable. The context of feminist critique is gender. Its other is patriarchy. The context of black critique is race. Its other is white supremacy. In a similar manner, the context of Critical Islam is modernity. Its other is 'the West'. Or more precisely, it is the West defined as those descriptions, expectations and evaluations of the modern world, and of its pasts, presents and futures, that rely on a shared library of experiences and often also a common vocabulary that is peculiarly Western. Just as there is no single Muslim way of speaking about the modern world, there is no single Western way of speaking about it either. Yet just as patriarchy and white supremacy are no less problematic on account of their complexity, neither is the West. In this reading, as a way of describing Islam and its proper place in the modern world, the West is one name for that set of socially constructed descriptions and debates that render Muslims insufficiently or incompletely human. It depoliticizes them and in so doing dehumanizes them.

Introduction

To depoliticize someone is to render a political relationship with them untenable. It is to demand compliance, not consent. And domination need not imply any self-conscious ill will. One can have friendly, even loving relationships that are nonetheless not political – think *Uncle Tom's Cabin* or "Stand by Your Man." They are not political because the depoliticized party has no capacity to meaningfully engage the terms of their condition. The depoliticized party can accept these terms or reject them. There is no middle ground. So depoliticization is at best some version of the white man's burden. At worst, there is outright and unapologetic domination, and often violence. Of course, there have been feminist critiques of patriarchy that veer toward a complete rejection of masculinity itself – 'a woman needs a man like a fish needs a bicycle' – and forms of black identity politics that favor separation from whites over engagement with them. Alternatively, there have always been women and black people who subscribe to their own inferiority and assent to being dominated and being told what to do, what to say, and how to live. But these are endpoint perspectives on a spectrum of critique. In the middle is the realm of politics and of debate in the open agora of a shared humanity. Depoliticization is the hollowing out of this middle until the idea of being in the middle with someone becomes wholly illegible.

As with patriarchy and white supremacy, legibility demands that debates in the West about the meaning of Islam naturally gravitate toward descriptions of it that either assimilate Islam to being a familiar but insufficient version of the West (Islam needs a Reformation, Religion of Peace, 'modernist' Islam, real Muslims share our values, etc.) or banish Islam to the outside as a wholly unfamiliar and/or dangerous ideology (political religion, Religion of Violence, 'fundamentalist' Islam, real Muslims do not share our values, etc.). This is because non-political relationships do not recognize a complex other, but instead are largely self-referential. In the mirror of the West, Muslims appear as friends or enemies, but not critics. Of course, there are Muslims who accept or reject the West summarily and in whole. But these are endpoint perspectives on a spectrum of critique. They are not definitive of Muslim experience as such. Still, like infantilizing talk of 'mothers and daughters' and good negroes, on the one hand, and Jezebels and black sexual predators, on the other, Muslims have come to occupy a similar binary in the Western imagination. Amidst these eithers and ors, there is little room for Critical Islam to make any novel contributions to debates about the meaning and nature of the modern world. In practical terms, this means that Muslim ways of speaking about the world are largely illegible in the world-making accounts of the West unless they either conform to or reject these accounts. Good Muslim, Bad Muslim. The middle space of critique, of politics and of shared humanity is not available. Hence, Muslims often become objects of observation and evaluation but seldom subjects in fabricating a world that they nonetheless still have to inhabit. And the

Introduction

sense of futility this engenders is a paradigmatic feature of the Muslim experience of the modern world. This sense of being observed, being measured and evaluated but not recognized is not unique to Muslim experience. Not long ago, women and black people were in a similar situation. As were Catholics and Jews and the various others that the West has generated for itself over all these years. We see hints of a similar futility in W.E. Dubois's discussion of "double-consciousness ... of measuring one's soul by the tape of a world that looks on in amused contempt and pity."[1] And also in Betty Friedan's critique of infantilized womanhood, "the problem that has no name" precisely because the available language only offered coherence to the binary choice between a happy housewifery and an unhappy careerism.[2] Setting aside for the moment the obvious danger associated with Godwin's law, anti-Semitism in nineteenth- and twentieth-century Europe has obvious affinities with the Muslim futility of contemporary times. 'Muslim' is not uniquely futile as an identity, nor is it inevitably and permanently futile. In each of these other cases, a simple non-politics of dual inclusion/exclusion (separate and unequal, different but equal, separate, different and unequal, free but with limits, etc.) eventually proved untenable and a more robust politicization of these identities instigated extensive and ongoing re-evaluations of ostensibly settled consensus on the meaning of freedom and equality, the public/private distinction, and the very nature and practice of politics itself. The West is more humane on account of these ongoing re-evaluations. And the world is a better place. It is for this reason that Western accounts of the world that describe politicized Islam as a problem have it exactly backwards. Muslim ways of speaking about the world need re-politicization, not depoliticization.

* * *

Like Muslim and Western ways of speaking about the world, there is no single 'modern' way of speaking about it either. Modernity is an amorphous concept. It is many things to many people. But as with Muslims and the West, there are distinguishing aspects that separate the modern world from its predecessors. This world has evolved on a universal scale in the last two centuries through the development of certain common features such as the nation-state, the bureaucratization of political institutions, the globalization of economic and financial networks, and the internationalization of rights discourse. In the realm of ideas, modernity was instigated by European reformulations of classical concepts such as freedom, democracy and reason, and modified versions of reformed Christian notions such as equality, progress and *self*-determination. European imperialism let these ideas loose on the rest of the world and that is where we now stand. These master concepts form the discursive field on which everyone now plays. At the level of global public discourse, there is no other game in town. Few argue against freedom and equality. Even despots hold elections.

Introduction

And 'growth' is the gold standard by which individuals and nations alike measure their progress against each other. To be modern is to speak about the world in the vocabulary of these ideas. But there has never been universal agreement on what they actually mean. In fact, the engine of modernity runs on constant contest over the many meanings that can be associated with these ideas and over the hierarchy among them.

Consider, for example, that twentieth-century anticolonial movements invariably relied on the idea of national self-determination, of freedom from foreign domination and equality with their rulers as justification for their struggle. In an earlier era, this would have made no sense. Of course, the colonizers' ideas of freedom, equality and self-determination did not always match up with those of their wards, inflected as they often were with claims of the colonized's lack of progress up the ladder of civilization and of reason (or of humanity). Slavery was justified in antebellum America using some version of the same ideas that animated the struggle against it. And activists for civil rights and for women's liberation choose from the same menu of options as populists, communists and even fascists. The difference is how they prioritize these options and what meanings they assign to them. There is nothing particularly insidious about this, nor anything new. As a general rule, newly dominant societies have always restructured the lifeworlds of their conquered peoples along with those of their own using new norms and ideas that buttress this dominance. What's different this time around is that this modern world is for the first time a world in full. The hydra of modernity touches everyone not just with its networked institutions and globalized markets, but also with its proprietary ideas. And partly as a consequence of European imperial expansion itself, the story of no part of this world can now be properly told without reference to other parts, and to the whole.

To be fully human in this world is to have the capacity to legibly speak the truth of these modern ideas, informed by one's history, identity and experience, into the ether of public debate about the pasts, presents and futures of this world. To be fully human is to be seen and to be heard as a political being. Slaves can debate their understandings of freedom among themselves in their quarters and women can discuss equality from their various perches chained to the kitchen. But this does not make them political beings. Neither does being merely freed from slavery or being finally able to drive a car. Political beings speak to and are recognized by other political beings. There is no politics without reciprocal recognition. Are Muslims political beings? Another way of asking this question is: Can Muslims speak about these ideas from a Muslim-centric perspective and be heard? The short answer is no. In fact, Muslims are often portrayed in public as either dismissive of freedom and equality or, in essence, having nothing new to say about these ideas. Yes, there may be some conversations going on in the ghetto of Islamic

Introduction

Studies, or perhaps some other arcane theological discussions, fully self-referential and sealed off. But the public façade of Islam remains trapped in the either/or of mimicry of the West or a rejection of modernity. The middle has been hollowed out on account of Islam's ostensibly native incapacity to contribute anything novel to the master concepts of the modern age.

But there is in fact a long tradition in modern Islamic thought of critical engagement with modernity that is neither a rejection of its master concepts nor a wholesale acceptance of them. Such engagement has instead produced intense contest around the meaning of these ideas. Consider the case of freedom as an organizing principle for life in the modern age. Islam's commensurability with any regime of individual rights based on freedom as non-coercion is often deemed uncertain. In conjunction with the concept of reason, the status of free inquiry as an end in itself is made to concede little direction to any external ethical standard suggested by Muslims and other religionists. And in recent years, various actors in the West have obsessively employed freedom of speech to ridicule Muslim concerns about blasphemy, and have doubled down on a freedom to insult as an inalienable cultural right of all civilized people. And yet, contra Hegel's oft-repeated claim that freedom is a distinctive attribute of the Western mind, Muslim thinkers from at least the mid-nineteenth century onwards routinely represent freedom as an essential, constitutive feature of the 'good life'. They offer accounts and evaluations of freedom that are often in conflict with dominant Western interpretations but are also always an engaged response to these interpretations. Muhammad Iqbal (1877–1938), for example, explicitly extends the Nietzschian critique of Enlightenment notions of freedom as a negative right in his formulation of *khudi* (selfness or ego) as an Islamic alternative to both liberal and communitarian accounts of the self.[3] Sayyid Qutb's (1906–1966) Muslim reinterpretation of modern notions of freedom and sovereignty leads to a practical utopianism that stands in stark contrast with a Western tradition littered with the impractical utopias of anarchism, fascism and communism.[4] And when Tariq Ramadan (1962–) calls for civic (not legal) denunciation of willfully insulting behavior toward Muslims, he imagines free speech primarily as an attendant value to solidarity and discernment of truth in pluralistic societies, and only secondarily as a legal right to speak one's mind.[5] How have these complex interpretations of freedom been received in the global public mainstream as constituted in and by the West? Iqbal is usually labeled modernist and assimilated to the West. Qutb is usually labeled fundamentalist and deemed a philosopher of terror. Ramadan is a source of constant controversy in his native Europe and was once denied a visa to the United States. Do their ideas inform how we set up international institutions or devise global regimes of rights and norms? Are they taught in philosophy departments as saying something meaningful

Introduction

about the human condition as such, and not just provincially relevant to their religion or region? Would we ever hear them spoken about in the same breath as a Kant, Hegel or Nietzsche? No. If a tree falls in the forest ...

And the above list is, in any case, an extraordinarily short list. The archive of modern Islam is literally teeming with critique. What is the self that determines itself, and is it an individual or a collective self? How does one reconcile the norm of equality with the fact of increasingly unequal distribution of resources, wealth and capacities? Is the use of reason to organize our worldly lives an inherent good? What is the meaning of progress for Islamic lifeworlds that have seen their share of power and prestige in the world regress in the modern age? Is the proper demos the nation, the *umma* or the world itself? Muslims have been vigorously debating these kinds of questions in the open agora of a globalized public sphere from the very beginning of their long tryst with modernity, and they have not stopped. They have always been modern. And yet their modernity remains an open question for much of the rest of the world. Consider that the historical archives of black and female voices also remained hidden from public view until furious social movements and intellectual mobilizations pulled them out into the open. And once the dams broke, these hidden transcripts flowed out into the world like gushing rivers of information, experience and critique. Inasmuch as it is a way of reading the archive of Muslim experiences *sans* the constraints imposed on it by the West, the dam is yet to break on Critical Islam.

Why is this dam yet to break? This is a complex question that requires much of the rest of this book to sort it out. For now, suffice it to say that the answer lies both literally and figuratively in 'the West'. Just as unexamined patriarchy prevents feminism from being a discursive possibility, and unexamined white supremacy does the same to black critique, the West left unexamined makes Critical Islam impossible. Both the feminist revolution and the civil rights movement were made possible by earlier generations of women and black intellectuals and activists who first investigated not just the parameters of their liberation, but the nature of their oppression. To understand why the archives of modern Islam remain unexamined and contemporary Muslims have such a hard time being heard, we must first examine and investigate the West. But how can this be? Is 'the West' not one of the more well-examined concepts in all of academia? It would appear so from how often we use the term and how seamlessly it enters into our conversations. But this is not true. If you ask ten people what it is, or where it is, you'll get twenty answers. This does not mean that it's not real. It only means that we must thoroughly examine what makes the West peculiarly Western in any given context and with regard to any given issue. It is to this end that I argue that regarding Islam and its proper place in the modern world, the West is that set of socially constructed descriptions and debates that render Muslims insufficiently or incompletely human. It depoliticizes them and in so doing dehumanizes them.

Introduction

This depoliticization is the cement that holds the dam together. And it is strong cement indeed.

* * *

The West did not create the modern world but is rather a creation of the modern world. So is the Muslim world, and the countless other worlds-within-the-World that modernity has birthed. The West is one evolving set of accounts of this World, the accounts that the West aggregates as signs of 'civilization'. To be civilized at any given point in time is to at least minimally ascribe to some version of these accounts as definitive. In the nineteenth century, for example, it was civilized to look down on Muslims for their supposed permissiveness toward homosexuality. In the twenty-first century, it is civilized to look down on them for the exact opposite reason. The West is not static or unitary. It is multiple and fecund. But when it comes to Islam, the narrative accounts of the West have remained in a holding pattern for quite some time now. So much so that Islam has now come to embody almost the entirety of what constitutes 'bad religion' in the Western imagination. Jews and Catholics were there with Islam too once upon a time, but they have long been assimilated to a common history and identity with the West. And 'Eastern religions' such as Hinduism and Buddhism have been repurposed as fonts of spiritual renewal for Westerners made uneasy by the overly materialistic veneer of their modern lives. But Islam remains the same, an exception to the rule of the modern West. To accept Islam as critique would be to relitigate history itself as it has been providentially grooved by the West for others to follow in its wake. It would be to take a step back on the road of progress and civilization.

This manner of understanding progress and civilization in Western accounts of the world is called by many names, but the most common are secularism and *laïcité*. These equate religion with propositional beliefs based on faith, not reason. But Critical Islam is no more narrowly theological than feminist critique is narrowly gynecological or black critique is narrowly dermatological. In fact, the idea that the Muslim identity is primarily oriented around unreasoned propositional beliefs and Muslim experience is mediated principally by faith is itself an artifact of the ideology of secularism. As is the notion that critique is by definition secular. It is for this reason that when confronted with Muslim objections to this or that Western interpretation of freedom, reason or civilization, Western positions harden into unbreakable concrete. The right to free speech becomes absolute. The right to cultural preservation becomes absolute. The right to national security becomes absolute. Not long ago, the regnant ideologies of white supremacy and anti-Semitism meant that the same could be said of black or Jewish objections. Even today, the fight for the right to say racist things and to preserve Confederate monuments in the United States or the recent Polish attempts at whitewashing the role of Poles in the Holocaust suggest that these ideologies are hardly dead

Introduction

and buried. But there is vigorous debate and pushback. The right to women's bodily integrity and control is similarly under threat. But there are viable and popular challenges, and a robust vocabulary is in place to resist. This is because white supremacy, anti-Semitism and patriarchy stand naked in the public square. They can be shameless, but they can no longer hide as common sense.

What would it take to remove the veneer of common sense from depoliticizing and dehumanizing talk in the West about Islam and Muslims? The answer to this question is not to be found in the theoretical musings of any one person, much less one as unqualified for such musing as myself. It is a political question and as such can only have provisional answers. And even then only those answers that are forged in debates and conversations, and in agreements and disagreements among the varied participants who must of necessity be part of such deliberations, and not in the theoretical musing of any one person. Such debates and conversations are already ongoing. There's a burgeoning literature on Islamophobia and on other forms of anti-Muslim animus in the West and elsewhere. Academic heavy hitters, journalists and activists all participate in the production of this literature. Ethnographic accounts that describe Muslim lifeworlds in their full complexity and diversity are becoming more common, especially in Anthropology and Religious Studies. And Muslim representation in Western media has now reached the bare minimum of the critical mass needed for better descriptions of their lived experience of this world and of their aspirations for it. Much work has been done to remedy the farce and futility of Islam in the modern world, but much more still needs to be done.

This book is my contribution to this work and to these debates. It examines the West's evaluations and descriptions of Islam along three major axes of modernity: the master concepts of freedom, reason and culture (or civilization). I call these three sets of descriptions and evaluations freedom talk, reason talk and (*pace* Mahmood Mamdani) culture talk. I argue that along each of these three axes, what we find is neither pure animus nor unbridled acceptance, but a curious melange of intermingling sentiments that nudge Muslims toward either/or descriptions of their experiences and of their identity. These either/ors are an artifact of the dizzying transformations of the long nineteenth century, and of those historical and ideological processes that gave rise to the West in the first place. These processes produced a curiously bifurcated form of Western identity that was at once both 'particular' as the evolving history of certain European peoples and 'universal' as the provident elaboration of essentially human principles, virtues and aspirations. Muslims have always been useful ciphers to either shore up the progressive credentials of this Janus-faced identity in their affirmation of its universalist aspirations or to serve as the archetypical nemesis in their rejection of them. The Muslim world as we know it today was born in the mirror of the West. This does not mean that it is not real. It just

Introduction

means that it needs examination and elaboration that can only be accomplished after a prior examination and elaboration of the West itself.

I am prompted to make this intervention because I am not fully satisfied with either the tenor or the content of the current conversation. I believe that simple theories of anti-Muslim animus provide only a partial explanation for the marginalization of Muslims in modern bodies politic. The depoliticization attendant to the clean binary – the either/or of Islam – demands a more robust analysis than is usually on offer. The ethical defects in Western descriptions of Islam, for example, are sometimes as evident in rosy proclamations of universal brotherhood and 'Muslims can be modern too' rhetoric as in theories of constitutive difference and of Western exceptionalism. We must therefore be careful not to counter a dehumanizing Islamophobia with an equally depoliticizing 'Muslims are just like us' Islamophilia. There is, in any case, a harsh polemicism at work in breathless accounts of Islamophobia and in the intense interrogations of Western power in postcolonial literature that often leaves little room for narrative constructions of the modern world in which all manner of actors from all sides can participate together. And the scholarly tendency to divide this world strongly between the either/ors of haves or have nots, colonizers or the colonized, and the West or the Rest seldom takes into account the underlying unity of the modern world beneath all of its obvious diversity.

To posit such a unity is to argue a hotly contested position. This is as it has to be. Political questions require constant debate and conversation, the agreements and disagreements of the many. The starting point of my investigation is the prior assumption that to be human is to be a political being that seeks recognition from other political beings. This is not a new insight. It is at least as ancient as Aristotle and likely much older than even that. The problem of living together in a rapidly shrinking world means that the question of the humanity of others is now immediate and immanent in a way that it never was before. And as the mixer of mass migration swirls ever-greater numbers of Muslims into Western polities and wars exacerbated by Western intervention in the Muslim heartland generate millions of refugees radiating out into the world, the question of the humanity of Muslims can no longer be localized to any one place. It is a global issue with global consequences. The events of 9/11 and the furious Western response to them clearly revealed that there is no here or there in this new world. Here and there are everywhere and under sway of an escalating globalization. Rather than the fractured descriptions that are so in vogue these days, it seems to me that the contemporary moment instead demands humanistic accounts of the world that highlight our shared histories and our common destinies. But no such accounts of our shared histories and common destinies are possible without critical Muslim voices in debates about the nature and meaning of freedom, of reason and

Introduction

of civilization. While all this talk of our common humanity may sound like a hackneyed cliché, it also happens to be true. After all, Muslims can be human too.

* * *

Before I proceed any further, let me offer some points of clarification about this project, and also deal with an obvious objection to the manner in which I have defined 'the problem' so far in this book. To the objection first, one could reasonably argue that I have been rather cavalier in my descriptions of categories such as 'women' and 'black people', to say nothing of 'Muslims' and 'the West'. After all, Muslims can be any of these other categories as well, as in American Muslims who happen to be black women, for example, or any combination or permutation thereof. Recent work by Sylvia Chan-Malik, for example, delves deep into the rich cultural history of Muslim women of color in America, and Sylvester Johnson's genre-defining research has shown that Islam has been an indelible aspect of American black religion from the very beginning of the slave trade.[6] To speak as a Muslim is never a simple affair and the category of Muslim is seldom a free-standing identity wholly and entirely exhausted in this identification. The same is true of the West. In fact, each of these categories of identity always exists in the real world not only as an aggregate of varied experiences in and of itself, but also nestled within an intersectional monad holding in provisional equilibrium the complex mottled whole of any subject position. And to speak of human beings without attending to this complexity is to diminish their humanity. In what sense, then, am I speaking here of 'Muslims' and 'the West' without reducing the humans contained therein to a parody of their complex intersectional wholes? The answer to this question lies in the first of the two clarifications about this project I teased above. My purpose in this book is to narrowly "identify 'Muslim' as one distinct (and aggregate) vector in the intersectional network of critique generated by peripherally positioned subjects in the modern world." The composite and intersectional reality of all identities "is no reason to throw up one's hands but rather to attend appropriately to each vector in the intersectional unity of said identity to properly resist oppression." Inasmuch as moving along the 'Muslim' vector of an identity can give us unique insight into otherwise obscure views of the world, it is a path well worth traversing.

In this reading, what I am calling 'the West' is at least in part that particular set of public discourses that block this path. It is "one name then for what the poet Audre Lorde calls 'the mythical norm', an abstract representation of what counts as 'normal,' and also the ideal normative standard against which all other claims to normalcy are to be judged." The West is not only this vector of ostensible normalcy associated narrowly with Euro-American culture, but is also more broadly a component internal to the intersectional identities of *all* modern peoples, including Muslims. Partly as a consequence of European imperial expansion and its postcolonial aftermath, the far-flung corners of this world have been "knitted together into a whole crisscrossed and interpolated by transformative encounters between peoples and ideas."[7] This is what Edward W. Said meant when he said that despite the obvious asymmetries and exploitations attendant to European colonialism, "most of us should now regard the historical experience of empire as a common one." He added that what needs "to be remembered is that narratives of emancipation and enlightenment [among the colonized] in their strongest form were also narratives of *integration* not separation, the stories of people who had been excluded from the main group but who were fighting for a place in it."[8] Such narratives often did turn sour under stress from an intensifying imperialism. But the core of their concern has always been finding a sense of belonging in this new world and a way to feel at home in it.

It is this desire for recognition, and for belonging, that engenders the near global preoccupation with modernity's proprietary ideas and its many proliferating institutions. It is also what makes the concept of the West essential to understanding the modern world as a meaningful unity and for properly grounding any notion of a common humanity. Yet the West is simultaneously also a way of talking about the modern world that undermines this humanity's particular instantiations when they run counter to its own transient consensuses. It is therefore the font both of a humanistic ether that continues to connect the world together *and* of dehumanizing impulses for its own narrative efficacy. It is this double bind, this Janus-faced duality of the West, that when projected onto Muslim subjects – and *into* their intersectional identities – generates the eithers and ors of their status vis-à-vis the West and restricts the possibility of critical forms of Muslim subjectivity in the global public sphere.

This global public sphere is the modern world's most consequential creation. Driven initially by the invention of print, intensifying with the use of powered rapid transport, and finally reaching its full worldly potential with a generalized prevalence of remote media technologies, it is now a webbed network of publics and counter-publics that jostle and compete for relevance in the global marketplace of identities and ideas. Talk about Islam and Muslims has always been ubiquitous here. Escalating almost immediately into essentializing theories of culture and reason, of deficient geographies and archaic ideologies, of religions of peace and religions of violence, it is often a dehumanizing and anti-political form of talk that seeks knowledge without understanding and explanation without cause. Muslims participate in such talk as well as non-Muslims, and those who defend and valorize Islam as much as those who decry it. Overt calls for violence by and against Muslims is also one species of such talk, as is the back and forth between unrestrained Islamophobia and visceral hatred of the West. But this mostly takes place at the fringes of the open agora, not at its center. And one need not hover over these dusky

Introduction

margins nor dive into the murky depths to find depoliticizing talk about Islam. No, it is everywhere, and everywhere it is common sense.

Herein lies the second clarification about this project that I teased above. This book is not about the margins and the depths of the global agora, but rather about its mainstream center. This is a space inhabited by noted journalists and public-facing academics, policy wonks and think tanks, politicians and civil society groups, religious leaders and activists, news organizations and other media outlets, public intellectuals of this or that variety, and, of course, 'influencers' of one sort or another that have wide-ranging and committed audiences. The world as we know it today is being made, remade and unmade in this space, in this babble of screens and radios, this clattering of typesets, this zooming of information. And in the numberless conversations across continents and centuries that each of us is having with the living and the dead as we try to make sense of this world and our place in it. It is here, in this global "space of appearance," to use Hannah Arendt's terminology, that is present "wherever men are together in the manner of speech and action" and "where [we] appear to others as others appear to [us], where men exist not merely like other living or inanimate things, but to make their appearance *explicitly*," that the nature and meaning of the modern world becomes most evident and the architecture of modernity most clearly defined.[9] What do people talk about when they talk about Islam in the open agora of our common world? Who does the talking and who the listening, and why? Which discursive routes are taken and which abandoned? What is made meaningful in these conversations and what is rendered illegible? These kinds of questions cannot be appropriately addressed within the narrow rubric of 'Islamophobia' or anti-Muslim animus, nor of polemics unleavened by amity. They demand a wide-angle view of the world and of those in it.

It is for this reason that I also do not intend this book to be a deep dive into scholarly literature on Islam generated in the Western academy, or in academies elsewhere. Instead, I will focus my attention on the intersecting vectors of identity and disposition in public debates about Islam. This book is therefore primarily a meditation on the questions surrounding Islam as they appear and are debated in the mainstream center of public life. How does the intersectional vector known as the West interact with the Muslim vector in the open agora of the new world created by European imperial expansion? Why do these interactions so often involve embedding Islam and Muslims into the binary architecture of the either/or? And is there a way out of this either/or trap? Of course, there are academic voices in this agora, but they do not dominate this space. Neither, for that matter, do the unambiguous Islamophobes or the incorrigible haters of the West. These margins and depths instead frame a dominant center of 'respectable' talk about Islam, where the parameters of this respectability are in a state of constant evolution over time

Introduction

as a series of ongoing but stable equilibria in Western public disposition. It is only here, at the center, that answers befitting the significance of the Muslim Question can be found.

Inasmuch as there is a prescriptive angle to this project, it is also animated by a simple question: What would it mean to imagine Islam as an immanent critique of the West? As I mentioned earlier, the archive of the Muslim experience of modernity is teeming with critique. Yet much of it is too often domesticated to the restrictive architecture of the either/or in public talk about Islam. To humanize Muslims and to re-politicize their existence in the global public sphere would mean populating this sphere with voices that have been hitherto silenced, ignored or, at best, only available when sieved into pre-existing boxes of commensurability (or lack thereof) with the West. In addition to paying attention to such critical Muslim voices in the present, we must also undertake the long overdue task of excavating the voices of Muslims long dead and buried for salutary contribution to our conversations in the present. What would it mean to imagine the events of 1798 in Egypt and 1857 in India as being as relevant to the making of the world we live in today as the events that took place in France in the 1790s or in America in the 1860s?[10] And the disappearance of the Caliphate in 1926, and Muslim reactions to this occurrence, being as significant as the Great Depression? These are merely the more obvious examples where Muslims were never mere spectators of history, but fully involved in its movement, and active interpreters of this movement's nature and meaning. There are countless others, of course, and all awaiting publicity.

In this reading, what I mean by Critical Islam is, at least in part, a new way of *reading* and *organizing* this archive of Muslim experience and thought over the last two hundred years or so. I take no strong position on the content of the archive other than to say that it is not narrowly theological, but rather constituted by reactions to the broader experience of being Muslim both in relation to other Muslims and to the West. Critical Islam here refers to (re)reading this archive in critical engagement with Western views of concepts such as freedom, reason and civilization (among others), but *sans* the binaries that attend to commensurability talk. This critique is immanent precisely because the West, both as a concept and as a way of looking at the world, is not external to these Muslim identities, but rather a part of their intersectional reality in the modern age. And the mirroring resonance made possible by the existence of a genuinely global public sphere means that the opposite is also, in fact, true. That Islam is an *internal* aspect of Western identities as assuredly as the other way around.[11]

* * *

A chapter summary is customary for introductions, so let me lay the book out for you. For ease of following the argument of this book – which on account of a global context spread over centuries will sometimes of necessity veer

Introduction

this way and that – a version of these chapter summaries is available at the beginning of each chapter as well. In Chapter 1, I focus on rhetoric about Muslims in the time immediately following the events of September 2001, and in the years since, as indicative of certain basic ideological patterns in Western treatments of Islam. These patterns eschew proper political analysis of events and focus instead on essentialized readings of Islam as both explanation and prescription for what ails the Muslim world. From President George W. Bush's famous "Why do they hate us?" speech, to the widespread derision of Muslim critics such as Tariq Ramadan among the learned classes in the West, to the intellectual drift of ostensibly progressive intellectuals toward an identarian politics that rejects Islam as critique as a matter of basic principle, this chapter clarifies what the either/or of Islam actually looks like in the contemporary discursive practices of the West. But why does such talk cling so persistently to the clean binaries of the either/or? The events of 9/11 themselves and the various iterations of the 'War on Terror' are obvious candidates for an explanation. Perhaps the causal soup of 9/11 was far too thick with historical and political entanglements to parse out each ingredient for edifying consumption by an anxious public. So shorthand cultural and theological explanations served the rhetorical purposes of well-wishers and adversaries of Muslims alike. This is true to a certain extent. But scholars and public intellectuals had been indulging in such forms of talk for decades in advance of the twenty-first-century explosion of Islam into mainstream public consciousness; 9/11 merely weaponized pre-existing dispositions toward these essentialist treatments of Islam and Muslims and of their proper place in a world order dominated by the West. The dispositional binaries themselves are in fact of ancient vintage. They have their origins in the intertwined sentiments of civilizational mission and intense race consciousness associated with the nineteenth-century European imperial expansion that birthed the modern world as we know it today. And in the various Muslim responses to this fact of European 'superiority' over the last two centuries or so.

In Chapter 2, I track this historical waltz between the expansion of European power and the parallel diminishment of Muslim control over much of the Middle East and India in the nineteenth century as the most significant drivers in the emergence of essentializing accounts of Islam and its inferiority to an emergent West. These accounts became interpolated with the new language of race, reason and civilization in ways that fundamentally altered the previously existing status of Islam and Muslims in the European imagination (and vice versa). Both the Muslim world and, in part, the West are novel conceptual creations of what this new language made cognitively possible, ideologically coherent and politically desirable. There are, of course, no simple or final answers to be found, merely ideas proffered, considered and put to use in my analysis of these matters. Cognizant of the fact that theoretical considerations and

Introduction

individual opinions are no substitute for practical politics, I will mostly refrain from offering any concrete solutions other than to point to the felicity of politics itself as "the only activity that goes on directly between men without the intermediary of things or matter," and which corresponds to the human condition of plurality, "the fact that men, not Man, live on the earth and inhabit the world."[12] And inasmuch as the Muslim Question is a political question, and as a political question it is simultaneously a human question about the world, then the way we talk about the world and the Muslims in it must by necessity carry traces of the defects in the relationship between Islam and the West. The binding of Muslims into constraining talk about them, and imagining some of them talking back, is therefore the subject of the next three chapters in this book.

In Chapter 3, for example, I identify a set of conversational traps that together constitute what I call *freedom talk* about Islam. This kind of talk is primarily concerned with identifying Islam as a peculiar way of doing *politics* that is then judged as either commensurable or incommensurable with the West. Any critical Muslim perspective that frustrates this binary either becomes conceptually conflated with the most militant political instantiations of Islam (notice the panoramic reach of the term 'Islamist', for example) or is reassessed as a confirmation of modern liberal values (albeit with caveats concerning another panoramic term, 'reform'). In its inclusive, totalizing architecture, freedom talk transcends the usual dichotomies of the right and the left, of liberal and conservative. Those who judge Islam as familiar but underdeveloped kin to the West come in many shapes and sizes. And some make for strange bedfellows. They run the gamut from 'moderate' Muslim intellectuals, to liberal philosophers, to neo-conservative thinkers and politicians, to modernization theorists, to internationalist utopians of all kinds. Those who judge Islam otherwise, as a form of politics that is decisively incompatible with Western values, can similarly count among their ranks a panoply of multiculturalist and left liberals, conservative historians and political scientists, the (so-called) radical or fundamentalist Muslim thinkers, a whole bevy of political realists, and moral relativists of one sort or another. Debates and disagreements between contending parties in their enactment of freedom talk focus ostensibly on the twin issues of democracy and secularism in the Muslim world, and on the attendant value of self-determination. But this focus only masks what is in reality the underlying utility of the trope in depoliticizing the Muslim subject as either wholly familiar or wholly unfamiliar.

Yet freedom as a political idea can have valences other than democracy and secularism. And even valences within the rubric of democracy and secularism that do not match the West's transient consensuses on what constitutes self-determination. In the regime of servitude in colonial India in the nineteenth and early twentieth centuries, for example, Muslims had to reimagine political sovereignty from the ground up *sans* the prevailing conditions that gave rise to "a secular age" in Western Europe.¹³ This chapter concludes with a brief discussion of *khudi* (selfness/ego), Indian Muslim poet Muhammad Iqbal's novel identification of political freedom not with self-determination in the regular sense, but rather with a prior determination of the character of the proper Muslim *self* itself before it can freely determine the nature and character of its reality in the *polis*. Iqbal's formulation is deeply informed by both the fact of Western domination and the reality of a disaggregated Muslim self in the regime of such dominance that requires a 'reconstruction' neither wholly subservient to the West's moral lexicon on freedom nor entirely free of its influence altogether.¹⁴ Breaking free of the either/or, Iqbal's vision soars in its peculiarly Muslim exposition.

In Chapter 4, I argue that public discourse on the problem of Islam is replete with references to reform and rationality because such discourse bends to the strictures of what I call *reason talk* about Muslims. This kind of talk is primarily concerned with identifying Islam as a *religion* that is then judged against the West's own peculiar historical experience as a normative ideal for evaluating all iterations of religion as such. The generic, fully privatized, and historically suspect ideals rooted in this experience have long served to highlight the deficiencies of Islam in its impartial ecclesiastic divestment from politics and in its inability to accept the public supremacy of reason. But particularly punitive tropes from the nineteenth century are enjoying a renaissance post-9/11. At least since Ernest Renan's famous lecture on "Islam and Science" (1883), the scientific, reasoned outlook of Westernized moderns has been contrasted with the Muslim's surfeit of religious enthusiasm that not only prevents material progress, but also boils over into zealotry and violence.[15] These same themes have been picked up and developed further by the (so-called) New Atheists and critical ex-Muslims who demand that Muslims conjoin their faith to the established trajectory of the European Enlightenment. In this reading, Islam ceases to be an independent category of historical or intellectual analysis. It can either regurgitate an established role, acting out the necessary reformations and revolutions in a replaying of European history. Or it can decline the invitation to do so and remain unreasonable, irrational and obscure. In reason talk about Muslims, the only good Muslim is an ex-Muslim informant.

But the notion of reason as rooted in the overcoming of religion is an artifact of the peculiar history of the Enlightenment and of a Scientific Revolution that often pitted men of reason against the clerical establishment in Europe. In this telling, the story has a clean and simple arc, with the age of reason rising in parallel with the decline of religious forms of subjectivity that hitherto constrained human intellect. This story is not entirely untrue, but it has gaping holes in both its logic and its lack of attention to context. When applied to Islam and Muslims, for example, it naturally engenders Kafkaesque treatments that are at best farcical, and often deadly. Consider instead an account of reason by noted nineteenth-century Indian

Introduction

Muslim polymath Sayyid Ahmad Khan that identifies reason *not* with the overcoming of the constraints of religion, but as naturally engrained *in* this constraint itself. Sensing not a surfeit of zealotry in the Indian Muslim population, but rather an enervating cynicism under colonial subjugation, Khan reinterpreted the classical theological idea of *taklif*, or the condition of being put under obligation by God, more generally as the state of being constrained as such by the fact of human finitude. And, additionally, this condition of being constrained not as a burden on human beings, but rather the very source of their free will and their capacity to reason. As a corollary to the notion of *taklif*, Khan's reason is not the overcoming of religion at all, but rather a native capacity of finite beings to contemplate their reality in the regime of divine infinity. Sidestepping the teleological narratives of progress along the enlightenment(s), reformation(s) and revolutions of European history, Khan's account of reason feels eerily anachronistic in its religiosity and yet also uncannily modern in its sensitivity to context. It is a Muslim exposition, to be sure, but not so Muslim as to be incomprehensible to others.

Chapter 5 picks up this notion of Muslim 'incomprehensibility' and takes it one step further. Fed in equal parts by theories of biological evolution, Comtian positivism and eugenics, social Darwinism had its heyday in the late nineteenth and early twentieth centuries. But the idea that cultural norms associated with Euro-American societies are an ever-evolving apotheosis of human social development has been a consistent feature of Western thinking right up to the present. This idea is the basis of what I call *culture talk* about Islam, a way of cognizing and articulating the proximate presence of Muslims that I examine in this chapter. This kind of talk is primarily concerned with identifying Islam as a *culture* that is then judged against the vanishing contemporary, the cultural consensus of the West that is constantly on the move and hence difficult to pin down as a theoretical ideal. Unlike freedom and reason talk, this kind of talk is animated by "structures of feeling" and impressions of unease, a sense of being wronged by the presence of difference.[16] Its effects are evident in an abiding repugnance of Muslim cultural symbols and in attempts to coercively re-engineer ostensibly private spheres of Muslim life such as clothing, speech, dietary codes and physical appearance on the European continent. Such punitive tendencies have historically been weaker in the United States, but suspicion still runs deep that any unmonitored private Muslim spaces are *ipso facto* cauldrons of radicalization. Culture talk imagines the historical, and ongoing, development of Western cultural norms as co-produced with its material and political supremacy and as therefore so many signs of its superiority. The Islamic equivalents of these norms (variously imagined and immediately essentialized), of food and drink, of clothing and personal hygiene, and sometimes even music and literature, are therefore inextricably tied with lagging development, regression, disorder and violence. On the left, culture talk is a principal feature of benevolent cultural and

Introduction

political paternalism. On the right, it often takes the form of nationalistic chauvinism. In either case, some version of a cultural conversion is a prerequisite to an adequate integration of Muslims into Western societies and the expedient evolution of the Islamic world along Euro-American lines. But since the evaluative standard is a moving target, there is also an asymptotic quality to culture talk in that it can never meaningfully reach a resolution unless the historical development of Islam as culture is directly pegged to some generic Western counterpart and Muslims become master mimics. Once again, we find ourselves in the realm of farce, not politics.

This sense of farce was also evident, for example, in the joy that some Muslims clearly experienced in the immediate aftermath of 9/11. This joy is a version of what Homi Bhabha calls a "resort to dreaming, imagining, acting out, embedding the reactive vocabulary of violence and retributive justice in their bodies, their psyches," in the absence of "a public voice" for those rendered futile in their experience of modernity.[17] But nothing is more futile than summary rejections and retributive reversals because these merely reinscribe the pathologies they seek to destroy in their inversions of power. Reversal may have symbolic signification, but in the end it solves nothing. And dehumanization, whether effected by an oppressor or a victim, is still dehumanization either way. We need alternative, humanistic accounts of this world and of those who inhabit it if we are to overcome the pathologies of this world's presents. Consider, for example, Edward Said, an avowed and unrepentant humanist throughout his life, who always seemed guided by that old dictum "nothing human is alien to me."[18] Although his work did much to enhance the appeal of postcolonial studies, Said never made for a particularly comfortable denizen of this new field. He decried the "rhetoric of blame" and "the hostility between Western and non-Western cultures that [lead] to crisis. The world is too small," he said, "and too interdependent to let these passively happen."[19] He advocated instead what he called "a contrapuntal approach" to harmonize the intertwined, overlapping and in the end shared historical experience of a common world in the wake of empire. As Said put it, this approach tries to juxtapose into concurrence "those views and experiences that are ideologically and culturally closed to each other and that attempt to suppress other views and experiences."[20] "To read Austen," for example, "without also reading Fanon and Cabral – and so on and on – is to disaffiliate modern culture from its engagements and attachments."[21] In being a Palestinian Christian, Said also embodies the complexity of Islam as a language of critique not strongly tied to a particular theology, but rather more broadly to an experience of the world rooted in, and along, the Muslim vector.

It is with Said's expansive humanism in mind that I begin the conclusion of this book with a discussion of Hannah Arendt's idea of *Amor Mundi*, or love of the world. More than any other modern theorist perhaps, Arendt is

Introduction

responsible for a revival of the classical Aristotelian notion of humans as political beings, and of politics at its core as the exchange of speech acts in public between free peoples. I have adopted this understanding of the human being and of politics itself because it makes for the clearest exposition of the problems besetting the relationship between the West and Muslims and it provides the firmest ethical handle for a possible solution to these problems. For *Amor Mundi* is not the flattening love of *eros* or *agape*, nor even the comforting love of empathy and community, but rather the challenging political love of plurality, of "the fact that men, not Man, live on the earth and inhabit the world."[22] It is also the affective response to an acknowledgment of the humanity of others and to reconciling oneself with the world as it actually is, and not as we wish it was. The opposite of *Amor Mundi* is not hate, but a kind of lazy indifference toward the facts of the world as mere irritants, as largely irrelevant to the smooth elaboration of this or that theory about this world rather than engagement with its lived history and with its continuously differentiating reality.

Like Said and Arendt, the German philosopher Hans-Georg Gadamer theorized the possibility of understanding across distance measured in both centuries and difference through what he called "a fusion of horizons."[23] "Thus it belongs to every true conversation," Gadamer argues, "that each person opens himself to the other, truly accepts his point of view as valid and transposes himself into the other to such an extent that he understands not the particular individual but what he says."[24] Our discrete "horizons of experience," the particular historical and cultural embeddedness that necessarily limit the view from our own vantage point, can still provisionally merge in the generation of meaning about each other, "an event in which a world opens itself to [us]."[25] For Gadamer, this is possible precisely because of our "belongingness" to language, to the fact of our shared humanity as speaking beings.

Iqbal's poetic self-reflections, Khan's theological rationalism, Said's grand humanism, and Gadamer's dialectic of dialogue – these all provide ways for situating the Muslim as a viable subject of an Arendtian politics of appearance in the public square, and for breaking out of the conversational traps discussed in previous chapters. I offer no sustained meditation on the life and work of these figures, just small "pearls" of their wisdom dove for and retrieved from the ocean of 'Muslim' thought, mere trinkets to attract the reader's attention. The hope is that the strange and unfamiliar splendor of these pearls would also encourage the reader to revisit and reconceive the writings of Muslim thinkers over the last two hundred years absent the constraining taxonomies of 'modernist' or 'fundamentalist' as engaged criticisms instead that are neither a rejection of modernity nor a wholesale acceptance of the West's accounts of it. Muslims have offered alternative cartographies for a world emergent in this modernity as the common context for diverse human experiences,

Introduction

and these maps are no more provincial than those offered by the West. And if modernity is to be rescued as a general category of analysis, it must be reimagined precisely as the emergence of this common world as an *event* that generates contesting "horizons of expectation" about this world's past, present and (especially) future.[26] Aaron Hughes has argued that what scholars refer to as various different "Islamic ideologies" are in fact often "Islamic interpretations of global ideologies" embedded universally in the experience of modernity itself; "rather than envisage *an* Islamic take on the modern world, it might make more sense to imagine Islam as an interpretive strategy that can be used in the service of numerous local and global agendas."[27] In this reading, contemporary intellectuals such as Tariq Ramadan belong to a long tradition of Muslims for whom "the challenge of modernity [has been and] is the overwhelming fact of their lives."[28] Interrogations of these Muslims as relics of some old and fearful religious technology bent on contaminating modernity are not only misplaced, but insulting. Or as the journalist Christopher de Bellaigue puts it, "there is something wonderfully earnest and yet wholly irrelevant about Westerners demanding modernity from people whose lives are drenched in it."[29]

* * *

But to be drenched in modernity is hardly being at home in it. I have called this state of being drenched a *depoliticization* of Muslims and focused on the either/or structure of its manifestations in the global public square. But it has been called many other names over the years and given many other descriptions. Back in the day, it was simply called imperialism. The term 'colonialism' was in vogue in the early years of the twentieth century and then switched to 'neo-colonialism' following the wave of mid-century decolonizations. In recent years, postcolonial theory has conjured up its own varied assemblage of terms and concepts (too numerous to list here) to describe the reality of an ascendant West and the social, cultural and political consequences thereof. 'Empire' continues to hold sway with some folks (including myself) both as a concept and a description of the lived reality of many peoples around the world as well. But the closest theoretical analogue for the 'drenching' I wish to describe in this book is the concept of *coloniality* from the emerging field of decolonial studies. I am generally allergic to *-ity* neologisms (secularity, glocality, governmentality, etc.) because to me they usually signal an inability or unwillingness to describe things simply and clearly. But I mention coloniality here both to acknowledge an intellectual debt to folks such as Walter Mignolo and Hamid Dabashi, and also to distinguish my project from important work in postcolonial studies, for example, and from more activist literature on Islamophobia. Coloniality here refers not to the condition of being colonized as such, but rather to the truth-claims, institutions, practices and discourses designed to sustain a particular architecture of power. Mignolo has called coloniality "the darker side

Introduction

of modernity," or those aspects of the West's rise on the global stage that are often overlooked in the West itself as only being incidental to its lived reality – namely racism, imperialism, genocide, ethnocide, and peculiarly Western forms of knowledge hierarchies and political domination.[30] In this reading, decolonization did not eliminate coloniality as an architecture of power, but rather only tinkered with its "outer form" while the innards remained largely intact in their structure and operations. The eithers and ors of talk about Islam are together one aspect of how coloniality continues to operate in the modern world, *sans* the oeuvre of explicit empire, to constrain Muslim speech and stifle Muslim ideas about this world. Decoloniality as an obverse set of epistemologies, institutions, practices and discourses therefore requires us to imagine the world and its near history anew in a manner that is not endlessly trapped in the feedback loops inherent to 'the West and the rest' thinking or simple universalizations of what are clearly provincial moral lexicons.

It is for this reason that in writing this book, I have often caught myself being guided by old-fashioned modernist clichés that nonetheless seem to me to be increasingly relevant in the world we live in today. This is partly because the cynicism of much postmodernist thinking often appears deeply anti-political to me. And I find postcolonial theories similarly difficult to digest in whole. The breaking down of this or that system, the constant interrogations, the persistent excavations and deconstructions all have the feel of worlds being made to fall apart as a kind of intellectual exercise. Of course, postmodernist and postcolonialist insights inform my work as they should all good scholarly arguments. But I have this sense, more than a feeling but less than an idea, that something new must be imagined to break the cyclical futility of folks cheering the destruction of towers or the demonization of others. That these times demand an avant-garde. In response to this imperative, therefore, I will be relying largely on early to mid-twentieth-century figures for intellectual inspiration rather than more contemporary thinkers. It is folks such as Arendt, Fanon and Gadamer who had come out of the carnage of world wars and the horrors of racist imperialism with great suspicion of grand narratives but who were still not yet entirely jaded into a rejection of "something new" for the world. Their modernism was perhaps reluctant (as Seyla Benhabib said of Arendt's), but it was animated nonetheless by a humanism that is in short supply these days.[31]

The choice of Khan, Iqbal and Said as the critical 'Muslim' interlocutors is similarly motivated by their inherent optimism about the future, and not cynicism in the face of it. As will become evident in the ensuing chapters, each of them recognized modernity not as an affliction visited on them by others, but rather as a connective tissue that binds together people and ideas from disparate backgrounds into an often unsettling but common whole that demands an enlarged imagination on our part, and not a summary rejection of its compartmentalized unity.

Introduction

Already in 1974, for example, the Tunisian Muslim philosopher Hichem Djait had intuited as much when he proclaimed that:

> Modernity has sprung free from its country of origins and is now in *universal* orbit. To grasp it in its universal dimensions, to integrate it and make it ours, to add to it and express it in the language of our own particularity, this is our primary goal: it is the dialectic of perpetuity in renovation.[32]

A perennial cynosure for me, then, is Marshall Berman's seminal insight that modernism is "any attempt by modern men and women to become subjects as well as objects of modernization, to get a grip on the modern world and to make themselves at home in it."[33] We are living in an age of rapidly changing circumstances, of unprecedented movements of peoples and goods, of technology that was science fiction less than a generation ago. And in a world that is too small and becoming smaller. We cannot talk our way out of the problems of this age. But we can certainly begin by speaking it better.

1

The Slanted Abyss

In this chapter, I focus on rhetoric about Muslims in the time immediately following the events of September 2001, and in the years since, as indicative of certain basic ideological patterns in Western treatments of Islam. These patterns eschew proper political analysis of events and focus instead on essentialized readings of Islam as both explanation and prescription for what ails the Muslim world. From President George W. Bush's famous "Why do they hate us?" speech, to the widespread derision of Muslim critics such as Tariq Ramadan among the learned classes in the West, to the intellectual drift of ostensibly progressive intellectuals toward an identarian politics that rejects Islam as critique as a matter of basic principle, this chapter clarifies what the either/or of Islam actually sounds like in the contemporary discursive practices of the West.

* * *

In an obvious sign of 'peak Islam' in the public imagination, academic libraries in the West now flow over with books about fundamentalist and jihadist Islam or liberal and modernist Muslims. Talking heads on cable news television indulge in endless debates about whether Islam is a religion of peace or of violence. Harrowing tales of ex-Muslims absconding the astringent constraints of religion rub shoulders on real and virtual bookshelves with 'moderate' Muslim calls for reform of their faith. A pervasive fear of Muslims competes in the public square with concerns about Islamophobia and its enervating effects on modern bodies politic. Disagreements about the nature and meaning of wearing the hijab turn on whether it is a free expression of faith or an indelible sign of cultural inferiority. Countless texts pairing Islam with the West, democracy, human rights, feminism or secularism, and so on, argue either affinity between the two or a lack thereof. And of course, intellectuals and activists of all stripes incessantly deliberate the potential for a reformation in the Muslim world or the dangers of radicalization in it. Bickering over the essence and future of Islam is the tic-tac-toe of debates. And the ink spilt on such discussions would fill a proverbial ocean.

I have no interest in feeding into what is already this deluge of talk fixated on the eithers and ors of Islam's compatibility with the West or with this or that version of what counts as modernity. Or, for that matter, in tedious enumerations and analyses of 'Islamophobia' or 'reform'.

The Slanted Abyss

In this chapter, I will argue instead that the ostensible back and forth of these so-called debates often functions as a discursive straitjacket that ensnares Muslims into futile, dead-end conversations about 'Islam' and 'the West'. This chronic reliance on ever-evolving tropes of Western vintage to evaluate and explain Islam forecloses any possibility of critical novelty from Muslims and sieves these discussions into the restrictive either/or of Islam's familiarity or difference with the West. In the discursive regime of this kind of talk, then, Muslims can be friends or foes but not critics. Here, a professed and sincere love of Muslims can serve to inhibit complex elaborations of Muslim subjectivity just as effectively as overt Islamophobia. And Muslims can render themselves irrelevant to critical participation in the affairs of this world just as proficiently as non-Muslims often do.

I focus on the West not because Muslims play no role in their futility (they obviously do), but because Western discourses set the stage for anything that follows. This is what it means to live in a world that European imperial expansion has created but which all of humanity now calls home. This creation is, of course, an ongoing process. The world is imagined and made anew in countless debates and happenings every day, through iconic events such as 9/11 but also the writing of books, the making of films and the movement of peoples. To argue that this world is the common context of our shared humanity, that it is in fact now one world with one future, may come across as an old-fashioned modernist cliché, a quaint idea whose time has come and gone. We live in what Pankaj Mishra calls an 'age of anger', of alternative modernities, multiculturalism and postcolonial angst on the left and Western exceptionalism and triumphalism, of resurgent religion and nationalism on the right. But the idea that this world is meaningfully divided between the West and the rest is a dangerous diversion. And although a liberatory politics of difference is a necessary corrective to the failed universalisms of the past, it offers no ultimate reckoning with the thoroughly globalized nature of the present moment. Even as far back as 1968, Hannah Arendt had already intuited that:

> For the first time in history, all peoples on earth have a common present ... Every country has become the almost immediate neighbor of every other country, and every man feels the shock of events which take place at the other end of the globe.[1]

But this collapsing proximity generates what Arendt calls "negative solidarity" when "individuals with very different pasts find themselves herded by capitalism and technology into a common present ... [with] grossly unequal distributions of wealth and power."[2] This is what Frantz Fanon meant when he called this "a compartmentalized world ... inhabited by different species."[3] Power in this new reality properly refers not just to military might or economic advantage, but that most ancient of human privileges, the power to name. To set the terms of the debate, so to say, to posit the truth of things. The immediacy of the global present is interpolated with vast discrepancies in the practice of this privilege. And if the neo-liberal world order and the 'War on Terror' are any indications, the West jealously and often violently protects its turf, this hard-won privilege.

It is in this sense that the modern world sometimes begins to resemble a kind of global household, and on the classical model where women, children and slaves properly belong in the *oikia*, the private realm of necessity, and only the *despotikon* is freed from necessity, by the labor of his wards, to debate the good life with free and equal men in the *polis*. This capacity to discuss the common good, the past, present and future of a common communal life in the open agora, is the essence of politics itself for Aristotle, and its practice is the very actualization of our humanity. Or as Arendt put it rather more evocatively:

> The world is not human just because it is made by human beings ... [rather] we humanize what is going on in the world and in ourselves only by speaking of it, and in the course of speaking of it we learn to be human.[4]

Locked in the prison of particularity, of essence and difference, of being spoken about and looked into, not at, the Muslim can only really ever be an object of politics in this common world, never a subject. And this rationing of discourse about the world not only dehumanizes the one being rationed out, but depoliticizes the world itself, and in so doing dehumanizes it. The Muslim Question, then, is ultimately and always has been a political question, which is to say a question about the humanity of others. But it is also in this sense always already a question about what kind of world we imagine this world to be and what manner of futures we make available for it in speaking it continuously into existence.

It is for this reason that the discursive asymmetries that generate this world of Muslim children and slaves never offer a durable panacea for the ongoing problem of Islam and the West. In this discursive regime, any exposition of Islam's critical edge must be surrendered to the so-called Islamists who definitively reject the West while 'moderate' Muslims all but cower in apologia, bidding validation for their liberal and progressive credentials. But if the last twenty or so years are any indication, these pious comforts continue to make us ever-more somnolent as the complexities of the world we inhabit overwhelm our senses and blind our half-open eyes. Writing in the mid oughts some years after 9/11 and well into the proverbial War on Terror, Mahmood Mamdani argued that when "President [George W.] Bush moved to distinguish between 'good Muslims' and 'bad Muslims' ... [his] presumption that there are such categories mask[ed] a refusal to address our own failure to make a political analysis of our time."⁵ These refusals of history and failures to understand our present political moment mean that there is little acknowledgment of the need for a politics that conforms to neither enmity nor acquiescence. And as ISIS, al-Shabab and Boko Haram take hold in the very hearts of Muslim lands and radicalized Westerners threaten to turn their own homelands into shooting galleries, perhaps it is time to admit that our regnant paradigms have done little to win hearts and minds and our political calculations regarding the future of the Muslim world have been deficient and inadequate. That a humble curiosity about modern Muslims, bereft of affirmation or rejection, seeking political engagement, not observation, evaluation and judgment, may well be the proper order of the day.

But though it does sometimes appear here and there in current debates on Islam in the West, such humble curiosity is desperately rare. Instead, every Tom, Dick and Harry feels qualified to actively theologize Islam's true essence and to opine definitively on its real meaning. Muslims are not entirely absent from these kinds of discussion, but they tend to play along to get along. Or they confirm the infernal character of their religion in the minds of many in the West by blowing this or that thing up here and elsewhere. And all the while, negative solidarity gains more momentum. Most Muslims are mere spectators to these discussions when they are not being targeted on account of them. Their depoliticized selves are extras in the stories being told and histories being written about them by others.

* * *

Of course, some may be tempted to retort that bringing down the tallest buildings in the metropole (to say nothing of hitting the nerve center of the imperial military) were acts of tremendous political agency. Insofar as Muslims planned and executed these attacks, they clearly demonstrated their willingness and capacity to act against the West in furtherance of their own ends. They continue to pursue these ends even today, despite the trillions that Western governments have now spent in the ongoing, never-ending struggle against Muslim insurgencies, and the billions they continue to spend on 'hearts and minds'. These Muslims may be the villains of history but their renewed influence on the affairs of the modern world is not contestable. They are once again actors on the world stage. How else to explain the clear signs of their impact everywhere one looks. Islamist partisans are resurgent in Muslim lands. Veiled women confidently stroll the streets of European capitals. Young men strap bombs to their chests and their limbs and gladly embrace their own death in return for visiting it upon countless others. Strident mullahs openly preach violent jihad against the West to ever-expanding audiences. Insurgencies are ubiquitous, spattering the blood of their victims across the globe in crescent arcs of destruction from Southeast Asia to Europe to the homeland itself. In eighteen short years, al-Qaeda has metastasized into Boko Haram, al-Shabab and countless other outfits operating with near impunity. There was for a time even a so-called Islamic State in the Levant, stubbornly persistent against staggering odds, that even in its absence still remains a "shining city on the hill" for jihadists everywhere. And closer to home, the West is embroiled in endless debates concerning moral and political principles that, until recently, were considered irrefutable foundations of modern civilized life. There is even talk of negotiating with the Taliban so that an unwinnable war can be brought to a face-saving end that, in the end, will end nothing. If agency is the capacity to create change, then surely these Muslims have had a greater impact on the world in the last twenty years than anyone could have anticipated not so long ago. In what sense, then, is this axiomatic of the futility of Islam, and not its renewed agency?

One obvious response to this question has been to deploy a kindly euphemism that is popular among the so-called enlightened political classes here and elsewhere. This is the notion that true Islam is a religion of peace. It has been hijacked by a small group of extremists, wolves in sheep's clothing, who fiendishly dress their depraved ideological ends in the fabric of Islam. They are at best misguided and ignorant, oblivious to the true nature of the religion they ostensibly profess. Or worse, they willfully twist Islam in service of their own destructive agenda. The most telling iteration of this paradigm is George

W. Bush's speech to a joint session of the United States Congress on September 20, 2001, in the wake of the 9/11 attacks. Widely regarded even by his detractors as a high point of his presidency, this speech set out to explain to the American people who had attacked them, and why. Bush asserted that "[these] terrorists practice a fringe form of Islamic extremism that has been rejected by Muslim scholars and the vast majority of Muslim clerics; a fringe movement that perverts the peaceful teachings of Islam." Bush then addressed the Muslim world directly in a display of deep empathy and remarkable statesmanship (rare during the rest of his presidency):

> We respect your faith. It's practiced freely by many millions of Americans and by millions more in countries that America counts as friends. Its teachings are good and peaceful, and those who commit evil in the name of Allah blaspheme the name of Allah. The terrorists are traitors to their own faith, trying, in effect, to hijack Islam itself. The enemy of America is not our many Muslim friends. It is not our many Arab friends. Our enemy is a radical network of terrorists and every government that supports them.[6]

With the precision of a surgeon, Bush theologically amputates al-Qaeda from the healthy body of Islam and then defines this body as the very antithesis of what al-Qaeda represents. When the story is told this way, Muslims appear as much the victims of al-Qaeda as those Americans targeted on 9/11. Like a diseased limb that could ravage an entire organism if left unchecked, the fringe extremism of al-Qaeda and its ilk infects the Islamic body politic. Re-envisaged in this manner, the attacks of 9/11 are properly understood not as signs of Muslim agency, but of futility, not of healthful vigor, but a sick body.

Like all effective euphemisms, this one too rests on a partial sort of truth. Al-Qaeda's brand of Islam is clearly detached from any mainstream understanding of the religion. Inasmuch as the short-lived Taliban government in Afghanistan could be said to represent a test run of this philosophy, it lacks credibility with the vast majority of Muslims.[7] ISIS has fared little better.[8] There are also no traditional standards by which people such as Osama bin Laden or Abu Bakr al-Baghdadi have any religious authority to speak about Islam or for Islam in any meaningful sense. They are not theologically trained, have been conferred no titles except those they confer on themselves, and have no formal education in Islamic law or jurisprudence that is recognized by the established religious authorities of Islam.[9] They have won no elections and lead no political parties. They are affiliated with no institutions except ones they themselves have created for ends they themselves uphold. The fact that they are able to mobilize enough men and resources to simulate authority, to conjure up voices and bodies that appear to speak for Muslims and to act on their behalf, is an indisputable tragedy. George W. Bush is on solid theological and sociological grounds, then, when he calls them "traitors to their own faith." To be spoken for and done for by those with whom one shares little is to have one's agency to speak and do for oneself wrested away, or as Bush cleverly put it in a clear reference to the events of 9/11, hijacked!

Still, this speech should leave the discerning reader with a sense of unease. What is this true Islam that Bush calls the religion of peace? It is easy enough to establish that it is not the religion of the terrorists. But what is its positive content? What does it stand for? And against? The speech provides little guidance, but whatever it does provide is exceedingly instructive. Inasmuch as it stands for "good and peaceful teachings," true Islam must stand against the terrorists. And if it stands against the terrorists, it must stand with its true friends, those who were attacked on 9/11 by the same malevolent force that seeks to undermine it. In a particularly evocative moment in the speech, Bush asks the now famous question:

> Why do they hate us? They hate what they see right here in this chamber – a democratically elected government. Their leaders are self-appointed. They hate our freedoms – our freedom of religion, our freedom of speech, our freedom to vote and assemble and disagree with each other. They want to overthrow existing governments in many

The Slanted Abyss

Muslim countries, such as Egypt, Saudi Arabia, and Jordan. They want to drive Israel out of the Middle East. They want to drive Christians and Jews out of vast regions of Asia and Africa. These terrorists kill not merely to end lives, but to disrupt and end a way of life. With every atrocity, they hope that America grows fearful, retreating from the world and forsaking our friends. They stand against us, because we stand in their way.

Bush rhetorically blurs the distinctions between true Muslims and Americans by identifying both as being under attack by the same foe, and perhaps for the same reasons. The empathetic tone of the entire speech is powerful and undeniable. And Bush deserves much credit for the lack of overt violence against Muslims in America following 9/11 because he explicitly exhorts his countrymen to:

> Uphold the values of America, and remember why so many have come here. We are in a fight for our principles, and our first responsibility is to live by them. No one should be singled out for unfair treatment or unkind words because of their ethnic background or religious faith.[10]

But empathy too has its price. In Bush's reading, there is a chasm between true Islam and its twisted counterpart that is as wide as it is deep. Its depth separates the normative concern for human dignity from a willful indifference to it. It denotes an existential break between two incompatible ways of being. Its width separates civilized life from tyranny and barbarity. It signifies the distance between an enlightened modernity and a diseased obscurantism. *Either with us or against us.* For between the either/or is a slanted abyss. And atop this chasm is no safe place to float. One must choose sides. This is an odd reversal where the picture of Islam so constructed is a perfected mirror image of the West, beautiful, resplendent with timeless values and ageless virtues, while out there in the world Islam grows ever-more hideous, deformed and ancient by the day. Bush's ostensibly sympathetic "real Muslims are just like us" response to 9/11 is therefore a paradigmatic demonstration of Muslim futility precisely in its salutary sheltering of Islam into the snug bosom of the West. I am not suggesting that George W. Bush was operating on multiple levels of philosophical nuance or theological complexity. But after all, when offered the hot embrace of familiarity, what else is it to be a religion of peace than to turn the other cheek?

* * *

Religion of peace talk is that particular species of theological theater wherein self-engagement masquerades as dialogue to loud applause from all and sundry. Consider, for example, that 'peace' has very peculiar connotations in the modern Western lexicon. These include 'the condition of peace' (lack of violence), 'leaving each other in peace' (toleration) or 'being at peace' (spiritual contentment). Ever since the wars of religion ravaged Europe in the sixteenth and seventeenth centuries, the association of religion with violence has been a strong one.[11] The modern European state's insistence on monopolizing the use of force emerged first as a response to the supposed threat of uncontrolled and irrational violence from religious zealots. Precisely because religious adherents can be compelled by the commanding sentiment of belief, they must renounce the possibility of actualizing such sentiment as coercion. This is what Richard Rorty has called the "Jeffersonian compromise," whereby "democratic societies, should, in the manner of Jefferson, think of themselves as having exchanged toleration [of religion] for an assurance that the believers would leave their religion at home when discussing political questions in public."[12] Those who commit violence in the name of religion lose the right to be tolerated by the state and by society in general. Moreover, even the appearance of religious reasons in political debates can raise the possibility of irresolvable conflict. Mixing religion and politics is asking for trouble. It is bad form. The state's toleration of religion is therefore complemented by tolerance of another kind. Adherents of different religions must tolerate each other, leave each other be, in matters of belief, morality and ritual practice. Their public interactions concerning religion or morality must be framed by the gentle claims of either mutual affirmation or mutual indifference. Polite conversation demands that no one ask another of their faith unless they bring it up themselves. And even then, to tread softly, cautiously, for this is dangerous ground. The private sphere of religion is sacrosanct, just as its public manifestations are strictly regulated. This is because it is only in the private sphere that the believing individual is fully free from all intrusion, manipulation or regulation. It is only here that the legitimate concerns of religion, moral development and spiritual contentment can be properly realized. Outside lies the world, the domain of reason, expertise and utility, of social contracts and legal strictures. Of peaceful coexistence. If not profane, then the world is not properly sacred either. By dividing human existence into the public and the private, the secular and the sacred, the Jeffersonian compromise seeks to make the world safe from religion and religion safe from the world.

This particular compromise is one way of describing the more general sociological processes by which the religious veneer of the European public order has been gradually readjusted since the late Middle Ages. The older unity of order and orientation that bound the imperium to the *sacerdotium* in a mostly stable normative configuration (what Carl Schmitt has called the *respublica Christiana*) became disaggregated under the relentless pressure of rapidly changing circumstances.[13] Schmitt focuses on the European discovery of the New World as the primary causal event in this story.[14] Others have looked to the Reformation, the wars of religion, and the soul-searching that followed the carnage.[15] Still others argue that it was the rise of the capitalist economy, the Industrial Revolution and the modern state that undid the old order.[16] There is also the obligatory mention of the Enlightenment and the Scientific Revolution as interlocked pliers restraining religion within the limits of reason alone or even divesting it of movement altogether.[17] The specifics need not concern us here yet. Suffice it to say that through some combination of these forces, the nature and meaning of religion, and its legitimate stations in society, underwent a radical transformation in early modern Europe.[18] The Jeffersonian compromise is one way of describing the new order that coalesced after this transformation. It is a good description because it evokes an evolving paradigm shift of conflicting interests reaching ongoing stable equilibria where the public primacy of reason, the cultural values of freedom and toleration, and the institutional infrastructure of the modern state emerge as requisite features of a new order.[19]

To speak of Islam as a religion of peace, then, is to demand that Muslims break definitively from their pasts and bind themselves theologically and historically to the normative parameters of something akin to the Jeffersonian compromise. But they must also put aside any active intellectual and political participation in the continuing evolution of these norms. They must do this well enough to ensure the peace. And all that such peace entails. It is for this reason that for all its empathy, Bush's rhetoric is backed by an implicit threat of violence – conform, or else.

Incessant talk of reform in Muslim societies is similarly menacing underneath its impatient smiles of encouragement and hope. In a 2010 article for the *The American Prospect*, for example, the political theorist Andrew March suggests that the term 'moderate Islam' is a conceptual chimera with which European intellectuals often entertain themselves. It provides them with an idyllic vision of the future where moderate Muslim voices gradually drown out the strident shrieks of their radical co-religionists and reform Islam into a modern, tolerant religion. But at the heart of this fantasy lies a contradiction: moderate Islam has very little to do with Islam. Instead, its main referents are the (so-called) values of the Enlightenment. Moderation is the standard by which we judge Islam's distance from these values. March finds this rather odd. Since the term 'moderate Islam' is itself incoherent and disaggregated (its meaning has nothing to do with the words that comprise it), it presents Muslims with absurd ethical choices: "You are either pro-Enlightenment or you are soft on stoning."[20] It holds Muslims to an evolving set of standards wholly devoid of any engaged participation on their part in these standards' continuing development. In this sense at least, 'moderate Islam' demands as much a kind of divestment from Islam as an engagement with it.

This explains why the conceptual lines between an invitation to reform and a demand for outright conversion are always blurred in such rhetoric. March's article was occasioned by Paul Berman's then recent book *The Flight of the*

The Slanted Abyss

Intellectuals in which Berman assails European intellectuals for not taking a harsher line against Islamism.[21] Berman is especially critical of the Swiss Muslim theologian and reformer Tariq Ramadan, "a double-talking confidence man who by refusing to make a complete break with his Islamist heritage is merely offering an Islamism with a human face." It is certainly true that Ramadan cuts an interesting and controversial figure in European Muslim life. This is because his critique of the status quo cuts both ways. He berates his Muslim co-religionists for their insularity and obscurantism, demanding instead that "rather than recoil[ing] into self-protective ghettos, Muslims should bear witness to Islam's universalistic values while committing themselves morally to European societies." But he also refuses to distance himself from his tradition and his genealogy. As the grandson of Hasan al-Banna, the founder of the Muslim Brotherhood in Egypt (and the father of modern Islamism), and the son of a close associate of Sayyid Qutb (the foremost philosopher of modern Islamism), Ramadan has a lot to live up to (or to live down). When Europeans demand that he unequivocally repudiate the politics of his ancestors, Ramadan refuses to play along. As March points out, Ramadan is an internal critic, who seeks to "push [his] community to change, but [he does] so from within it, out of love."[22] Islam is like his family tree; it grows on the roots that are already there. So, Ramadan demands instead that European societies accept and nurture this tree as their own, and to engage constructively with it rather than impulsively seek its destruction. His refusal to pull the tree out from its roots and plant a new tree fit for European soil is seen by many as indicative of his unwillingness to moderate his Islam. And so the beat goes on.

Interestingly, even Berman admits that Ramadan is no extremist. It would be hard to argue otherwise. As a European Muslim, Ramadan's primary concern has always been engagement with the West.[23] While he does not opine against political Islam explicitly and often enough for some Europeans such as Berman, there is nothing in either Ramadan's politics or his philosophy that suggests that he condones violence. It is for this reason that Berman directs his most piercing critiques not at Tariq Ramadan, but rather at those in the West who find in Ramadan a serious and reasoned conversation partner, a worthy interlocutor. These are the *intellectuals* of the title of Berman's book. Many of these intellectuals are skillfully skewered by Berman, but it is Ian Baruma who emerges as the archetypical villain of the narrative. Particularly vexing for Berman is Baruma's otherwise unrivaled credentials as a liberal critic of Islam. But when he was commissioned by the *New York Times Magazine* to do a profile of Tariq Ramadan, a task to which Berman thought Baruma was "supremely suited," the latter chose nuance over the knee-jerk, a complex assessment of his subject, and not a simple skewering of his character. The last paragraph of Baruma's appraisal is particularly instructive in this regard:

The Slanted Abyss

Ramadan offers a different way, which insists that a reasoned but traditionalist approach to Islam offers values that are as universal as those of the European Enlightenment. From what I understand of Ramadan's enterprise, these values are neither secular, nor always liberal, but they are not part of a holy war against Western democracy either. His politics offer an alternative to violence, which, in the end, *is reason enough to engage with him, critically, but without fear.*

Baruma is rather puzzled by the lack of verbal fireworks during his interviews with Ramadan or during a public discussion between the two sponsored by the French magazine *Le Point*: "Perhaps I didn't push hard enough. We agreed on most issues, and even when we didn't (he was more friendly toward the Pope than I was), our debate refused to catch fire."[24] Berman clearly thinks Baruma did not "push hard enough," for if he had Ramadan would have revealed himself as the purveyor of a worldview that has nothing at all on offer. Worse, it is hardly even intelligible. Berman is by turns amazed and aghast by the possibility that anyone should take Ramadan seriously. As he argues in *Intellectuals*:

This is the oddity about Tariq Ramadan – as his triumphs [become] ever greater and his thinking more widely known, no consensus whatsoever

[has] emerged regarding the nature of his philosophy or its meaning for France or Europe or the world.[25]

There is nothing here that should concern us, Berman seems to be saying, except that we should be concerned by it. Baruma's great sin is to suggest the mere possibility that there may indeed be something worthwhile to talk about "critically but without fear," and that Ramadan is allowed to offer complex assessments of historical Muslims and of Islamic ideas without conforming to the defective binary of affirmation or denouncement. After all, Euro-Americans do much the same in their complex assessments of their own histories. This, then, may well be Ramadan's great sin, that he harbors the not-so-secret hope of being European and Muslim at the same time, in equal measure and without contradiction. For reasons never stated nor made clear, Berman appears to believe that this is a contradiction in terms.

Andrew March is a scholar of Islam and a Rawlsian liberal. More specifically, he is interested in the possibility of discovering an "overlapping consensus" between the demands of liberal citizenship and Islamic law.[26] It is not surprising, then, that he finds Berman's views on this matter rather difficult to digest: no overlapping consensus is possible if one starts with the thesis that there is nothing to talk about. But there is more to March's concern with Berman and with others like him in the Western intellectual mainstream. It is the subtle premise that "Muslims in *their* mainstream intellectual and religious traditions do not deserve internal critics. They deserve only apostates."[27] Berman is not only upset with the rather warm reception Ramadan receives in some (and only some) European circles.[28] He also argues that real Muslim allies such as Ayaan Hirsi Ali and Salman Rushdie routinely come in for harsh criticism by too many of his colleagues in the press and in the academy. So much so that their views on Islam are often suppressed by the intellectual classes in the West. March correctly points out that these two famous critics of Islam are in fact self-declared apostates, and in that sense not Muslim at all. What does it mean to define one's true Muslim allies as only those who themselves do not believe they are Muslim? Even more tellingly perhaps, what is implied by the fact that Berman sees no contradiction in this position?

It is important to point out here that neither March nor Baruma do anything more than acknowledge Ramadan's existence, and suggest the abstract possibility of a coherent, critical conversation with him. Neither claims to agree with what Ramadan says or does. March has written extensively on Ramadan's work, but he evaluates it as a scholar, not a judge. It is true that in their agreeableness toward Ramadan, both March and Baruma do appear to be signaling that as fellow citizens, as human beings for that matter, Muslims be allowed to speak. If Ramadan offers an Islamic critique of the normative values that dominate the West and structure the international order, we must engage "critically but without fear." It is not as if the regnant values of the West have been set in stone or have existed outside of history itself impervious to change. In fact, exactly the opposite is true. The content, scope and subject of these values have all evolved at a dizzying pace over the last two centuries. The meaning of terms such as 'rights', 'equality', 'freedom', 'democracy' and 'secularism' has been subject to rigorous, rancorous debate, and has oftentimes transformed beyond recognition. Even at any given point in time, the West can hardly agree with itself about these many meanings, nor the hierarchies of priority among them, nor even the human subjects to whom these meanings apply. Nor for that matter on the meaning of 'the West' itself, what it is and where. The intellectual, political and cultural processes that undergird these disparities in space and time have not suddenly ceased in their movement, nor have the drivers of history become arrested in the present moment. Even if we grant that there is a contemporary consensus on what constitutes Western values (there isn't), and accept a historically suspect tale of their exclusive origins and evolution in lockboxes of hermetically sealed Western societies (which is nonsense), even then the source of Berman's consternation cannot reasonably be that Western *intellectuals* are engaging with an 'outsider' (he isn't) or taking someone with a religiously informed worldview seriously. The Western canon is replete with both kinds of agents of change. And whatever values Berman espouses, these would have no existence without them.

No, Berman's issue with Ramadan appears to be that he exists at all, and with the manner in which he has chosen to define this existence – his desire for a seat at the European table, for critical participation in the ongoing development of norms and values, for an active engagement in processes of history without divestment from Islam. Berman tries to thread the needle in his repeated disclaimers that he is critiquing Islamism as an ideology, and not Islam as a religion or Muslims as a people. But his descriptions of the imminent threat are often so outlandishly panoramic, and his use of guilt by association (across oceans and centuries) so prevalent, that this feels like a distinction without a difference. Berman minces no words. Mere acknowledgment of Ramadan is already a bridge too far. He must "make a *complete* break from his Islamist heritage" or "he's a double-talking confidence man." Nowhere is it clear what such a break would look like or what degree or frequency of denouncement would be enough for Berman. Has Berman made a complete break from the racist, misogynistic, anti-democratic excesses of his own philosophical antecedents? What are we to think of his progressive credentials if he does not preface everything he says with a denouncement of Aristotle, Augustine, Hegel and Marx? There is indeed a con at work here, but it is Berman who is the con man.

March recognizes the Kafkaesque quality of this interrogation: "Because Ramadan refuses to define himself negatively in terms of what he has denounced, Berman's Ramadan becomes a shadow on a cave wall: *a figure defined primarily in terms of what he has not denounced.*"[29] And if a man whose actual self-stated agenda is wholesome integration of Muslims into European societies by "[dissolving] the psychological antagonism toward non-Muslims and the West on the part of believing Muslims," if such a man is not allowed a seat at the table, what of Muslims in general?[30] What of their capacities for political participation in the affairs of the world? What of history being animated by their concerns and receptive to their needs? What of their desire for a destination, a resolution, *recognition*? Those Muslims who felt pleasure at the events of 9/11 were clearly not celebrating the death of innocents. And certainly, they were making no declarations of animus toward freedom, equality or democracy. No, they were merely being icons of Muslim futility, of symbolic satisfaction in the absence of any real reversal of fortune. Given the option between absolute compliance at the pointy end of a bayonet and experiencing remote pleasure at mere signs of resistance, they were choosing the latter. And as such, for those in the know, such a response to the towers' destruction was hardly even surprising, or requiring any profound explanation.

* * *

How did it come to this? Normative glosses aside, the genealogy of Muslim futility is not obscure in its historical record. We could begin by pointing to secularism (the more general term for the Jeffersonian compromise) as only one among many broader processes of material, political and cultural restructuring that have beset Muslim societies around the world in the wake of the rapid expansion of Euro-American power in the last two centuries. From the British encroachments into Mughal India in the middle of the eighteenth century to Napoleon's invasion of Egypt in 1798 and all the way to the present, Muslim thinkers have sought to address the novelties of this new age by deploying both dynamic resources made available from within their own traditions and newer forms of knowledge emanating mostly from the West. Muslim polities such as the Ottoman Empire and the Mamluk kingdom in Egypt were the earliest to recognize the need for reform not just as a reactive response to European power, but as salutary for the development of their own communities. But any early intellectual and political successes at reform were quickly overwhelmed by the pace of change associated with the Industrial Revolution, the globalization of European capital, and the eventual conquest of many of these societies by European imperial powers.

Loss of political power and economic clout also meant the gradual erosion of extant languages of moral action and social organization in Muslim societies. These diverse languages together constituted what Marshall Hodgson has called the *Islamicate Weltanschauung*, an overarching system of signs and symbols, of ritual, culture and norms, a *sensus communis* that loosely bound together the bewildering varieties of peoples living under Muslim rule. By the beginning of the eighteenth century, a worldwide system of Islamicate societies stretching from Northwest Africa to the Indonesian archipelago in the east had emerged from a long and complicated interaction of the Middle Eastern Islamic state, religious and communal institutions, and local cultures. And "in each case the interactions generated a different type of Islamic society." Despite the discrete trajectories of their unique evolution, these societies "remained interconnected through political and religious contact."[31] Together they constituted a distinct world system of Muslim societies, though not yet a Muslim world in the contemporary sense of the word. Over the next two centuries, the evolution of these societies was interrupted by European intervention. The old orders, with their concomitant political, intellectual and religious elites, and local industries and economic practices, were everywhere swept away. It was clear to the ruler and the ruled, the elites and the masses, that Muslim societies as reservoirs of cultural, economic and political power could no longer compete.

Following mid-twentieth-century decolonization, the institution of the modern nation-state in such societies has also often disaggregated modernizing elites from the masses and spawned countless crisis of authority that have mostly frustrated attempted resolutions. The latest of these attempts, the Arab Spring of 2011, has only served to reinforce a status quo that now ironically appears to

The Slanted Abyss

be both untenable and inevitable at the same time. And nearly everywhere one looks, these societies are to varying degrees still peripheral in the new world system. In their generalized inferiority of resources to handle the change, they also remain uniquely susceptible to the fragmenting effects of an escalating globalization. The Princeton historian Muhammad Qasim Zaman has noted that "no *rupture* is greater in the history of Islam than that brought about by the impact of Western modernity."[32] European powers did not just take over Muslim lands; piece by piece, they disaggregated the integrated edifice of the Islamicate world. It was as if a long, dark shadow had descended on this world. And it still hangs there today.

What has risen to take the place of this now disaggregated *Weltanschauung*? Nothing in particular. Like Frankenstein's monster, Muslim societies are a hodgepodge of this and that. Dead flesh brought to life by the magic of Western ideology, and careening through modernity like the monster staggering through town, terrorizing the population. But anyone familiar with Mary Shelley's classic knows that the monster is a rather pathetic figure. In being hideous and ill-formed, it is less than the sum of its parts. It is alive and self-conscious, even articulate, but the unwillingness of other humans to give it reciprocal recognition forever denies it the possibility of being fully human itself. It is odious, repulsive and inexplicable. And its rage stems from this pain of inexplicability. It is a being simultaneously appropriated into existence by human ingenuity and expropriated out of humanity on account of his liminality: Is it alive or dead? Is it man or beast? Is it to be pitied or feared? Is it to be acknowledged or obliterated? In manner and form, if not in content, Muslims have become subject to similar questions and the same type of interrogations. The languages in which Muslims historically constructed their identities have been atomized to their constituent parts, to single words such as 'jihad' 'ijtihad', '*umma*', 'Quran' and 'sharia'. And a burgeoning crisis of authority means that lacking a definitive grammar to animate its peculiar form and structure, the vocabulary of Islam now stands emptied and available for appropriation.

Such appropriation is evident in George W. Bush's active theologizing of Islam and its meaning, but no less so in Berman's rejection of Ramadan as a double-talking con man. And it is certainly also evident in the proclamations of Osama bin Laden and in the state-making utopias of Abu Bakr al-Baghdadi's imagination. Each appropriates the emptied signifiers of Islam, infuses them with historical, ideological and theological meanings, and breathes life into his own version of a Muslim golem. In this new world, essentialized appropriations of Islam are hardly limited to the West, or to non-Muslims. In fact, the relentless back and forth between Muslims and non-Muslims is the requisite modulation that energizes this engine of appropriation, these endless inscriptions and re-inscriptions of the meaning of Islam: Is it good or evil? Is it to be pitied or feared? Is it to be recognized or rejected? Is it the problem or the solution? And in the post 9/11 proliferation of global talk about Islam and Muslims, these dueling appropriations have congealed into a unified language of near universal coherence and powerful simplicity. Pankaj Mishra was pointing to precisely this language when he suggested that the "rash of pseudo-explanations [for events involving Muslims] – Islamofascism, Islamic extremism, Islamic fundamentalism, Islamic theology, Islamic irrationalism – makes Islam seem more than ever a concept in search of some content," while the world's nearly 2 billion Muslims are caught in the middle of absurd philological battles concerning the 'essence' of their suspect identities.[33]

* * *

Religion of peace is one particular kind of appropriation of this Muslim identity and experience, religion of violence another. The liberal, modernist and tolerant competes with fundamentalist, obscurantist and fascist in the marketplace of ideas about Islam. Some seek to breathe new life into the monster, others seek to kill it for good. Still others are ambivalent. Of course, this is not to say that there is something inauthentic about these various new meanings of Islam, as though one could peal back the curtain of appropriation to reveal an authentic Muslim essence of this or that sort. All identity formation involves appropriative and meaning-making processes, and a piecing together of coherent narratives from out of available ideological and historical resources. Muslim futility does not stem from a lack of authenticity of this or that Muslim identity (although stories of this sort are ubiquitous in contemporary debates on the meaning of Islam). No, Muslim futility is a necessary corollary of the peculiar architecture of these modern constructions of Islam, and what that architecture allows and what it inhibits. It is that particular set of discursive parameters that compel talk about Islam, and about Muslim identities, inevitably toward an ever-evolving set of either/or propositions: Is Islam compatible with modernity, or not? Will Muslim societies accept modern Western freedoms, or not? Can Muslims living in the West integrate, or not? Or as March put it, are you an Enlightenment liberal or are you soft on stoning? The same kinds of questions first generated in the West then often arise in reverse among the Muslim publics. Here, it is the West being interrogated for its commensurability with Islam. It is for this reason that so much of even the best popular and scholarly literature on Islam naturally hues to topics that accentuate either its familiarity or its unfamiliarity to the West; think hijab vs. human rights, jihad vs. the Arab Spring, ISIS vs. Rumi, etc. Not to summarily dismiss the value of these kinds of projects, but too much ink has already been spilt on domesticating Islam and Muslims within this either/or framework, reanimating dead flesh only to render it mute toward anything other than the question of its essence, the definitive yes/no meaning of its existence in the mirror of the West.

The Slanted Abyss

Such regurgitations of the same old formulas, the same old expositions and interrogations, would be considered farcical if applied to aspects of the West's own evolving norms, politics and history. And yet they have the force of common sense when applied to Muslims. The reason for this discrepancy is the definitive affirmation of total humanity for one side, and a subtle provision of only a liminal humanity for the other. March clearly has this in mind when he ends his review of Berman's book with a series of poignant and searching questions:

> Are all good and decent people destined to converge on the same secular, Enlightenment principles? Is every encounter with strangers about sizing them up as friends or enemies once and for all? How should outsiders seek to influence the moral struggles of other communities, especially religious ones?

March then adds that "these are not easy questions, and Berman is hardly the first to blink in the face of them and choose comforting pieties over curiosity, complexity, and humility."[34] This rather ordinary suggestion, that 'Muslims are people too', falls on deaf ears precisely because for neither Berman nor Bush is this a settled matter. The only difference is that where Berman senses an inexplicable monster, Bush perceives a familiar-looking child being terrorized by an inexplicable monster (who happens to be related to the child). Monster or child, one past its humanity, the other not yet grown into it, are metaphors of liminality, the rhetorical ingredients that make up the discourse of Muslim futility.

The idea that these issues under our consideration are not provincial or proximate to Muslims alone, that they are in fact human issues and worldly issues and must be dealt with as a common concern, is a prerequisite for making a proper "political analysis of our time." Consider, for example, how in addition to Muslim futility, the either/or architecture of talk about Islam has an alarming corollary that hits closer to home in the West. Anti-Muslim animus has often been simplistically conceived as bias rooted in religious, cultural or ethnic differences that lead to personal and structural discrimination, discursive and political marginalization, and sometimes even violence directed against Muslims. But such animus has a long history conceiving of Islam as the very *antithesis* of Western civilization such that an active hostility toward all public signs of Muslimness have often served as a necessary marker of Westernization. The trajectory of Western modernity is therefore intimately tied to the Muslim Question as it plays itself out in various contexts around the world. While 'othering' discourses on Islam have been a consistent historical feature of Western self-imaginings, Islam has now definitively usurped Catholicism's old role as the paradigmatic 'bad religion' refusing to submit to the supremacy of reason *and* of the Jews as the visible, cultural other of the Euro-American imagination. It is in this sense that various appropriations of Islam formulated as *antitheses* exert enormous influence in the continuing evolution of Western societies even as Muslims themselves are increasingly marginalized and rendered ever-more futile.

This suggests that the problem of Muslim futility is not just a Muslim problem. If the continuing development of the normative and cultural underpinnings of Western modernity has now become inextricably intertwined with their appropriations of Islam, then Muslim futility could well be a canary in the mine, a harbinger of troubling times ahead for the regnant world order. As eithers and ors about Islam proliferate in the Euro-American metropoles, they also generate sinister new conceptions of Western culture and identity, and its own attendant values, as completed events – "fully arrived," to use Wendy Brown's formulation – no longer amenable to intervention.[35] In the dark mirror of Islam, Western identity is itself being increasingly assimilated to the binary architecture of the either/or. The signs of such assimilation are everywhere. In London, Paris, Berlin and Washington, DC, battle lines are being drawn around the carcass of Islam and on the bodies of Muslims. But the battles themselves may very well consume these societies as well. A politics of anger and futility is hardly a stranger to the modern history of the West – there are, of course, innumerable examples, but one need look no further than the carnage of the Second World War. And in its latest iteration, such politics is evident as much in the crowds cheering for Donald Trump and Marine Le Pen as in the smiles of those cheering the towers' destruction. The grandee of French Islamicists Oliver Roy worries that "one of the cornerstones of modern democracy is at stake in the debate about Islam ... [when] Islam is perceived as the absolute other whose very presence requires a rethinking of what constitutes a political bond."[36] It is becoming increasingly clear that "anti-Muslim narratives [are] becoming more formulaic and narrow on both sides of the Atlantic since 2000 ... giving rise to convergent lines of questioning," and an otherwise elusive common Euro-American public space "is being created in a negative, paradoxical way as a result of the standardization of polemical debates over Islam."[37] Where the Cold War can be credited with congealing the West as a viable unity into existence, this new supposed clash of civilizations is playing out in conflicts as much inside each contestant as between them. And with the election of Donald J. Trump in the United States and Britain's impending exit from Europe, there is every indication of even more unsettling days ahead.

* * *

There is a scene in the final pages of Tayeb Salih's seminal novel *Season of Migration to the North* (*Mawsim al-Hijrah ilá al-Shamál*) where, in a most explicit manifestation of futility, the Muslim narrator finds himself trapped, floating literally in the middle of the River Nile. The book ends

The Slanted Abyss

with him shouting "Help! Help!" to no one in particular and *sans* any explicit resolution of his predicament.[38] Unwilling to decide between either having him try to make it to the far shore or to swim back to the safety of the near one, Salih leaves his narrator suspended in hesitant stasis over an abyss. This is a fitting conclusion to a story set in mid-1960s Sudan as the country and its people grapple, often ineffectually, with the perplexities of their postcolonial modernity and with the nature and meaning of their existence both as individuals and as a community. The narrator himself, and the main protagonist, are both English-educated 'traveled and returned' men slowly losing their sanity (and, in the case of the protagonist, also visiting insanity on others in both England and Sudan) as the monstrous liminality of their in-between existence causes them to either behave badly or not act at all. The novel is too complex for me to render a suitable precis here – the reader is free to look it up. But suffice it to say that Salih's book effectively evokes the futility of Muslims (and in this specific case, black Africans as well) in the face of the eithers and ors of the West vs. Islam or modernity vs. tradition or religion vs. reason, and the countless other either/ors of contemporary coloniality, as the river of time pushes them inexorably into an unknown future over which they have little control.

It is this same metaphor that the Indian/Pakistani novelist Qurratulain Hyder deploys in her epic *River of Fire* (*Aag ka Duriya*) as she recounts over two thousand years of Indian history through the narrative device of using the same characters being born and reborn, reincarnated again and again in different guises over time until they stumble out into India's imminent vivisection by British colonial authorities in 1947.[39] This Partition (and the capitalization is warranted here), and in particular the 'Muslim' Pakistan that it augured, was a source of agony and consternation for many Indian Muslims such as Hyder who saw their own complex historical identities being obliterated in the either/or of choosing between an ostensibly 'secular' India or a 'Muslim' Pakistan. As with Salih's book, Hyder does not absolve her Muslim characters of guilt altogether, but points to the discursive binaries within which their actions are necessarily embedded and which inevitably prop up figures that conform to these binaries rather than those who reject them. It is this same dread of history cascading down a river of fire that likely triggered the Indian/Pakistani poet Faiz Ahmad Faiz to describe the creation of Pakistan in his elegiac and ironically titled "Dawn of Freedom – August 1947" (*Subh-e-Azadi*) as:

> These tarnished rays, this night-smudged light –
> This is not that Dawn for which, ravished with freedom,
> we had set out in sheer longing,
> so sure that somewhere in its desert the sky harbored
> a final haven for the stars, and we would find it.
> We had no doubt that night's vagrant wave would stray

The Slanted Abyss

towards the shore,
that the heart rocked with sorrow would at last reach
its port.

Friends, our blood shaped its own mysterious roads.
When hands tugged at our sleeves, enticing us to stay,
and from wondrous chambers Sirens cried out
with their beguiling arms, with their bare bodies,
our eyes remained fixed on that beckoning Dawn,
forever vivid in her muslins of transparent light.
Our blood was young – what could hold us back?

Now listen to the terrible rampant lie:
Light has forever been severed from the Dark;
our feet, it is heard, are now one with their goal.
See our leaders polish their manner clean of our suffering:
Indeed, we must confess only to bliss;
we must surrender any utterance for the Beloved – all
yearning
is outlawed.

But the heart, the eye, the yet deeper heart –
Still ablaze for the Beloved, their turmoil shines.
In the lantern by the road the flame is stalled for news:
Did the morning breeze ever come? Where has it gone?
Night weighs us down, it still weighs us down.
Friends, come away from this false light. Come, we must
search for that promised Dawn.[40]

As an astute theorist of his own moment in history (and much as Fanon would do some years later), Faiz recognized the futility of the false dawn of 'independence' as any sort of panacea for what ailed the colonized soul. Yet (and again, just as with Fanon) Faiz was ultimately inspired not by despair, but by hope for "something new," "for that promised Dawn" that is evasive but must be searched for. Still, as this chapter has hopefully made clear, this promised dawn remains elusive even after all these years. And, in fact, the "false light" now appears to be fast bleeding out from under Islam's grim shadow and into the world at large. The forces of negative solidarity are gaining steam everywhere one looks, and abiding hatreds are taking terrifying new forms. It sometimes appears as if the world itself, and in whole, is now floating perilously above a slanted abyss that can no longer be sated by the drowning of Muslim children and monsters, and which is demanding instead a more universal sacrifice worthy of its plunging depths.

So, what is to be done? In *The Human Condition*, Hannah Arendt (a contemporary of Salih, Hyder, Faiz *and* Fanon) bemoaned "the heedless recklessness or hopeless confusion or complacent repetition of 'truths' which have become trivial and empty" in the modern world. What she proposed in response was a "reconsideration of the human condition from the vantage point of our newest experiences and our most recent fears." This, she said, is "nothing more than to think what we are doing." This awkward formulation, "to think what we are doing," is surely one of the more enigmatic remedies for the recklessness, confusions and repetitions of the modern age. For in one sense, it is no remedy at all. Arendt herself concedes that to "the preoccupations and perplexities" of modernity, her "book does not offer an answer" because "such answers ... are matters of practical politics, subject to the agreement of many; they can never lie in theoretical considerations or the opinion of one person."[41] But no amount of political deliberation can furnish answers if the right questions themselves are obscured by a prior "failure to make a political analysis of our time" as per Mamdani or "choosing [of] comforting pieties over curiosity, complexity, and humility" as per March. Such answers will continue to elude us in Fanon's "compartmentalized world ... inhabited by different species" for a politics adequate to reconciling this world requires at least an acknowledgment of our shared humanity. "To think what we are doing" is then an inducement to linger on first-order problems before hurtling mindlessly, recklessly in Arendt's formulation, into the same confusions and repetitions, the futile banging of heads on walls, the exasperations with the other that define the relationship between the Muslim world and the West. Which is to say, to first think through what we mean when we refer to a 'Muslim world' and to 'the West'. What are the historical, ideological and political bases of the common-sense reality of these categories and why do they exert such oversized influence in our contemporary deliberations?

The same goes for terms such as 'modernity', 'progress' and 'development' that form the backbone of Western self-understandings, and undergird the language in which Muslims are often spoken about and evaluated. It is to these foundational questions that we must now turn first.

2

Mirror, Mirror ...

Why does talk about Islam cling so persistently to the clean binaries of the either/or? The events of 9/11 themselves and the various iterations of the 'War on Terror' are obvious candidates for an explanation. Perhaps the causal soup of 9/11 was far too thick with historical and political entanglements to parse out each ingredient for edifying consumption by an anxious public. So, shorthand cultural and theological explanations served the rhetorical purposes of well-wishers and adversaries of Muslims alike. This is true to a certain extent. But scholars and public intellectuals had been indulging in such forms of talk for decades in advance of the twenty-first-century explosion of Islam into mainstream public consciousness; 9/11 merely weaponized pre-existing dispositions toward these essentialist treatments of Islam and Muslims and of their proper place in a world order dominated by the West. The dispositional *binaries themselves are in fact of ancient vintage. They have their origins in the intertwined sentiments of civilizational mission and intense race consciousness associated with the nineteenth-century European imperial expansion that birthed the modern world as we know it today. And in the various Muslim responses to this fact of European 'superiority' over the last two centuries or so. In this chapter, I track this historical waltz between the expansion of European power and the parallel diminishment of Muslim control over much of the Middle East and India in the nineteenth century as the most significant drivers in the emergence of essentializing accounts of Islam and its inferiority to an emergent West. These accounts became interpolated with the new language of race, reason and civilization in ways that fundamentally altered the previously existing status of Islam and Muslims in the European imagination (and vice versa). Both 'the Muslim world' and, in part, 'the West' are novel conceptual creations of what this new language made cognitively possible, ideologically coherent and politically desirable.*

* * *

G.W.F. Hegel's master–slave dialectic has confounded philosophers for decades and it is not my intention to adjudicate its *true* meaning here.[1] But surely most would agree with Robert Brandom's attendant insight that "asymmetric recognitive relations are metaphysically defective [because] the norms they institute aren't the right kind to help us think and act with."² This metaphysical defect is evident in Hegel's intuition that neither master nor slave is free, just subjected by the relationship in different ways. Contra Immanuel Kant, Hegel does not equate the experience of true freedom with the rational autonomy of the individual, but with recognition by another rationally autonomous being. So, neither power nor responsibility, in themselves, offer durable panacea against the constitutive pathology of lordship and bondage. Only a recognitive synthesis can (provisionally) resolve the problem.³ Frantz Fanon gives his own normative gloss on this aspect of the dialectic by declaring that "the white man is locked in his whiteness" in his (post)colonial relationship with his black subjects.⁴ In his condescending contempt for non-European stock, "[a] white man talking to a person of color behaves exactly like a grown-up with a kid."⁵ And a child can only evidence the adult's authority over him; by definition, it lacks standing to give the adult any reciprocal recognition. The futility of this relationship provokes Fanon to assert that "something new must be created – neither a resuscitation of their historical culture nor an imitation of the colonizer's culture"⁶ – "if [the colonized] want humanity to take one step forward ... to another level than the one where Europe has placed it." Fanon clearly rejects the latent naturalism in Hegel's idea of history. But he still relies on a dialectical mechanics for the slave's liberation in the fabrication of a "new man" synthesized from an agonistic encounter between the colonized and the colonizer.⁷

Fanon's political reading of Hegel's phenomenological myth has had a profound impact on revolutionary movements in the postcolonial world, exerting enormous influence on figures as diverse as Ali Shariati in Iran, Che Guevara in Cuba, and Steve Biko in South Africa. There are even echoes of Fanon's creative agonism and his "new man" in Malcolm X's militant black nationalism. It is no mystery why Fanon has such great appeal in sociopolitical contexts still riven by (real or perceived) arrangements of neo-colonial or racist subjugation. His advocacy of violence against the colonizer as "a cleansing force [that] rids the colonized of their inferiority complex, of their passive and despairing attitude" is modular in its relevance to any and all approximations of an oppressive master–slave relationship.[8] And few can match Fanon's combination of lyricism, pathos and righteous indignation for the wretched of the Earth in the political vortex of the twentieth century's middle years.

Still, it begs attention that Fanon is read primarily as a worthy tribune of the dispossessed, not more widely, and simply, as a philosopher of the modern age. To be sure, he does cut an interesting figure in contemporary academic discourse but mostly as "an object either of worship or hatred and fear," quoted often by leftists who have mostly not read his work, "an old-fashioned third-worldist and antimondialist" with a quaint "revolutionary theory that apologizes for violence" and not much more.[9] In this sense at least, Fanon sadly epitomizes, in his own person, the very condition of being locked out that he describes in his work. And such a rendering is hardly a one-off affair, being of a piece with the general provincializing of non-Euro-American thinkers or the reduction of their contributions to the specifics of their context.[10] But, à la Hegel, Fanon identifies self-consciousness as an emergent property of the encounter between self and other. His particular emphasis on the psychopathology of colonialism is in this sense at least as instructive about the nature and meaning of whiteness as it is of blackness. Or as Lewis R. Gordon has pointed out, Fanon's "profound social existential analysis of antiblack racism ... led him to identify conditions of skewed rationality and reason in contemporary discourses on the human being."[11] This "skewed rationality" preventing "humanity from taking one step forward" is symptomatic of the asymmetric recognitive relations attendant to modern racism and imperialism. The dialectic processes that move history forward break down in the regime of such asymmetry. Self-consciousness hardens and identities become locked in a perverse mirroring resonance between self and other. And with no recourse to a Hegelian rationality of the real, or a self-steering history, Fanon imagines cathartic violence as necessary to reignite the dialectic engine of history, to move humanity "to another level than the one where Europe has placed it." Fanon is clearly concerned about more than just the fate of the black man; the common context of human existence made small in the age of empire and science, the world itself needs rescue and rejuvenation.

This is a very different sort of story than the usual, triumphalist narrative of progress we are all familiar with. Fanon is rejecting the premise that independence will allow the colonized to join the march of modernity and catch up, so to say, with his erstwhile captors in a new bonhomie of equals. From his perspective, something is ineluctably broken about this world that Europeans have created and which all of humanity now calls home. To mimic whiteness, then, is to peddle in self-hate. But worse, it offers no permanent escape from the malaise. Fanon is not interested in provisional solutions, but a total "elimination of the vicious circle ... [of] dual narcissism" that locks the colonizer and the colonized into a feedback loop masquerading as an open circuit.[12] For the norms and values, the institutional and cultural forms generated in such a feedback loop "aren't the right kind to help us think and act with." *Sans* a revitalizing dialectic intervention, the making of something new, the history of this world will keep moving in circles. It will not move on.

This futile moving in circles is clearly evident in the West's relations with the Muslim world. Even to the extent that the very categories of 'the West' and a 'Muslim world' are themselves a kind of miasmic froth agitating atop an asymmetric recognitive relationship breaking endlessly on the same shore, year after year. Zareena Grewal has argued that the Muslim world is at its core "a Western idea built on the faulty racial logic that Muslims live in a world of their own – that Islam is an eastern, foreign religion that properly belongs in a distant, faraway, dusty place."[13] It is a world inhabited by Muslim hearts and minds, steeped in Muslim culture, populated by hijab-clad Muslim women and bearded Muslim men. Most importantly, it is a world apart, addressed often in whole by American presidents with benign condescension just as it was theorized about with apprehension by colonial administrators in yester-years. This place, this idea, even in its most benevolent renderings, has always served as a marker of "an exotic but inferior culture ... as weak, decadent, depraved, irrational and fanatical," and as one of the many contrasting mirrors in which the West gave birth to itself as "civilized, dynamic and superior."[14] The modern world, then, a world created by Europe and inhabited by all, a world made small and immediate with crisscrossing lines of commerce, information, people and bombs, is at once both singular and plural. Fanon called it a "compartmentalized world, this world divided in two ... inhabited by different species" where the singularity of the context is coextensive with the regimes of difference it necessarily entails.[15] This is a world enclosed as one by the expansion of European power but always experienced as fractured because the mechanism of said enclosure is the superimposition of a very specific form of alterity. It is in this sense that when "Americans refer to the 'Muslim World' they reproduce, amend and complicate Colonial Europe's moral geography of the Orient."[16] But the logic of these amendments and reproductions is to always continuously lock and relock this place *in* place, like a tidally locked moon showing its host planet the same differently familiar face in spite of its endless rotations and revolutions.

* * *

This face of Islam, a disclosure of unity in the enclosure of another unity, has been a familiar one only since around the waning years of the nineteenth century. Writing for *Aeon* magazine, Faisal Devji cautions that while "the ideal of universal agreement in Islam might have existed before … it seldom constituted a political or even religious project beyond fairly circumscribed arenas of debate."[17] Other recent scholarship has definitively established the modern vintage of this idea. In an excellent new monograph, the historian Cemil Aydin has identified its origins in the epochal transition from the age of imperial rivalries to an increasingly racialized conflict among nations and civilizations in the political *imaginaire* of the nineteenth century. Islamic empires and Christendom had, to be sure, faced each other across the Bosporus and the Mediterranean often (though not always) as enemies since the Middle Ages. But the mutual suspicion was predicated on mutual understanding and recognition. As sovereign imperial orders competing for subjects and wealth, they spoke the same political language. Though never entirely absent, the rhetoric of religious difference was incidental and instrumental to other core concerns. "Jihad," for example, "may have been part of the language in some of these conflicts, but the logic of Muslim friend and Christian enemy did not apply." And in any case, no Muslim ruler imagined war with Christian enemies as defense against "a Western threat to a shared Muslim world."[18] Even as European powers began to encroach and then penetrate into lands previously under Muslim control in the seventeenth and eighteenth centuries, the context was trade, not a "European" civilization at war with an "Islamic" civilization.[19] The cosmopolitan empires of this era could well harbor great prejudice against Muslims or Christians depending on the polity involved, but "neither made geo-political distinctions between the Muslim world and the West." And certainly, "even when pre nineteenth-century Muslim writers distinguished Muslim lands from others, they had no concept of Muslims the world over unified in civilizational and religious unity against a common enemy."[20] Whatever enmities there were between Muslims and Christians, they were horizontally aligned in complex patterns of interest, ideology and power. Going all the way back to the Middle Ages, this relationship had been deeply agonistic, and punctuated by periods of great violence. But its "mixture of fear [and] bewilderment" was often leavened by an "uneasy recognition of a kind of spiritual kinship."[21] And in any case, it lacked the kind of constitutive recognitive asymmetry described by Hegel or Fanon.

The earliest phase of the modern military encroachment of European power and ideas into Muslim lands, which began with Napoleon's invasion of Egypt in 1798 and ended roughly with the Sepoy Mutiny in British India in 1857, was also markedly different from what followed. Beginning with developments in Cairo, one Muslim polity after another recognized the superiority of European models of military and government organization. And Muslims generally, and worldwide, quickly became attentive to the advances in science and technology emanating from across the Mediterranean. Still, "the imperial reforms that followed were not necessarily identified with secularism and pro-Westernism" in any meaningfully relevant sense but with imperial self-strengthening. The Ottoman reform process, called *Tanzimat*, was designed primarily "to secure the empire's place in the Concert of Europe, thereby also strengthening European imperial norms." Similar reforms were quickly taken up in Egypt, Tunisia and Iran. These early reformist elites certainly drew "inspiration from civilized Europe" but they "did not see themselves as victims of Europe [or] as outsiders seeking entry into European society."[22] The journalist Christopher de Bellaigue argues, for example, that although the centers of Muslim power were clearly "caught up in a vortex of change," reformist elites were keen to engage the outside world in "a sustained intellectual and social correspondence," and to integrate new ideas about governance, science and industry for the salutary development of their own societies.[23]

On the European end, Napoleon's "proclamation following the invasion [of Egypt] contained encomia to

Muhammad and Islam [and] he later claimed that the prophet himself had come to him in a dream."[24] Further belying any narrative construction of these events as a clash between Christianity and Islam, Napoleon was so eager "to endear himself to the Muslim population that his officers asked Egyptian clerics whether his conversion to Islam would legitimize his rule."[25] Farther east, British advances into India escalated primarily in preservation of their economic and commercial interests. Some company officers even went native, producing an entire class of Euro-Indian 'White Mughals' whose fascinating late eighteenth- and early nineteenth-century lives augured an intriguing future that unfortunately never materialized.[26] The eminent Middle East Studies scholar Albert Hourani claims that even Enlightenment treatments of Islam were decidedly mixed, alternating between "the use of the career of Muhammad as an oblique way to criticize Christianity ... [in his] excesses of enthusiasm and ambition" and depictions of Muhammad "as preaching a religion which was more rational, or nearer to purely natural faith, than Christianity." There was no general and uncontested identification of Muslims with barbarism or Islam with resistance to reason. And in the 50th chapter of Edward Gibbon's magisterial *The Decline and Fall of the Roman Empire*, which reflected the thinking of many of his contemporaries, "Muhammad appeared in as favorable a light as any religious leader could" and, at least early in his prophetic ministry, as a man of "original and superior genius."²⁷ While Europeans were convinced of their newfound material superiority over many of their Muslim neighbors and subjects, an ideological basis for the superiority of 'the West' over the 'Muslim world' was nowhere self-evident.

This all began to change in the nineteenth century when a series of momentous developments in Europe gave birth to an embryonic form of the contemporary relationship between Islam and the West. First, an intellectual project "ongoing since the Renaissance, to create 'Europe' as a transcendental idea, composed of a set of Enlightened ideals" reached its political apogee in the 'Eastern Question', which furnished the European public with "a unified and separate geography differentiated from 'dark' lands lying outside it."²⁸ Paradigmatic also of the increasing 'Christianization' of imperial frontiers was "the romantic notions of Greece's place in the history of Europe, and Russia's arguments for freedom of Orthodox Christians from the [Ottoman] sultan" during the Greek War of Independence.²⁹ It is in this context, and coupled with an Enlightenment critique of religion gradually shifting its attention to the Orient, that Islam first emerged as a self-evident "cultural unity with a ... central core," a religion antithetical to Christian Europe, and bereft of reason, lacking in vigor, addled with superstition.³⁰ Already by 1853, the Count Arthur de Gobineau, "a curious mixture of frustrated nobleman and romantic intellectual," had theorized a grand history of mankind where "the fall of civilizations is due to the degeneration of race and the decay of race is due to a mixture of blood."[31] But it was Darwinian notions of evolution that finally provided firm scientific scaffolding for the continuing construction of racialized others in Europe's burgeoning colonies as not only different, but biologically inferior and less evolved. Buttressed by the works of noted polymaths such as Herbert Spencer and Gustave Le Bon, this scientific form of racism was to prove incredibly effective as a public, intellectual and respectable discourse among European elites about their Muslim subjects as "an inferior, colored race" of Semitic ethnicity who on account of their religion were "prone to rebellion against global white hegemony."[32]

In addition, the concept of 'civilization' went through an impressive and consequential evolution from a provincial eighteenth-century French reference to judicial processes "extending out from the courts to wider reaches of society," to its widespread use in nineteenth-century European metropoles to "identify a *transnational* group of Enlightened civilized nations in opposition to their colonies."[33] Voltaire had already set the stage for a comparative historicization of the world based on civilizational development (with Europe at its apex).[34] But Lewis H. Morgan's scientifically sophisticated theory of social evolution furnished civilization with taxonomies of difference that rendered colonial subjects 'savage' or 'barbarian' in their lagging development. In the aftermath of the Darwinian revolution, there also emerged a picture of the world as populated by different species of people, of civilizations in the plural, locked in a struggle for the 'survival of the fittest' where material, economic and political domination conferred superior status on the Europeans.[35] In the regime of this complementary schema, Muslims began to be imagined either as passive racialized objects of a civilizing mission by enlightened Europeans, or as members of a distinct and inferior civilization in terminal decline, and sometimes both at the same time. And in the mid to late nineteenth century, they were therefore subjected to a "new style of empire starkly inflected by race, the borders of which were drawn along multiple lines, not just physical features of human bodies but also religion and perceptions of shared history and political loyalty."[36]

Just as significant was the post-Enlightenment development of a lay form of messianism that had much of Western Europe's learned public in its thrall during the middle decades of the nineteenth century. Contrary to received wisdom, in its heyday "nineteenth century positivism was not a 'value free' scientific method … [but] rather in the 'myth of science', positivism was the expression of an inner-worldly faith in human welfare and progress in replacing traditional religion by rational science."[37] This "cosmology of progress" is a recurring, and requisite, feature in the works of a diverse set of writers and thinkers who together constitute the pulse of their age.[38] It is evident in the romanticized, post-Christian positivism of philologist Ernest Renan, who developed a "philosophy of history in which science came to play a divine role."[39] In Karl Marx, the salvific process is powered by the laws of historical materialism, but his eschatology is clearly tied to the progress of humanity's mastery over the natural world as a kind of ordained mandate that culminates in the absolute destruction of evil and a heaven on earth. Even Auguste Comte fancied himself pope of the new "Religion of Humanity" and Oeuvres de Saint-Simon dreamed of temples dedicated to Newton. The neat periodization of religion, enlightenment, romanticism and positivism in the linear development of ideas is belied by the bewildering combination of impulses and aspirations in the whirlpool of nineteenth-century Europe.

What emerges from these disparate and often conflicting inclinations is the idea of a singular world, populated by a singular humanity, subject to a universal, natural history and fueled by the laws of universal progress as revealed by the magic of modern science. Yet this world is also compartmentalized in the parallel development of the European as a kind of World-Subject par excellence, the eyes and ears of humanity, investigating from his universal vantage point all the different objects of this newly discovered world in order to engineer its salvation. In this reading, Islam is a deficient and retrograde mechanism for observing and organizing this world and is therefore, as such, something "sordid and repulsive."[40] And while science and reason are in fact universal, the primacy of the European subject is predicated on the provident peculiarities of his ethnohistorical trajectory that has not, and perhaps cannot, be replicated elsewhere without salutary supervision. The Muslim world is one such 'elsewhere' in a plural universe of provincial backwaters that all reside, uncomfortably, within a European 'World' in the singular universal.

Although it would blunder on till the end of the First World War, the old cosmopolitan imperial system was rendered ever-more untenable in this new world of race, nationalism, progress and civilization(s). The Ottomans did their level best to "uphold the universalism of the Concert of Europe" throughout much of the nineteenth century, but they increasingly became "identified with a distinctive Muslimness in both European metropoles and Muslim colonies," possessed by a peculiar form of "Muslim despotism unworthy of alliance and in need of further division."[41] Navigating this complex new reality provoked a variety of responses and counter-responses that eventually congealed into a standard European identification of Muslims with uniquely high levels of piety and devotion, and on account of this exceptional attachment to their religion, as constituting a single world community bound together by the nature and essence of their faith. The bewildering variety of actually existing Muslim societies were merely discrete manifestations of the same Islamic genus, their racialized Muslimness now being the operative condition and explanation of their history, culture and motivations. Islam's civilizational inferiority was confirmed with each European encroachment into lands under Muslim political rule, and any resistance to European interests was quickly folded into a standard account of the 'Muslim peril'. In seeking an explanation, for example, for the 1857 Sepoy Mutiny in India against British East India Company rule, "British colonial officers openly discussed whether Muslims, as opposed to Hindus, could be loyal subjects of the empire."[42] A best-selling account of these events was W.H. Carey's suggestively titled 1857 book *The Mahomedan Rebellion*, followed later by W.W. Hunter's alarmist 1871 book *The Indian Musalmans*. The latter text's ostensibly provincial concerns are belied by its panoramic treatment of "Muslims [as] everywhere the same because Islam was some kind of trans-historical force that [determined] their thoughts and actions [and therefore] posed a trans-regional threat."[43] It is with this uniformity of faith, and especially with this threat in mind, that many European imperial powers became increasingly embroiled in the religious life of their Muslim subjects, generating new classes of specialized intermediaries to manage Muslim communities in their far-flung empires, and creating separate regimes of legal and political participation based on specialized knowledge about Islam.[44]

As Christian missionaries poured into formerly Muslim principalities across the globe, they also "embedded their theological claims in imperial and racial hierarchies by portraying European imperial hegemony and scientific progress as signs of God's favor to Christians" over Muslims.[45] And bolstered in equal parts by tales of traveling adventurers and of colonial administrators (and sometimes also of their wives), it was during this time that the Orient first became fixed in the European imagination as an idea of essentialized difference, at once effeminate, decadent and arrested in its development, but also menacing, ominous, a kind of surrogate other for Europeans, or even, as in Edward Said's formulation, an "underground self."[46] With this notion of the Orient as cipher for continent-wide debates on the causes of Muslim inferiority, threat and/or decline, the scholarly study of Islam was not immune from all manners of theories mixing philology, philosophy and phrenology, essentialized accounts of 'desert mentalities' and deficient geographies, racialized affinities (or lack thereof) for science, reason and religious commitments. But always looming as the catch-all explanation was "Islam … [a word] that [appeared] rarely in premodern titles, but after the nineteenth century … [was] everywhere."[47] The Eastern Question did not morph definitively into the Muslim Question until the final dissolution of the Ottoman Empire in the 1920s. Still, Islam was already locked in as a polyvalent signifier of tremendous explanatory power by the end of the nineteenth century. And in many ways, it is still locked there today.

* * *

The Muslim world is another name, then, for this Orientalized, essentialized and/or racialized view of Islam as a totalizing authority in the lives of its adherents. Predicated on the "powerful orientalist pretensions of a principle of epistemological and ontological difference between the East and the West," it also often hints at an "enduring cultural essence, the fundamental and unchangeable attributes of ... Islam."[48] The dynamics of its construction, its resident manifestations in the culture, literature and *governmentality* of the colonizing West, and of course the sinews in which it resides to this day in the global body politic, have all been well covered by Edward W. Said, Talal Asad and their legion of acolytes. For our purposes and for now, it must be noted that this Muslim world is no myth, fable or fiction. The polemical temptation to paint it as such is strong among some scholarly well-wishers of Islam and Muslims. But this often leads them down a slippery slope to a futile rhetoric of authenticity that stubbornly refuses the discursive reality of an idea that has global relevance and operates well beyond the confines of its European birthplace. Edward Said acknowledged, for example, that:

> [Even if] Orientalism is more valuable as a sign of Euro-Atlantic power over the Orient than it is as a veridic discourse about the Orient ... any system of ideas that can remain teachable wisdom (in academies, books, congresses, universities, foreign service institutes) from the period of Ernest Renan in the late 1840s until the present in the United States must be something more formidable than a mere collection off lies.[49]

No, not a collection of lies, not even merely a system of ideas about the Orient per se. Instead, it is something much more complicated and durable precisely because it establishes the terms on which any intelligible discussion of Islam could hitherto take place. Not a unified system of ideas, then, but rather an evolving constellation of either/or options, shifting with time but maintaining its binary architecture, such that even a rejection of any particular proposition about Islam is locked into playing on the same discursive AstroTurf as any affirmations.

In *The Origins of Totalitarianism*, for example, Hannah Arendt decries the simplistic theory of the Jew as an abstract, generalized and powerless scapegoat during the rise of anti-Semitism, "a story dear to the heart of many liberals," for it erroneously "upholds the perfect innocence of the victim, an innocence which insinuates not only that no evil was done but that nothing at all was done which might possibly have a connection with the issue at stake."[50] Edward Said has often been rightly criticized for making this very same error, of rendering the Oriental himself entirely incidental to the story, and almost as effete in Said's treatment of him as he is in the Orientalist imagination.[51] As Said himself admits in his later works, the historical record clearly suggests otherwise. Consider, for example, the undeniable popularity among turn-of-the-century Muslims themselves of the idea of a Muslim world; or of the narrative of civilizational decline, and the need for reform and rejuvenation of Islam; or of the oft-repeated twaddle that Islam is not a religion but a way of life; or of the nostalgia for a unified *umma*, and political glory for Muslims qua Muslims. I could go on. These notions may have begun their life in the collective minds of colonizing Europeans, but from the mid-nineteenth century onwards their potency derived as much from Muslim appropriations, amendments and revisions of these same ideas in a discursive feedback loop with their European interlocutors. It is important to note here that reform as such is "neither an innovation nor a novelty" in the Islamic tradition, which has often "[conceptualized] human history as a continuum of renewal, revival, and reform (*tajdid, ihya', and islah*) ... for safeguarding and ensuring the continuity of a moral community."[52] Reform movements are in fact ubiquitous in Muslim history, bubbling up often in times of crisis, and especially during periods of political uncertainty or conflict with foreign powers. Engagement with and assimilation of new forms of knowledge from Greek, Persian, Indian and Chinese sources have also been, from the very beginning, ongoing and integral aspects of the development of Muslim societies. But before the nineteenth century, Muslims in various parts of the world, with their admittedly diverse worldviews, had not as a whole been confronted by a challenge with the ideological, epistemological and political vigor of colonizing Europe. The polemical back and forth between Muslim men of religion and Christian missionaries that had energized the mid-century public squares from Delhi to Cairo and Istanbul gradually gave way to a sobering retreat by Muslim apologists into a defensive posture against an unceasing evaluative glare that judged Islam deficient. And stretched thin by the spaghettifying forces of an escalating asymmetry, Muslim thinkers increasingly began to theorize the religion of Islam and a world of Muslims in terms that shared hue with those of their European inquisitors.

Up until the 1840s, for example, "Mirza Asadullah Ghalib and Syed Ahmad Khan, two prominent Indian intellectuals, could [still] weigh the merits of the British and Mughal empires" in a comparative perspective without overt reference to religion.[53] But by 1879, so dire was the situation for Islam itself in this new regime of European power that their countryman Khwaja Altaf Hussain Hali lamented "the dilapidated halls of the true religion, whose pillars have been tottering for ages [and] which will remain in the world only a few days more."[54] Over in Istanbul, Şemseddin Sami Frashëri worried that "today civilization seems to belong exclusively to the Christian nations" and chided his co-religionists for making a mockery of Islam in their fanaticism and backwardness.[55] The peripatetic Sayyid Jamal al-Din al-Afghani sounded decidedly positivist in arguing that "it is science that everywhere manifests its greatness and power [and] ignorance has no alternative to prostrating itself humbly before science and knowledge."[56] Still, he deflected European attacks on Islam by claiming that "the Islamic religion is the closest of religions to science and knowledge … [which are] the foundation of the

Islamic faith."⁵⁷ Afghani's Egyptian acolyte Muhammad Abduh (re)discovered the principle of 'the survival of the fittest' in the Quran itself and explained the inferiority of Muslim societies, "the social illnesses in the Orient" as he called them, "the humiliation of nations" as the turning away from *true* Islam, which was naturally in accordance with reason, and "the source of power, glory and happiness to its [original] followers."⁵⁸ Having lost most of his Christian subjects to nationalist movements in the Balkans, and both Tunisia and Egypt to European powers in the 1880s, the Ottoman Sultan AbdulHamid II finally abandoned the pretense of the Concert of Europe and began to encourage the new idea of an Ottoman Caliphate as a pan-Islamic entity with filial relevance to all Muslims. The political questions of imperial subjecthood had gradually given way to an existential crisis of identity. From India to the Maghreb, Muslims were mired in a collective mood of looming jeopardy and furiously debated what had gone wrong with their common history.

In her most recent work, India-based historian Seema Alavi has traced the movement of people and ideas across the imperial frontiers in the aftermath of the Sepoy Mutiny of 1857. She argues that already by the beginning of the nineteenth century, the unraveling of the Mughal political order had instigated reformers such as the Delhi Naqshbandi Sufi Shahwaliulla to imagine "an alternative political imperium for Muslims via the universal appeal of the scriptures and individual agency" and to begin to ground their new political theologies firmly in the Arabic canonical texts, the Quran and the Hadith. Under the sway of an Indo-Persianate imperium, the Arabic sources had great ritual and symbolic significance but little theological or political relevance. These canonical texts, and concepts such as *tauhid* and *umma*, came to the forefront in the religious and political imagination of Muslims in India as a direct consequence of the erstwhile imperium being in tatters and the successor states being picked off one by one by the British East India Company. After the rebellion, as colonial officers turned their suspicious gaze onto Indian Muslims and pursued many of them right out of the country, the "spirit of 1857" and its concomitant "political culture [that was] both global and Arabist in its orientation" circulated in the wider Muslim ecumene as these exiles and emigres made their way to the cosmopolitan centers of Mecca, Cairo and Istanbul.[59] These nodes of imperial power and influence were all awash in European ideas such as Orientalism, race, social Darwinism and Eurocentric accounts of history that amalgamated into novel formulations as they mixed with Muslim thinking from various parts of the world. Alavi describes how trade networks spawned by the new market realities of European capitalism and a booming publishing industry greatly facilitated the development of a shared Muslim consciousness in this cosmopolitan milieu as information and people moved across the globe with ever-increasing ease and the perilous "fate of Muslims seemed more unified than ever."[60]

The Muslim world may well have been a European construct. But its innards were of decidedly local vintage in the native lands of Islam.

So, as the century drew to a close, some clear patterns were beginning to emerge in the thinking of Muslim intellectual elites. The theme of civilizational decline was everywhere common sense, as was the collective culpability of Muslims as authors of their own sordid fate. Dislike of European powers was tempered with a sober admiration for their highly evolved societies. The need for reform, renewal and rejuvenation was being preached from all corners. The terms 'Islam' and 'Muslim' had acquired a kind of abstract general validity as references to something identifiably unitary and requiring exposition and explanation. It was only here, at this point of exposition and explanation of the nature and essence of Islam, that Muslims consistently disagreed with their European counterparts. They reimagined the early centuries of Islam as a golden age of science and reason, of the progressive spirit of philosophy and great works of art and architecture. They discovered democratic and constitutionalist norms in the Prophet's community in Medina, and a regime of rights in the Quran to match the European canon. They even theorized that Europe itself owed a debt of gratitude to Muslims for its Renaissance rediscovery of the classics. In less than a century, Islam had brought a Bedouin people to the very apex of world-historical power and made Muslim civilization the greatest of its time. No, the problem was not with the Islamic DNA, but its corruption by Muslims of later years. But the idea of an Islamic DNA itself, of a racialized Muslim people, of a world organized around and through the political, cultural and historical essences attendant to these realities, was by this time a prerequisite to any further conversation.

This discovery of Islam as an animating essence, a code or doxa through which Muslim life as such can be organized, had profound implications for further articulations of the Muslim world in the twentieth century. As Europe's imperial hegemony became a settled fact of life, many Muslims also began to imagine the essence of Islam in direct opposition to the West and its values and institutions. In the inverse mirror of their so-called modernist counterparts and antecedents, this fundamentalist form of Islam also reached back for a golden age of Muslim ascendancy to decipher what had gone wrong with Islamic civilization. But instead of excavating the history and sacred sources of Islam for signs of familiarity with the West, they fashioned their beatific visions of renewal in the rejection of it. Writing in the middle years of the twentieth century in pre-partition India, Sayyid Abul A'la Maududi claimed that "the various phases of Islamic life and activity flow from [the] fundamental postulates exactly as the plant sprouts forth from its seed," and that "unconditional faith [in these fundamentals] is the first and foremost requirement of Islam."[61] Maududi easily mixed biological metaphors and Quranic literalism with a self-consciously anti-Western political theory of Islam that was still deeply embedded in Western ideas about the state, sovereignty, law and rights. Over in Iran, Jalal Al-e Ahmad in Iran explicitly speaks "of being afflicted with 'Westitis' the way [he] would speak of being afflicted with cholera."[62] And Sayyid Qutb perfected the "Manichaean lines of destructive mutual opposition" in identifying the West with *jahilliyyah*, and demanding a revolutionary vanguard to plot the overthrow of Muslim despots who kowtow to it.[63] These rejections of Western claims of superiority were also dismissals of the possibility of a political relationship between Muslims and Westerners. The fear of the other had been internalized, and the other's sense of privilege inverted to produce the vision of true Islam as the anti-West, and similarly universalist in its aspirations for total domination.

It is in this sense that whether it is imagined in its modernist varieties or articulated in the fundamentalist manner, all talk about the Muslim world continues to be derivative of the essentializing accounts first generated in nineteenth-century Europe. And by the beginning of the twentieth century, such accounts had taken firm root in Muslim communities worldwide. The contours of contemporary debates on Islam were already in place. These debates would undergo shifts in emphasis over the next century, switching terms and changing frills around the edges. And the later emergence of a Muslim form of modern anti-modernism and a Euro-American form of Islamophilia have added new wrinkles to the still endlessly repeating backs and forth. But the basic discursive architecture of these debates has remained remarkably resilient.

* * *

What explains this resilience? Fanon's contention that the "white man is locked into his whiteness" offers one clue. His additional insight, that "Europe has placed" the world at the level where "[a] white man talking to a person of color behaves exactly like a grown-up with a kid," offers another. There is something about the modern configuration of Euro-American power that is both resistant to adjustment from outside itself and condescending toward those subject to its continuing control. Such condescension is evident, for example, in the French treatment of its conquered peoples as "both ... brothers and ... subjects – brothers in the fraternity of a common civilization and subjects in that they are disciples of French light and followers of French leading."[64] This manner of dual inclusion/exclusion is paradigmatic of the more liberal trends in early Euro-American imperialism, best exemplified by Rudyard Kipling's poem "The White Man's Burden" but evident throughout much of the twentieth century, even up to the present. This pedagogical model imagines the world as a classroom occupied by teachers and pupils, where the instructors always remain the same, locked into their creedal roles, their salvific obligations. In this theatre of perpetual beatific instruction, no pupil is allowed to act out of role, to graduate, so to say, out into the real world. "We don't need no education," Fanon seems to be saying, "We don't need no thought control."[65] For the architecture of the relationship between the white man and the black man is resilient precisely because, in every ostensibly benign iteration, it cements its confining apparatus into place, walls the black man in and leaves the white man on top with a switch.

But Fanon's possible anticipation of the Pink Floyd hit by over a decade has a kink in it that needs adjustment. Already by the time of Fanon's mature writings, explicit race talk had become unfashionable among the educated classes of Europe and North America. This was partly in response to the self-consciously racist political program of Nazi Germany and the devastation it had visited on the world. Partly also "a desire to challenge the global influence of the Soviet Union whose anti-racist credentials were taken seriously, even by anti-communists."[66] The scientific basis for discrete races had already been undermined by current research in genetics and heredity by the 1930s, and biologists such as Sir. Julian S. Huxley and Alfred C. Haddon were recommending that "the word *race* should be banished, and the descriptive and non-committal term *ethnic group* should be substituted ... [so as to avoid] connotations of homogeneity, of purity of descent, and so forth."[67] Liberation struggles across Europe's imperial holdings had also exposed the tensions between ostensibly liberal political orders at home and racially oppressive ones in the colonies. And a form of reactive race consciousness disaggregated from white supremacy had emerged in writings about the distinct genius of Islamic, Indian, Asian or African peoples by a diverse set of non-European thought leaders such as Mohandas Gandhi, Rabindranath Tagore, Liang Qichao and Marcus Garvey. Racism was hardly dead as a social, political and legal phenomenon. But by the middle of the twentieth century, its time as a discourse of justification for the Euro-American world order had largely come and gone. Fanon's framing of the issues in terms of black and white, his deployment of slaves and masters, was therefore a self-conscious provocation of his audiences. Behind a new façade of enlightened civility still lurked the same old prejudices of constitutive, racial difference seared into the very skins of non-white folks, corrupting their minds and making their bodies mere objects of extraction and exploitation. Fanon was not fooled. The white man was still locked into his whiteness. He had just given it a different name.

In reality, this new form of whiteness has had not one but many different names. But the most enduring and effective in also being the hardest to pin down is the idea of 'the West'. An "old word for a new idea," the West has been ascendant in the global discourse of Euro-American exceptionalism and supremacy at least since the 1920s, although its apotheosis dates back to the new threat of Soviet communism, from 'the East', following the Second World War.[68] In contemporary Western discourse, the West is meant to evoke liberal democracy and free-market capitalism, technological advancement and cultural refinement, the rule of law and secular nation-states allied against the perversions of tyranny, theocracy and authoritarian governments everywhere. This was not always the case. In its earliest iterations on the European continent, the West meant precisely, and literally, the western lands of the empire centered on Rome just as the eastern lands were around Constantinople. The disintegration of the empire and the later schism in Christianity overlaid the earlier Roman division with the robust distinction between Western and Eastern Christendom. When the Protestant Reformation shattered the unity of the Catholic Church in the sixteenth and seventeenth centuries, the West became increasingly identified with the Atlantic-facing ascendant powers such as Britain, the Netherlands and France, and also with regions of the continent most affected by the wars of religion. It is at this point that the story gets more complicated. Writing for *The American Interest* back in 2011, Peter Berger argued that the German romanticist "reaction to the French revolutionary ideas carried into Germany on the bayonets of Napoleon's armies" was to contrast their own "deeply spiritual *kultur*" with the "merely technological *Zivilisation*" of "the West (France and England lumped together)." "It was clear," he points out, "*the West was on the other side of the Rhine.*" Russian Slavophiles "repeated the exercise with minor variations" in the nineteenth century, distinguishing between "the depths of the Russian soul [and] – yes, indeed – the superficial, only technologically sophisticated West (Germany definitely included)." Now the West was on the other side of the Russian border. Similar sentiments in Catholic and conservative circles of Spain, France and Latin America concerned about the increasing individualization and fragmentation of traditional society have, since the nineteenth century, placed the West, respectively, "*north of the Pyrenees ... west of the English Channel ... [and] north of the Rio Grande.*"[69] The West was still a moving target but its association with what are now well-established aspects of modernity was becoming stronger.

Hegel was probably the first widely read thinker to definitively conflate the geographical designation of 'the West' with the Renaissance notion of 'Europe' and with the political, economic and social transformations taking place in the aftermath of the French Revolution. His philosophy of history confidently proclaims that the "history of the world moves from East to West, for Europe is absolutely the end of History."[70] This oft-repeated phrase, "the end of History" itself, the exhaustion of all previous iterations of civilization in its apotheosis in Europe, would someday serve to sacralize the evolving normative paradigms of a particular Western peoples as the unique path to global salvation. In the meantime, some three decades later, Karl Marx would be the first to use the phrase "the Western world" in direct reference to European colonial adventures in Asia.[71] In his mid-nineteenth-century work, Marx would revisit Montesquieu's eighteenth-century interpretation of a peculiarly "Oriental despotism" as rooted in the "Asiatic mode of production" that renders these societies stagnant and unchanging, lacking the vigor of the modernizing West.[72] According to Marx, "Asia fell asleep in history" until it was rudely roused by the intervention of the "Western world" in the nineteenth century. These new depictions of the West were clearly contrasted with an East, the Orient of Edward Said, as an inverse mirror image, substantiated in precisely those ways in which the East was hollowed out. It is with such thinking as prologue that in 1880, the radical British MP Joseph Cowen could coherently argue on the floor of the House of Commons about "the conflicting civilizations of East and the West – the one iconoclastic and progressive, the other traditional and conservative."[73] The West had come a long way from the western lands of the Roman Empire. This evolution of the West from a term of geographical direction to its loose association with Christianity into a full-blown signifier of tremendous explanatory power has been a gradual one. But it picked up steam in the beginning years of the twentieth century both inside and outside the West, and is now firmly established as a reference to some identifiable unity of ideological, cultural, political and epistemological concerns.

The key to grasping this contemporary notion of the West is understanding its evolution from within pre-existing turn-of-the-century discourses concerning imperial Europe and the 'White race'. The period in question is the three decades of gestation that Hannah Arendt calls the 'age of imperialism', at the end of which a nineteenth century already pregnant with change since the scramble for Africa in 1881 finally gave birth to the twentieth century proper in the onset of the Great War. The "stagnant quiet in Europe" of this period was complemented by "breathtaking developments in Asia and Africa." And, as Arendt points out, "some of the fundamental aspects of this time appear so close to totalitarian phenomena of the twentieth century that it may be justifiable to consider the whole period a preparatory stage for coming catastrophes." Buoyed already by social Darwinism since the middle of the nineteenth century, it was during this time that race consciousness evolved swiftly into full-blown imperial racism of the modern kind as European power lorded over virtually the entire surface of the planet. And the burgeoning demand for imperial possessions, a kind of existential 'need for empire', was itself "born when the ruling class in capitalist production came up against national limitations to its economic expansion" by the last quarter of the century.[74] This entanglement of race, capital and empire had existed before, but never with this level of mutually reinforcing justification, what William Apple Williams called:

> Empire as a way of life ... [wherein] there was virtual unanimity [in the imperial metropoles] that subject races should be ruled, that they *are*

subject races, that one race deserves and has consistently earned the right to be considered the race whose main mission is to expand beyond its own domain.⁷⁵

The master race was born not in Germany, but in the jungles and deserts of Africa, in the Southeast Asian countryside and the decaying urban centers of India, and in those complex "structures of feeling" that domination over these lands and these people engendered among Europeans as all together members of a White race with a provident sanction to rule.⁷⁶ The Muslim world and this imperial version of the White race came into sharp relief at around the same time, frothing into existence atop the same tides of change that Europe had unleashed on itself and the rest of the world. The West followed shortly thereafter.

* * *

There are three discrete but often intermingling sentiments, intertwined structures of feeling, that are most relevant to the genesis of the West from these entanglements of race, capital and empire. The first of these is a kind of *noblesse oblige*, equal parts exasperation with the natives and a sincere desire born of an unassailable sense of racial privilege to enable their development toward some semblance of civilization. That this sometimes required ruling the natives with an iron fist, or forcing them against their will toward salutary ends they themselves could not comprehend, was a basic fact of imperial life, the white man's burden "to serve [his] captive's needs ... [the] new-caught sullen peoples, half devil and half child."[77] Like the God of the Hebrew Bible, the White man will often smite out of a deeper affection, destroy for the sake of recreation, for he can see through to the true meaning of things to the ends of history. The academic study of 'world religions' also came of age in this imperial setting that provided hitherto unthinkable access to non-European peoples. For the first time, ambitious translation projects created a world canon of scriptures and other seminal texts. And the counting, classifying and cataloguing of their rituals, beliefs and practices led to intense theorizing about the essential nature of these societies and instigated the development of new disciplines such as anthropology and sociology. In turn, this burgeoning of knowledge about the natives was constantly folded back into supporting the imperial mission of civilizing rule.

Armed with science and reason, and a cosmology of progress, this civilizing mission came to dominate the European public imagination. Rudyard Kipling's varied works provided the sincerest expositions of this mission, just as Joseph Conrad's noted the futility of the task and the constitutive corruptions that it inevitably entailed. But the task itself, the bringing of light into darkness and the playing of 'the Great Game' toward universal 'Progress' were all the White man's prerogative, if only he were up to the task. The half devil and half child was asleep in history, unable to move without provocation. It is for this reason that Kipling could both render India with such skill, with such purity and genuine affection, yet also persist in the "belief that the Indian reality required, indeed beseeched British tutelage more or less *indefinitely*."[78] And why, for all the pathos of his texts, Conrad could never quite manage to write a proper speaking role for the native; the dark masses were extras in the unfolding of their own destiny. To unreservedly call either Kipling or Conrad a *racist* in the contemporary sense of the term is both misleading and deeply inappropriate. But their views of the world, their feelings and aspirations and exasperations about its future were structured by race in a manner so elementary it seldom even needed explicit mention. It is this set of sentiments, of not just benign but constructive condescension, which Fanon has in mind when he talks of the White man treating his subjects like children. This pedagogical model of the world had room for only one kind of teacher, and at the beginning of the twentieth century his credentials were evaluated in explicitly racial terms.

The second collage of sentiments is animated by fear, revulsion and sometimes also a morbid fascination of the lower races, the conquered peoples of the world. For just as soon as it was born, in the very moment of the zenith of its power, the master race was always already imperiled. Nazi Germany was hardly the first polity to become rife with fear of racial miscegenation and pollution by people of inferior racial stock. Such fear was rampant across the continent well in advance of the rise of Hitler, and in fact was the necessary context of his emergence in the first place. Enlightenment humanism had been clearly hierarchical with regard to different "specimens of mankind," but it was still animated by ideas such as the universality of the human condition, the singularity of the human species, and progress as the engine for the emancipation of man.[79] And political romanticism's "organic doctrine of a history for which 'every race is a separate, complete whole' was invented by men who needed ideological definitions of national unity as a substitute for political nationhood," and not, at least initially, for the purposes of racial animus or subjugation directed outwards.[80] But Darwinism biologized the politics of race. And empire weaponized it. No more mere fashionable science, the theory of natural selection rendered race competition the natural way of things, a zero-sum game with extinction both an ever-present possibility and a necessary cost of doing business. Survival of the fittest sometimes required that one "exterminate all the brutes" for the brutes would do the same if they could.[81] If speculation concerning the causes of the Sepoy Mutiny in India is any guide, the essence of the Islamic faith itself was a kind of racialized identity marker prompting rebellion and therefore requiring severe retribution.

In Herbert Spencer's studies of sociology, for example, social progress demanded racial conflict and "a continuous over-running of the less powerful or less adapted by the more powerful or more adapted, a driving of inferior varieties into undesirable habitats, and occasionally, an extermination of inferior varieties."[82] Racial panics in the colonies therefore often led to the bland-sounding 'administrative massacres' (a precursor to the equally innocuous 'collateral damage'). And the sheer numbers of the subjugated peoples, the hordes, the masses of savages peopling the Earth were a source of deepening anxiety in the imperial metropoles about the future of the White race. A widespread literature of 'White Crisis' emerged in the wake of this anxiety, with Max Nordau's dark fears of *Degeneration* (1892), Charles Pearson's number crunching in *National Life and Character: A Forecast* (1894), Putnam Weale's calls for White unity in *The Conflict of Colour* (1910), Sir Leo Chiozza Money's dawning realization of *The Peril of the White* (1925), and of course Lothrop Stoddard's seminal account of *The Rising Tide of Color against White World-Supremacy* (1925) being the most well-known examples. These respectable narratives operated in an ecosystem of ideas rife with race hatred and feelings of intense race consciousness. This fear of racial pollution as at once both a biological and political fear, and a world politics predicated on world domination as the only sure bet for survival, portended the coming catastrophes all over Europe.

Both these sets of sentiments, the *noblesse oblige* and race fear, are occasions of race as ideology for they "claim to possess," in the concept of race, "either the key to history, or the solution of all the riddles of the universe, or the intimate knowledge of the hidden universal laws which are supposed to rule nature and man." In turn-of-the-century discussions of race, the designation 'White' carried a whole host of information that had nothing to do with physical appearance or even geographical location. Everything was racialized. One could reasonably talk about White science and reason, a White way of doing politics, White history and values, White religion, culture, and civilization. In all of these different ways, Whiteness was the repository of all that Europe had achieved since the Renaissance and all that Europeans had become. It was simultaneously the old religion of Christianity and the Enlightenment critique of religion, both the culmination of a project of European solidarity and sanction for world domination, both omnipotent and fragile. And as for the White race, so too for all the other people of the world, their race identities were a complex mix of their physical features, their religious affiliations, their social histories, all iconic of their essential nature. That a single term could come to carry such vast oceans, such a baffling variety of signifiers and significations, symbols and worldviews, the very meaning and culmination of histories, is an ideological achievement of staggering proportions. Arendt would later claim that:

> Few ideologies have won enough prominence to survive the hard competitive struggle of persuasion [in the nineteenth century], and only two have come out on top and essentially defeated all

others: the ideology which interprets history as an economic struggle of classes, and the other that interprets history as a natural fight of races.[83]

It would take not one but two 'fratricidal' wars that killed hundreds of millions within White Europe, devastation on a scale unseen before or hence, the loss of empire and the continued political eminence of that other victorious ideology on the continent of Europe to drive a final nail into the coffin of respectable race talk. And even then, as we shall see shortly, most of its ideological infrastructure has survived the interment and continues to roam the world as 'the West'.

The third structure of feeling symptomatic of 'an empire state of mind' has little or nothing to do with race as such. That it often became intertwined with race is an inevitable consequence of its *mondialisme*. The economic historian Joel Mokyr has argued convincingly that the desire for a constant expansion of "useful knowledge" as a moving principle for rapid economic growth in eighteenth- and nineteenth-century Europe (what he calls the "Industrial" and "Commercial" Enlightenments) is the necessary corollary to the idea of progress.[84] The "Great Enrichment" has its roots in the cultural ascendancy of the values of 'growth' and 'improvement' that fundamentally transformed the relationship both between the present and the past, and between humans and their natural environment. In either case, the latter began to be seen as of primarily instrumental value to the progress of the former.

In the spheres of economic, material and technological development, growth therefore gradually came to be seen as the supreme organizing principle, an end in itself. Just as the *philosophes* had imagined the past as a useful repository for the present construction of improved futures, their mercantilist counterparts internalized the use value of new lands and new peoples for the constant expansion of their economic interests.

In the nineteenth century, the evolution of this sentiment naturally produced an "increasingly strong contingent of *homines novi*, for whom progress meant above all economic advantage for themselves"[85] – "patriotism ... [was] best expressed in money making and the national flag [was] a commercial asset."[86] "Expansion," said Cecil Rhodes "is everything." There is no better conveyor of this mood of empire than Rhodes, whose entire biography can sometimes read as a précis for imperialism itself. For those of Rhodes' ilk, the commodification of the already racially sub-humanized was seldom a function of simple racial animus, but rather of entrepreneurial spirit, clever manipulation of circumstances, and the prerogative of growth. "These stars ... these vast worlds which we can never reach," Rhodes despaired, "I would annex the planets if I could."[87] This yearning for growth and expansion, the endless churning of money begetting money, new markets and new innovations, the spreading out until all the space is filled and accounted for, and then spread out some more, the manic movement of stock markets that we are all familiar with in the neo-liberal present, has its origins in the imperialist appropriations of the mood of progress, substantiated as empire and counted in currency. The West as "a rhetorical invention" for coherently holding together these discrete yet intermingling sentiments, these often conflicting structures of feeling *sans* the embarrassment of empire and race, is the ideological progeny of the age of imperialism just as the twentieth century is its historical child.[88] Of course, the West in contemporary usage also has many other functions, other meanings. The West as a reference to liberal democracy and human rights has its roots in the Anglo-American war against Nazi Germany. The West as the primacy of freedom is a relic of a thousand years of Christian and post-Christian speculation but also of the Cold War and hot conflicts in twentieth-century Africa, Asia and Latin America. The West as the triumph of reason has the evolving history of knowledge in Europe as its most enduring foil; Bruno burning at the stake, Galileo muttering "*E pur si muove,*" and Descartes' skepticism, Bacon's optimism, Hume's doubt. The West as the rule of law, not men, has many fathers, many mothers, dating all the way back to the Magna Carta to the American constitution to the Third Republic. Likewise, the West as equality draws animation from the Revolution in France to the Emancipation Proclamation and the civil rights movement in America. Depending on the adversary, the constituting other, the inverse mirror, the West has been both the stronghold of true religion and the bastion of secularism, and sometimes both at once. It still is today. The West is both a new word for an old idea and an old word for a new idea. It is panoramic, fecund and multiple. So, it is not my purpose here to reduce it to its supposed sins. Nor to essentialize it as the root of all evil in the world today. Attempts to do so are almost always futile and ill-advised, no matter the presumed satisfaction of a righteous indignation. And inasmuch as Fanon is sometimes guilty of treading this way, it is a service to him to point out that what he probably meant by "the white man is locked into his whiteness" was precisely what he said. That Whiteness has clung to the new West. That for all else it may be, it is also still that rhetorical invention which allowed the post-imperial order to keep on being imperial without the embarrassment of white supremacy. It is these structures of feeling, the discrete but intermingling sentiments, that holding together of condescension *and* obligation, of the fear of the other *and* the desire to enclose the other, of endless expansion in a world being made small, these are the features of the West that are my primary concern. For together they constitute that incarnation of the West which faces the Muslim world in a mutually reinforcing glare of misrecognition, with one arm around the shoulders anticipating embrace and the other on the chest enforcing the distance.

* * *

This face of the West, the disclosure of a unity that enfolds other unities, is the final clue to the resilience of the basic structure of global debates about Islam over the last century or so. Divested of any explicit race and geography, the expansion of the West is no longer moored to the limits and constraints associated with those categories. It is in this sense that the West is also a Western word for the world itself. And it is for this reason that Western political leaders see no contradiction in calling on the normative consensus of the 'international community' to berate this or that recalcitrant actor on the world stage. The 'international community' is meant to denote both "a [particular] *transnational* group of Enlightened civilized nations" and an expansive claim to speak for the world as a whole, of being the properly human subject of a global politics. Perhaps the best articulation of this intermingling of particularism and universalism in the West's worldly aspirations is Arnold Toynbee's 'Christology' of the West evident throughout much of his work in the first half of the twentieth century. Toynbee famously had no patience with race talk, which he thought both unscientific and retrograde. But his accounts of a Western vanguard, heroically moving the history of the world forward in its brewing together of all the different cultures it has found into a unified amalgam, a world culture of Western vintage, provide "a less racially reductive but not necessarily less socially exclusive vision of community."[89] Toynbee argues that "by making history," Westerners "have transcended [their] own history." And this transcendence is most evident in the "progressive erection, by Western hands, of a scaffolding within which all the once separate societies have built themselves into one."⁹⁰ Toynbee's remarkable "combination of humility and arrogance" is a Christology in his insistence that the West's greatest triumph is sacrificing itself, erasing itself for the grand unity that it has created. For this is "a synthesis in which the West both disappears and finds its highest calling."⁹¹ Or as Toynbee puts it, "to be allowed to fulfil oneself by surpassing oneself is a glorious privilege for any of God's creatures."⁹² This appeal to divine providence allows Toynbee to effortlessly combine these discrete sentiments of expansion, of obligation to the world and of world domination as self-sacrifice, and hold them together without contradiction. It is a template that has been in use now for almost a century and its narrative vigor has scarcely diminished.

Toynbee's magnanimity toward this emergent world culture is not the only account of the West that has contemporary valence. The other structure of feeling, the desire to dominate the other, had its paradigmatic early theorization in the work of Benjamin Kidd, a British civil servant and champion of Western civilization extraordinaire. As with Toynbee, Kidd identifies the West not with race, but with a certain orientation toward a rapidly shrinking world and with being the vanguard of this world's future. But unlike Toynbee, Kidd's cosmology of progress is shot through with a Darwinian battle for supremacy from which the West is destined to emerge victorious. Already back in 1902, Kidd claimed that "we are par excellence the military peoples, not only of the entire world but of the evolutionary process itself." In an early echo of what would in our time become known as the clash of civilizations thesis, Kidd imagines a global context of zero-sum competition in which only the West is constituted by the making of history, "the potentiality of a principle *inherent* in it to project the controlling principles of its consciousness beyond the present." It is for this reason that only the Western mind is "destined, sooner or later, to rise to the conception of the nature of truth itself different from any that has hitherto prevailed in the world." It is therefore "the principles of our Western civilization ... and no others, that we feel are destined to hold the future of the world."[93] Kidd's West is not the Christ of self-sacrifice, but of the second coming, the harbinger of a militant millennium cleansed of the inferior specimens of mankind and made fit for the elect.

This version of the West is as familiar today as Toynbee's. And what makes the two distinct also in fact carries the trace of a family resemblance that allows the sentiments associated with each to coexist in the same body politic and sometimes even within the same person. For they both implicitly rely on the notion that the West is not just a Western word for the world, but also for history. That the West has an essence and a unity like all the other essences and unities associated with other peoples, other civilizations and other religions. But only the West's essence is movement, the making of history. Alone among the communal creatures that God has created, the West is that category of being that is not prisoner of its genus, but master of it, not subject to the whims of nature, but manipulator of it, not caught in the movement of time, but the mover of it in the grand design of human providence. And the particular ends of its history are therefore, and by definition, the ends of all other histories, and the unified culmination of the history of the world as such. These eschatological yearnings will be the subject of discussion in chapters to come. For now, suffice it to say that such yearnings indicate an orientation toward the world that is essentially theological. That the West is not just a Western word for the world and for history, but also a Western word for God.

And so we come to an end to this section of the story, the part that started with Hegel and Fanon and which I have tracked through the idea of the Muslim world, of reason, progress, empire and race all the way to the emergence of the West. The larger story, the one that began with crowds cheering the towers' destruction, continues in the chapters that follow. For now, it is time to take stock of what we have learned. The recognitive failures that underlie the West's relationship with Muslims are not just a function of power, but of ideology. And it is a very specific form of ideology. Inflected by race but not reducible to it, animated by reason but not prisoner to it, obligated by a sense of providence but not limited by it, both itself and the end of everything else, it is that particular evolutionary movement in which the very law of evolution is disclosed. No matter the inevitable failures in the unfolding of Western history, this history itself as a whole is the evolving perfection of time. It is difficult sometimes for those not in the West to recognize how much the history of the carnage of two world wars and the Cold War that followed is processed (especially by Anglo-Americans) not as failures of the Western project, but as instances of supreme sacrifice in which the West gave of itself to save the world from fascism and then communism. That these were 'world' wars in precisely this sense, of the West acting on behalf of a largely supine and ineffectual world "asleep in history" to rescue it from an apocalyptic derailment. It is for this reason that the West as the subject of world politics continuously enfolds the rest as objects into the safety of its bosom, and any resistance to such enfolding conjures up memories of fascism, communism, the wars of religion, and all those other ways in which the West has overcome the supposed failures of its own past.

As per Fanon, where Europe has placed the world, then, is in a tidally locked relationship with itself as the center axis around which all manners of objects revolve in endless, futile orbits. In the special case of Islam and Muslims, this locking in has had a profound impact on the world we live in today. The desire to enfold Islam has led from the very beginning to marking its lagging development with milestones from Western history. The incessant demand for a Muslim Martin Luther and a Reformation, for the privatization of Islamic faith and the latching of its history to the ideals of the European Enlightenment, Bush's salutary conception of a common world with a common cause, are all variations on Toynbee's optimism. So too in fact the rhetoric of Islamofascism, Islamic irrationalism, Islamic fundamentalism as regressive ghosts from the West's own sordid past that can be overcome in the future as they were by Western peoples. But these latter understandings also often bleed into instances of Kidd's triumphalist militarianism, of Islam's irreducible difference, of engulfment through competition and eventual destruction rather than enfolding into a common world history. But the primacy of the West is retained in either case. Recall that expansion, the third great imperative of imperial logic, is agnostic toward the guiding sentiment of obligation or competition. It can proceed apace either way. And it has.

Versions of Toynbee and Kidd have existed in each succeeding generation of the West. And their inverted mirror images have existed in each succeeding generation of the Muslim world. For every Leo Strauss, there is an Abu A'la Maududi; for every Woodrow Wilson, there is a Kemal Ataturk. Niall Ferguson, Michael Ignatieff, Maajid Nawaz and Irshad Manji line up opposite Bernard Henri-Levy, Sam Harris, Jalal Al-e Ahmad and Sayyid Qutb. Blair and Bush on one side, Khomeini and bin Laden the other. No exhaustive list is possible because these types are literally everywhere in the academy, in politics and policy circles, in the media and in popular culture. The great irony, of course, is that their ostensible disagreements are somehow counted as a critical confrontation between opposing sides in the global debate on Islam, its true meaning and nature, and the future of the West and the world. That the answer to the Muslim Question is sought in the resolution of these debates is the very condition of futility from which escape has become such a difficult proposition. Needless to say, these are not political debates, but the exact opposite of politics, in that the answers are pregiven, the destinations already in place before the journey has even begun. The absolute rejections of the West of folks such as Maududi, Qutb and Jalal Al-e Ahmad are mirrored perfectly by the absolute acceptances of Maajid Nawaz, Irshad Manji and Asra Nomani. But mirrors right side up or inverted are mirrors in either case. And mirrors can offer nothing more than that which we bring to them. They can only offer reflections, not recognition.

It must be mentioned that these types do not exhaust the entirety of the conversation and never have. Moments of novelty and clarity sometimes manage to issue through a context even as clogged with futility as this. I'd like to think that the conversation Tariq Ramadan and Ian Baruma would like to have is an example of such novelty. Although more difficult to stomach on account of his obvious political motivations, former Iranian President Mahmoud Ahmadinejad's 2006 letter to George W. Bush requesting a civilizational dialogue is another. Throughout the modern history of Islam, but especially before the imperial state of mind set in for good, there are countless examples of complicated, critical Muslims such as Jamal al-Din al-Afghani, Sayyid Ahmad Khan and Muhammad Abduh who defy easy characterization and resist being locked into a futile posture of affirmation or negation. This has been true throughout in the years since, even as the space for such novelty has diminished and the publicity of such voices has become harder to come by. I will investigate ways to remedy this state of affairs and rescue a form of Critical Islam from obscurity in the ensuing chapters. For now, it is first important to explore the mechanisms by which the either/or futility is realized in actual conversations about Islam. What are the specific ways in which Muslims are theorized, their actions and motivations are comprehended, and the manner in which their societies and histories are assimilated and locked into a futile relationship with the West? What frustrates the possibility of Critical Islam making an appearance in the global public mainstream? First up in the next chapter are essentialized readings of Islam as a distinct form of politics that may or may not be compatible with Western modernity. I call this *freedom talk* because these conversations all revolve around the possibility (or lack thereof) of fracturing sedimented tradition in Muslim societies so they can realize the two great political innovations of the West, namely secularism and democracy. I will describe how these debates hearken back to an earlier iteration of the notion of politics as loyalty to the sovereign, a Hobbesian rendering of the Muslim as a being in the state of nature who must bind himself to one god or another to escape the tyranny of rule by others of his kind. Needless to say, this is a deeply anti-political conception of politics that only amplifies the farce and futility of Islam.

3

Freedom Talk

In this chapter, I identify a set of conversational traps that together constitute what I call freedom talk about Islam. This kind of talk is primarily concerned with identifying Islam as a peculiar way of doing politics that is then judged as either commensurable or incommensurable with the West. Any critical Muslim perspective that frustrates this binary either becomes conceptually conflated with the most militant political instantiations of Islam (notice the panoramic reach of the term 'Islamist', for example) or is reassessed as a confirmation of modern liberal values (albeit with caveats concerning another panoramic term, 'reform'). In its inclusive, totalizing architecture, freedom talk transcends the usual dichotomies of the right and the left, of liberal and conservative. Those who judge Islam as familiar but underdeveloped kin to the West come in many shapes and sizes. And some make for strange bedfellows.

They run the gamut from 'moderate' Muslim intellectuals, to liberal philosophers, to neo-conservative thinkers and politicians, to modernization theorists, to internationalist utopians of all kinds. Those who judge Islam otherwise, as a form of politics that is decisively incompatible with Western values, can similarly count among their ranks a panoply of multiculturalist and left liberals, conservative historians and political scientists, the (so-called) radical or fundamentalist Muslim thinkers, a whole bevy of political realists, and moral relativists of one sort or another. Debates and disagreements between contending parties in their enactment of freedom talk focus ostensibly on the twin issues of democracy and secularism in the Muslim world, and on the attendant value of self-determination. But this focus only masks what is in reality the underlying utility of the trope in depoliticizing the Muslim subject as either wholly familiar or wholly unfamiliar.

* * *

In the wake of the successful ouster of Hosni Mubarak in 2012 by an unprecedented and, until then, unthinkable uprising of the Egyptian people, many observers failed to notice a peculiar feature of the coverage of these events in the American media. News organizations repeatedly raised the specter of the Muslim Brotherhood taking over in the absence of an organized secular opposition. At the same time, most pundits were at pains to point out that the protest for reform itself was a granular, grassroots movement largely secular in its concerns and orientation. The narrative hook of these intertwining stories was the danger of a secular movement being hijacked by politicized Muslims if the transition was not orderly, or if it was managed incorrectly; that the Muslim Brotherhood represented an anti-Western Islamic politics and the bulk of the protesters its secular pro-Western alternative. It was a simple dualism, and it was also simply wrong. The vast majority of Egyptians – those in Tahrir Square and elsewhere – would not have described themselves as secular in any meaningful sense. There were so-called secularists among them, of course, but most were animated by a peculiar mixture of concerns. Polling data by Pew Research and other organizations consistently showed their considerable support for the idea that Islam be a guiding concern for any government in their country. Anti-American sentiment also ran high among the protestors. Yet these data also confirmed their widespread support for democracy, freedom and human rights, and their concern with basic bread-and-butter issues.[1] Complicating the picture even further was Egypt's large Christian minority, which at nearly 10 percent of the population could hardly be described as incidental to the country's political future. Regardless, the comforting dualism of competing Islamic/anti-Western and secular/pro-Western commitments was the metanarrative that dominated the early media analysis of these events.[2]

Particularly instructive of this dynamic was the Director of National Intelligence James Clapper who tried to make the case to Congress that the Muslim Brotherhood had disavowed violence for participation in democratic politics by describing the group as now "largely secular!"[3] Although Clapper was immediately assailed by folks from the left and the right for this supposed faux pas, this strange formulation – calling the *Muslim* Brotherhood "largely secular" – was in reality an affirmation of the dualistic trope through which political action by Muslims is routinely evaluated in the West. Clapper used this formulation as a concise way to allay the fears of Congress-folk anxious about the possibility of losing another key Middle Eastern ally (the other being Iran in 1979) to an anti-Western revolution. In an echo of George W. Bush's salutary conception of real Islam, Clapper seemed to be saying that Muslims are not bound by their faith to rebel against us. If we manage the situation properly, even these formerly radical Muslims could perhaps be trusted to follow our lead. Like 'moderate' and 'religion of peace', 'secular' and 'democratic' are pithy qualifiers of Muslim political sentiment that have little to do with Islam, or the political complexities of Muslim lived experience, or even the evolving histories of Muslim-majority societies. Their main referents have always been of Western vintage, as are their primary audiences. In public and political discourse, they serve to signal familiarity, to ease apprehensions of existential conflict, and to point to the salutary potential for reform. Put another way, they hold out hope for the expansion of Western power, of an enfolding of the Muslim world, without the fierce antagonisms attendant to theories of absolute difference between Islam and the West. Notice, for example, that in such usage, both 'secular' and 'democratic' shed their disparate historical instantiations, the complex distinctions between their many variants and the diverse legal regimes they animate, to become a generalized reference evoking the obscurantism of premodern tradition, the carnage of religious fanaticism and the slow, deliberate climb out of such madness. They are rhetorical tools for the continuing utility of Arnold Toynbee's Christology of the West, an eschatological reading of history that retains great sanction among large sections of the learned elite.

Of course, theories about the irreducible difference of Islam also abound in the West – tales of danger and pollution, the fear of contamination, or even glum resignation over the feeble presents and pathetic futures of the lower peoples of the world. The ostensibly contrasting sentiments of antagonism and pity intermingle in the regime of such theories, and often take turns in the cyclical intellectual development of thinkers and polities dealing with the Muslim Question. This way of talking about Islam often betrays a *speciest* understanding of culture and religion and is peppered with ecological and biological metaphors. Extinction is a constant threat. Some proponents of this view imagine a grand unified future where the whole human race is literally swallowed up into the lockbox of Western history and the many become one.

Others reject such totalitarian universalism in favor of the preservation of civilizations much like environmentalists seek to preserve endangered species. But the allegorical reliance on ecology and biology is compelled in either case by a prior rejection of properly political engagements across this difference. The in-between spaces opened up by this difference are theatres of competition and domination, of the struggle for survival or, at best, of compromise on matters of utility, but on not much more. The evolving moral vocabularies of the West and Islam are too distinct, too specific to warrant any robust talk of a shared history or a common humanity. It is for this reason that a Darwinian fear of extinction is often also complemented in these theories by a more sophisticated fear of the world turning into the Island of Doctor Moreau.[4] Nothing good can come from the creation of abominable chimeras. Secularism and democracy are vital chromosomes in the genetic evolution of the West, uniquely and essentially so. Their realization among Muslims is never more than skin-deep. It is at best an exercise in facile imitation lacking any durable commitment. At worst, it is destabilizing of the Muslim mind and dangerous for the rest of the world.

Global debates about Islam and Muslims are dominated by the back and forth between contending parties in either one or the other of these two broad theoretical assemblages about the nature of the difference at play here. At issue is the meaning and essence of Islam as the name for a historically constituted practice of politics and the plausibility of its ensoulment by the West. This is the contemporary version of the tension between turn-of-the-century *noblesse oblige* and intense race competition. And true to the original intertwining of these discrete structures of feeling in the imperial imagination, their current variants also intermingle and cross-pollinate across ostensibly partisan political and intellectual lines. Certain segments of the neo-conservative right and the liberal left are, for example, equally invested in universalist accounts of Islam's coming transformation into what essentially amounts to a politics of acquiescence to the West. They share these sentiments with moderate Muslims and modernization theorists, and, oddly enough, certain far-left Marxists and internationalist utopians. On the other hand, those who judge Islam otherwise – as a form of politics that is decisively incompatible with Western values – can similarly count among their ranks a panoply of multiculturalist liberals, conservative historians and political scientists, the (so-called) radical Muslim thinkers, a whole bevy of political realists, and moral relativists of one sort or another. To paraphrase Edward Said, any preoccupation with the question of which one of these interpretations is a more veridic account of Islam only serves to obfuscate the fact that not only have the contending positions in this debate *both* been teachable wisdom across the political and intellectual spectrum for over a century, but also the dualistic trope of their contention itself is teachable wisdom! Quick, choose your side – this is the designated way to talk about Islam, in eithers and ors, in split screens of terror and democracy. And as with Orientalism, this manner of debating Islam is far "more formidable than a mere collection of lies."[5] It speaks the essentialized object of Islam into existence and then conjures into reality its dueling stations in the world. This is the powerful magic of Western ideology. It is no simple prevarication.

I am calling this back and forth, either/or banter on the status of Islam *freedom talk* because it often presents as an extended debate about the possibility and/or felicity of Muslim critical self-determination in the context of Western power. Those who believe that Islam can be made to conform to the demands of Western modernity ask the following questions: Under what conditions could Muslims be free to participate as full members in the global body politic, and under what circumstances will liberty be fully realized in Muslim life? Those who reject the possibility of such an overarching conformity deny the existence of any robust common context for a properly political engagement and argue instead for the exceptional quality of both the Islamic world and the West. These *conformists* and *exceptionalists* waltz their choreographed contentions year after year, generating oohs and aahs from newsreels and monographs. The veracity of one side or the other is not the relevant question here, as if a dance could be judged right or wrong. And again, this is not a matter of honesty or authenticity – there is no grand conspiracy to obfuscate the truth, at least none that is pervasive or self-evident. No, it is the particular architecture of freedom talk, and how its various parts play off each other in the appearance of contention, that frustrates the general cognition and realization of Critical Islam. And in the meanwhile, the prerogative of Western expansion becomes ever-more sedimented as a kind of globalized common sense.

* * *

This abstract discussion about conformists and exceptionalists clearly demands more meat on the bone, so to say, greater specificity as to their theories about Islam, its past, present and future. Who are these people, and what do they say? Let me begin by suggesting that in purely philosophical terms, contending participants in these debates tend to fall roughly on opposite sides of a perennial argument in the West about the source and status of moral values. Inasmuch as secularism and democracy are political values ultimately rooted in moral accounts of the human condition, where do these accounts come from and to whom do they apply?[6] Conformists usually begin with the premise that some version of the Enlightenment ethos that lies at the core of Western modernity is in fact universal and occupies a normative space underneath the particularities of different religions. The West's provident history has allowed it to discover the values that correspond to the human condition as such, and these values are modular in being essentially human values, not merely

Western values. They represent a kind of humanistic ether in which all other normative frameworks are embedded with varying degrees of commensurability. The important task, then, is to excavate the moral language of Islam for signs of such commensurability and to engineer reform on a grand scale. On the other hand, exceptionalists begin with the premise that cultural, historical and ideological differences are fundamental to the constitution of human identity. Systems of value reflect these differences and are as such not universal, but particular to the contexts in which they emerge and within which they develop and evolve. The temporary appearance of consensus on moral concerns across different systems of value can have an ephemeral, provisional character. More often than not, such consensus owes more to considerations of utility than morality. Attempts to reconcile Islam with the West are a fool's errand. There is utility in maintaining good relations with Muslims and their societies. And even perhaps in engineering their provident extinction through conversion to genuine Western doxa. But the difference of Islam is too robust to admit of middle ways.

Conformist thinking on Islam has had no greater champion in recent years, and certainly no better spokesperson, than the former president George W. Bush. In a speech given at London's Whitehall Palace in the aftermath of the invasion of Iraq and the toppling of the Baathist regime, Bush laid out what he called his "forward strategy of freedom" in the Middle East:

The United States must defend liberty and justice because these principles are right and true for all people everywhere. No nation owns these aspirations, and no nation is exempt from them ... Peoples of the Middle East share a high civilization, a religion of personal responsibility, and a need for freedom as deep as our own. It is not realism to suppose that one-fifth of humanity is unsuited to liberty; it is pessimism and condescension, and we should have none of it.[7]

It should surprise no one, then, that the most compelling contemporary accounts of the coming transformation of Islam into a politics of acquiescence to the West have tended to come from certain segments of the neo-conservative right. At least since Irving Kristol first coined the term in the 1970s, a basic feature of neo-conservative thinking has been to affirm the utility of religion as a mediating structure between the private realm of moral values and traditions and the public sphere of governance and civil society.[8] American democracy and secularism are not in opposition to American Christianity, but rather these are all together intertwined into a unified model for the robust experience of political liberty and economic growth. As an Abrahamic religion, Islam too is capable of such 'Christianization' in the mold of American Catholicism and Judaism. That so many Muslims continue to resist the urgency of reform is unfortunate. Islam needs rescue as much from their somnolence as from the excesses of radicals. The neo-conservative penchant for the use of hard military power to jolt awake those who are "asleep in history" is therefore rooted in beneficent condescension, the white man's burden "to serve [his] captive's needs ... [the] new-caught sullen peoples, half devil and half child."

Perhaps the most sanguine neo-conservative reading of Islam's coming transformation is Michael Novak's acknowledgment that while "liberty is the crimson interpretative thread of Western history," and that "the hunger for liberty has only slowly been felt among Muslims ... [this] hunger is [still] universal, even when it is latent, for the preconditions for it slumber in every human breast." In another one of those odd formulations that appear often in Western treatments of Islam, Novak suggests that political Islam is in fact a secular ideology, a perversion that threatens what he calls "majority Islam."[9] Politicization of Islam prevents it from being democratized precisely because it also prevents it from being properly Islam itself. Of course, the invasion of Iraq was also aided and abetted by a coterie of Muslim neo-conservatives aggravated by the slow pace of change in the Muslim world. Foremost among these is Irshad Manji, a fixture on cable television, elite universities and think tanks, and a best-selling author to boot. One of her books actually begins with the premise that when a French journalist jeeringly calls Islam "the most stupid religion," the appropriate response should be for Muslims to ask themselves, "Is the French guy wrong to write that Islam needs to grow up?"[10] As Fanon has taught us, this urge to infantilize the Muslim is not incidental to the *noblesse oblige* of the West, but rather an active assumption in the narrative of self-sacrificial domination. Manji's additional appropriation of ijtihad as 'independent reasoning' in the mold of Western reason but *sans* its historical emplacement within a complex set of philosophical and juridical concerns further atomizes an already fragmented vocabulary of Islam. This infantilization and fragmentation is not arbitrary, but in service of a subsequent reconstruction of Islam, of Muslims being compelled to abandon obscurantism, to finally "grow up." They must cease their incessant baying and complaining and familiarize themselves with the doctrine of double effect. The Muslim world is doomed without the West's salutary interventions. There is no other way.

The ideological vigor of this neo-conservative model of interventionist pedagogy is undiminished by repeated failures on the ground. In fact, each setback is a mere prologue to doing it better the next time: to expand the context of Western power faster, farther and longer into Muslim lands and the hearts and minds of the Muslim people. A classically liberal strain of humanism is sometimes so strong here that a general ignorance about the particulars of these peoples, their specific political contexts, their discrete histories, is in fact considered advantageous toward the reforming mission. Where the do-nothing liberals and paleo-conservatives get lost in the weeds of irrelevant detail, neo-conservatives tend to process the threat and promise of Islam almost entirely in analogy with recent Western history. Here, for example, are David Frum and Richard S. Pearle in the astonishingly titled book *An End to Evil*:

> Like communism, this [radical Islamic] ideology perverts the language of justice and equality to justify oppression and murder. Like Nazism, it exploits the injured pride of once-mighty nations. Like both communism and Nazism, militant Islam is opportunistic – it works willingly with all manner of unlikely allies, as the communists and Nazis worked with each other against the democratic West.[11]

Clearly and unambiguously central to the neo-conservative agenda of an abstract democratization of the Muslim world is the link between exporting democracy and the strengthening of U.S. security. There is little equivocation on the equation of democratization with pacification. Writing in the 1980s, for example, the ostensibly liberal political scientist Leonard Binder based his advocacy of an "Islamic Liberalism" in Islam's possible (but not necessary) "closeness and comparability with Western liberalism,"[12] but also warned that "as the basis of improving the human condition through collective action ... [political liberalism is] indivisible. It will either prevail worldwide, or it will have to be defended by *nondiscursive* means."¹³ And even as far back as 1958, the philosopher David Lerner had predicted that modernization involves "the infusion of a 'rationalist and positivist outlook' against which ... 'Islam is absolutely defenseless'."¹⁴ It is for this reason that freedom talk often makes democracy seem less like an exercise in Muslim self-determination and more a justificatory language for the forceful transformation of Muslim lands.

Like their neo-conservative counterparts, liberal conformists share a preoccupation with democracy and secularism, and with political reform in the Muslim world. And here again, the complex and often haphazard convulsions of modernizing Europe are rewoven for Muslim consumption into a simple and salubrious tale of ascent into the light. But the focus is on Muslim agency and self-transformation rather than intervention. Khaled Abou el Fadl – a much celebrated moderate Muslim – argues that "as history repeatedly teaches us, nothing is as corrupting of religion as politics."¹⁵ Even as Abou el Fadl admits that "a central conceptual problem [for Islam] is that modern democracy evolved over centuries within the distinctive context of post-Reformation, market-oriented Christian Europe," he still insists that "if we focus on ... *fundamental moral values*, I believe, we will see that the tradition of Islamic political thought contains both interpretive and practical possibilities that can be *developed* into a democratic system."¹⁶ In that most comforting of all historical analogies, Abou el Fadl contends that "Islam is at the current time passing through a transformative moment no less dramatic than the Reformation movements that swept through Europe at one time."[17] In the battle between Muslim moderates and what he calls "Muslim puritans," the former will surely emerge victorious.[18] The important task for Muslims everywhere is to prevent "the great theft" of their religion by extremists, and to excavate their tradition for a reconstruction of Islam fit for the modern age.

Similarly, the great liberal defender of Islam in the American academy, John Esposito, argues that:

> In the era of post-modern perspectives and institutions, the two most important issues relating to religious resurgence and political development are the potential democratic resources of the Islamic tradition and the ability of the new Islamic movements to operate effectively to meet the demand for both Islamic authenticity and popular democratic participation.

He goes on to add that concerning the role of Islam in modern polities, "the starting point of [this] discussion will be the conceptual and ideological resources available for programs of democratization in the Islamic tradition."[19] In another book, Esposito provides an analysis of the latest Pew Research survey data from the Muslim world to show that large majorities of Muslims are not only on board with democratic and secular forms of government, they also seem politically ready to take on the challenge of reform on their own, immediately. In fact, they have already been at it for quite some time. It would appear, then, that Abou el Fadl's exhortations to his co-religionists, that "Muslims take a self-critical and introspective look at their own tradition and system of beliefs ... to reclaim Islam and re-establish Islam as a *humanistic* moral force in the world today" are being heeded far and wide.[20] Both Esposito and Abou el Fadl believe that the Muslim world is capable of reform on its own and within the rubric of its own tradition without constant intervention from outside. This is the great challenge of contemporary Muslim life, to generate a reformation to match the one Europe had all those years ago. To even the score, so to say, and begin anew.[21]

Conformist thinking of one sort or another has been a staple among members of the modern Western academy, and in policy circles and the media as well for decades. In a recent monograph title *Islam in Liberalism*, the Columbia Middle East Studies scholar Joseph Massad has argued that this kind of discourse is in fact an unreconstructed continuation of colonial-era British and French aspirations for control of Muslim lands through either forceful accommodation or transformation from within.[22] And its bifurcation in interventionist and apologist camps provides the kind of internal disparity that makes for spirited debate and argument across ostensibly partisan lines. Some, such as Abou el Fadl and Esposito, argue for internal introspection among Muslims and demand patience from the West. Others, such as Novak, Bush and Manji, want to jolt Muslims out of their lethargy and force a transformation if none is forthcoming by itself on a timely basis. But even when conformists disagree among themselves about the mechanisms of change, conformism itself is an ideologically unified discourse. Its universalist reference point is always the humanistic ether of values and norms generated in the West and against which Islam is evaluated and judged. This reference point itself, this ether of Western vintage, remains above the fray, oblivious to any response from Muslims, or any critiques other than those that it may admit for itself, on its own terms. A politics of conformity therefore demands a prior acquiescence to an abstract set of parameters that are themselves inoculated from the practice of such politics. And the abstraction of these parameters (What manner of democracy? What kind of secularism?) means that conformity in practice plays out less as an intellectual or political exercise in reform than as a rolling proclamation of affinity for Western *normes du jour*. Consider, for example, that there is an almost insatiable market for books that investigate the ins and outs of such affinity (Islam and: Democracy, Secularism, Human Rights, Liberalism, Modernity, etc.) and for think tank policy papers on what Cheryl Benard of RAND unironically called "religion-building" in Muslim societies.[23] As one pole in the pixelated continuum of freedom talk, conformism is the lifeblood of academic careers and political (mis)adventures alike in its provision of coherence and conviction to the appropriative rhetoric of Islamic reform.

* * *

In his four-volume *Bibliographical Discourse Analysis: The Western Academic Perspective on Islam, Muslims and Islamic Countries 1949–2009*, Saied Reza Ameli notes that roughly 9 percent of the 23,872 works he analyzed belong to what he calls a discourse of *Islamophilia* in that they "are generally sympathetic towards Islam, emphasize its commonalities with other religions, and reveal its fundamentally peaceful nature." Another 13.4 percent evidence a constitutive "fear or dislike of Islam ... as a monolithic, inflexible, distant 'other' – a barbaric, irrational, primitive, sexist, aggressive, and intolerant religion." But a staggering 48.4 percent of these works are instances of the far more complicated discourse of *Islamoromia* in that they:

> contextualize Islam in the bosom of the Roman tradition embodying the West in general and from a historical perspective ... [and] try to compare [the] Islamic ethos with Western values; while the jury is still out on the debate, many works in this category – thinking, evaluating and comparing Islam with and in a Western mindset, pronounce their favor for Western values and norms as superior, the more practical and less ornamental side of the binary.[24]

Conformist thinking on Islam is often marked by this rhetoric of dual inclusion/exclusion, where the contextualization into the bosom of the West is simultaneously also an evaluation of developmental lag on the part of Muslims. But retardation is only one explanation for this difference. Another popular trope continues to be that Islam is exceptionally and inescapably foreign, irreducibly and essentially different from the West; either as exceptions to each other or exceptions as such, Islam and the West lack a common, underlying basis for a properly political relationship.

Nobody did more to popularize this exceptionalist thesis in the American academy than the IR scholar and public intellectual Samuel Huntington, whose 'clash of civilizations' thesis caused much uproar among the learned public in the 1990s. In words that appeared prophetic after the events of 9/11, Huntington warned that following the collapse of communism, "the great divisions among humankind and the dominating source of conflict will be cultural." Huntington proposed that the world can be seen as composed of several large and heterogeneous cultural entities that he called civilizations, where "a civilization is the highest cultural grouping of people and the broadest level of cultural identity people have short of that which distinguishes human beings from other species." Differences between these civilizations are "far more fundamental than differences among political ideologies or political regimes" because they are "not only real: they are basic." Huntington argued that religion is perhaps the most important of these differences in its provision of a normative language for expressing:

> the relationship between God and man, the individual and the group, the citizen and the state, parents and children, husband and wife, as well as differing views of the relative importance of rights and responsibilities, liberty and authority, equality and hierarchy.

Civilizational difference issues from centuries of development and evolution. It cannot be wished away by mere intellectual exertion or interfaith dialogue.

Huntington argued that the most important fault line between civilizations – and the most decisive in years to come – is the 'velvet curtain' that divides the West from Islam. Conflict is endemic to this fault line and has been since the birth of Arab Islam in the seventh century. In fact, the Islamic civilization is constantly at odds with all its neighbors. Or as Huntington infamously put it, "Islam has bloody borders."[25] Those who believe that Western values can be exported to Islamic lands are proponents of what he called "the Coca-Colonization thesis." They confuse the "consumption of material goods," such as Coca-Cola, with "the heart of a culture [which involves] language, religion, values, traditions and customs." There are others, equally misguided, who claim that "as civilizations modernize they also westernize, abandoning their traditional values, institutions and customs, and adopting those that prevail in the West." In Huntington's view, such conformists are "to varying degrees misguided, arrogant, false and dangerous."²⁶ The West is unique, not universal. Its attenuation by uncontrolled immigration or by overextension into a world of adversarial civilizations such as Islam will only lead to decay, not renewal.

Huntington wrote in broad strokes. His knowledge of Islam was minimal and he was always more adept at proclaiming the uniqueness of the West than at engaging with the specifics of Muslim societies. But the scholar who first coined the phrase "clash of civilizations" – Bernard Lewis – is of very different vintage. He is often skewered by the liberal intellectual establishment for the supposed anti-Muslim animus latent in his essentialized accounts of Arab life. His long-running feud with Edward Said did not help matters either. And his adoption by the neo-conservative foreign policy elite during the second Bush administration sealed his reputation as a nefarious Orientalist among left-leaning academics. But I do not share this assessment. His scholarly credentials are impeccable. And he has spent decades studying the texts and societies he describes in his work. That this work clearly and consistently peddles in Orientalist tropes is less a sign of animus than of the nature of the Western academy's treatments of Islam over the last hundred years or so. Lewis is an extraordinary historian and a wonderfully evocative writer. But his methodology is pretty standard for historians of the Middle East and he is ideologically a median scholar. He is no far-right crank. In fact, his reading of Arab history is often sympathetic to Muslims and deeply considered. Lewis argues that medieval Christendom and Islam were cut from the same Abrahamic cloth, and though there were obvious differences, they essentially "spoke the same language" and could therefore "disagree meaningfully" about this or that.[27] As the two civilizations faced each other across the Mediterranean and the Bosporus, they did so often as enemies. But the mutual suspicion was predicated on mutual understanding. As consecutive dispensations from the same God, they were competing for souls and had aspirations to a unified world order. In this, they mirrored each other perfectly.[28]

This symmetry was broken when Christendom went its own way and Islam stayed put in all significant respects. Secularism emerged in Christendom because there was practical need in Europe to "escape from the horrors of state-sponsored and state-enforced doctrine" during and after the wars of religion.[29] There were no such wars in the Muslim world and therefore no need to imagine an alternative. Lewis also argues that the persistent threat from Islam was a catalyst for the development of European social and human sciences, and the study of foreign languages and cultures.[30] For a thousand years, the Muslim world faced no such persistent threat, and developed no equivalent sciences of the study of the other.[31] As reformed and secularized Christendom has come to dominate the world order in the last two hundred years, it has made misguided attempts to reshape Islam in its own image. But lacking the historical and theological resources to internalize the political language of the West, Muslim societies have become schizophrenic and dangerous.[32] Lewis likens secularism to the prescription for a "Christian disease." Misprescribed, it can undermine and ultimately destroy the world of Islam.[33] He believes that if this were to happen, something remarkable and beautiful would be lost. A bastardized, half-baked version of the West in lieu for the exceptional fullness and essence of Islam is not an even exchange. For Lewis, this would be a travesty. It already is.

Similar sentiments have been put forth by a bevy of mid to late twentieth-century historians of the Middle East, most notably Eli Kedourie and Sylvia Haim. Even Marshall Hodgson's seminal work on Islam is sometimes prone to exoticizing and essentializing turns that share basic premises of Muslim difference with Bernard Lewis. And recent books by Shadi Hamid and Wael Hallaq point to the continuing utility of the trope of exception among Muslims themselves, even as it is now more commonly wedded to benevolent concern for Muslim societies or to a positive role for Islam in the modern world.[34] But as with the development of the idea of a Muslim world, the comprehensive reach of the trope of exception is most evident in its use by anti-Western Muslim thinkers and their militant counterparts. It is these Muslim exceptionalists that have received the most press in the West in recent years, and rightly so. Their actions have burst onto the scene in terrifying spectacles of violence. When Osama bin Laden officially declared war on the West in 1998, he did so with explicit reference to the presence of Western troops in Muslim lands. Although initially received as standard anti-colonial rhetoric coming from the global periphery, bin Laden's specific indignation at the mere presence of Western soldiers in "the land of the two holy mosques" was of singular importance in the fatwa. It was as if some fundamental norm of difference was being violated and a deadly virus had entered the body of Islam. This quasi-medical understanding of difference is a common feature in exceptionalist thought. In his last book-length manuscript, for example, Huntington decried the gradual disappearance of the Anglo-Protestant "American Creed" in the wake of an uncontrolled immigrant contagion from Latin America and elsewhere.[35] Paul Berman and his ilk are similarly concerned about the future of Europe.

The intellectual father of contemporary Muslim exceptionalism is Sayyid Qutb, the Egyptian dissident who was tortured, imprisoned and then executed by the regime of Gamal Abdul Nasser in 1966. Qutb argued that after centuries of domination by the West, "the Muslim community is now buried under the debris of man-made traditions of several generations and is crushed under the weight of those false laws and customs that are not even remotely related to Islamic teachings." The "whole world is now steeped in *jahilliyyah* [ignorance]" and the source of this ignorance is the modern Western claim that "the right to create values, to legislate rules of correct behavior, and to choose a way of life rests with man, without regard to what Allah has prescribed."[36] Qutb advocated for a Muslim vanguard to resist this anthropocentric value system and to regenerate the community by removing from the Muslim body politic those foreign elements that have infected it. Interestingly, Qutb's most trenchant concern was the Hobbesian problem of the rule of man over man and the violence, corruptions and curtailments of freedom that this necessarily devolved into. But unlike the socially contracted rule of a human sovereign, Qutb's solution was the voluntary surrender of *hakimiyyah*, of sovereign authority over other human beings, to God alone. The Muslim community, then, is that which willfully enters a social contract of submission to a theocentric source of law and "Islam is a declaration of the freedom of man from servitude to other men."[37]

Qutb's reading of the Quranic concept of *hakimiyyah* as sovereignty in the political sense is thoroughly nontraditional and modern, and it owes interpretive debt to a bevy of earlier Muslim thinkers such as Abu A'la Maududi who were themselves heavily influenced by Western concepts of state and society. And as with Maududi, Qutb refashions such concepts into imagining Islam as the very antithesis of the West. His two years living in America elicited only revulsion at the sin, depravity and corruption he found there.[38] Unlike the modernist elites and the modernizing state in Egypt – and in a curious mirroring of Paul Berman's exhortations against Tariq Ramadan – Qutb found nothing of value in America, nothing worth engaging with, but much to fear. He therefore offered a strident critique of Western understandings of freedom, even as he took freedom to be the primary goal of an Islamic politics. And this politics is as expansive and universalist as its Western counterpart, for "it addresses itself to the whole of mankind, and its sphere is the whole earth." Qutb's is the clearest exposition of an Islamic *nobelesse oblige*, the identification of "the very nature of Islam" with "initiative for freeing the human beings throughout the earth from servitude to anyone other than God."[39] This is Toynbee and Kidd in reverse, the dissolution of all difference into a harmonious and unified body of a renewed *Dar al-Islam* (abode of Islam), an Islamic melting pot in the inverse mirror of communist utopias and ends of history.

* * *

In an article suggestively titled "Of Mimicry and Man," Homi Bhabha quips that "the discourse of post-Enlightenment English colonialism often speaks in a tongue that is forked, not false."[40] True to its imperialist origins, this doublespeak of forked tongues is also evident in conformist and exceptionalist talk about Islam in the present contemporary. At the far end of the spectrum, such talk is respectively either liberal imperialist or fascist in its politics. But even in its ostensibly more reasonable iterations, either end of this discourse carries traces of early twentieth-century race talk and evolutionary theories of progress. Notice, for example, that although conformist thinking does imply an eventual solution, a perpetual peace in the *imago occidens*, in practice it nevertheless permanently defers any final resolution through the movement of Western history itself. Expansion here is the continuous unfurling of the meaning of freedom at the pace of the West, of a *Weltgeist* that can only be known in the concrete universal evolution of a particular *Volksgeist*. Enfolded into the bosom of this expansion, the Muslim concrete other is always a step behind, a minute late and a subject away from this expansion's farthest magnitude, its most current form, its latest extent. This is because as a structure of feeling, *noblesse oblige* is always intertwined with notions of constitutive difference, and conformism has no existence entirely independent of exceptionalism. European Jewry learned the hard way that the promise of assimilation *sans* the provision of a properly political integration is a ruse that ends in catastrophe. That no amount of conforming can decisively erase the exceptions attendant to the difference at play in such asymmetric recognitive relationships. A politics whose supreme and permanent aim is expansion is no politics at all for those being expanded into or around. It is in this sense that the eithers and ors of exception and conformity are ultimately neither genuine descriptions of Islam as a form of politics nor viable choices on how to proceed. They are instead the

Freedom Talk

various angled walls of an echo chamber that on account of their peculiar architecture turn the cacophony of different voices into a single, recurring, interrogatory drone.

Consider, for example, the case of the Sochi Winter Olympics in 2010 and the media outcry in the West about Russia's supposed mistreatment of its LGBT population. If the ink spilled on stories concerning the price tag, dirty water, malfunctioning showers and toilets, and of course the threat of terrorism was any indication, these were surely the most scrutinized of the lesser Olympics in history. Once the United States won its first gold medal, the storylines changed to more uplifting fare. Still, the media never did tire of venting its moral outrage at Russia's new laws discriminating against its LGBT population. This was, in a manner of speaking, as it should be. Although Russia had clearly stated that no visiting athletes would be targeted on the basis of the law, the moral concern was valid enough. But the relentless focus on this issue was never complemented by another germane concern: Would there have been such an outrage 20 years earlier? Ten? Five? This question is important because it points to the historical nature of Western moral consensus. When sprinters Tommie Smith and John Carlos raised their gloved fists in protest in the 1968 Summer Olympics, the moral valence of their act went unappreciated. *Time* magazine called it an act of "petulance," their silent remonstration a "theater of the absurd," and headlined its October 25 issue "Angrier, Nastier, Uglier."[41] In the decades since, most in the West have come to value this act of Smith and Carlos as a seminal moment in the civil rights movement. The political integration of African Americans into the American body politic and an accounting of the black experience of marginalization has been an indispensable factor in this transformation. But in 1968, the moral consensus was not particularly kind to these athletes or to their act. They were dismissed from the team and the Olympics, and forced to return home in disgrace. Their actions have not changed in the years since 1968, but the assessment of them certainly has. In a similar vein, the same laws in place during a hypothetical Olympics in Sochi in 1994 would have drawn little or no attention. Remember that this was a time *before* Ellen came out as the *first* gay character on American national television. Back then, the West's moral focus was elsewhere.

It is important to point out, though, that even back then, Smith and Carlos were hailed as heroes in the Global South. Folks in the formerly colonized world, and certainly also in the African-American community, were much better attuned to the moral concern of racism, exploitation and oppression on the part of the (mostly) white Global North. They did not have to wait a decade or two before recognizing the moral courage of these men. It would appear that a significant portion of the world was well *ahead* of the West in recognizing the moral danger of racism and the ethical consequences of oppressing a minority population through legal and other means. It took the intense political confrontations of a maturing civil rights movement and a furious international campaign of boycott and divestment against the South African apartheid regime to decisively shift the West's moral center on these matters. But even this shift has been internalized now as the timely self-flowering of the Western regime of rights, as though it were something internal to its essence only waiting to emerge at the opportune evolutionary moment. The political successes of the LGBTQ movement have now been similarly weaponized as cudgels of judgment on the rest of the world, while the political concerns emanating from this world are dismissed routinely as anachronistic or illegitimate if they challenge the West's current moral consensus.[42]

That particular iterations of the value and meaning of freedom, applied to particular subjects at particular times, can nonetheless present as a universalist moral model for normative evaluation is one way in which the rhetoric of liberal righteousness continuously bleeds into the proclamation of Western exceptionalism. Even in its most benign iteration, then, conformism is the premise that conversations across the difference of Islam lead not to the construction of ends constituted by a practice of politics, but to the confirmation of an ever-evolving *and* pregiven set of fundamental values. Conformists have therefore (at best) always served as sympathetic excavators of the Islamic tradition, mining texts, ideas and histories, seeking signs of familiarity. That this is an endless, asymptotic project is no sign of their lack of effort, but of the nature of the discourse itself. Suffice it to say that where conformists speak out of both sides of their mouth, exceptionalists also doublespeak in their incessant claims of cultural difference. This is true not only for those purveyors of Western exceptionalism who harp on about the superiority of their culture, but also for a certain kind of multiculturalist advocacy for preservation of 'other' people's lifeworlds, and of postcolonial and racial angst fetishized as an anti-political rejection of the culture of the oppressor. When practiced on strongly exceptionalist terms, this kind of politics also leads nowhere good.

* * *

Taken together, conformism and exceptionalism are the forked tongue of freedom talk, and they are in turn themselves forked into various units of conversation that still constitute a single, overarching discourse of depoliticization. Not always in the manner of malice or overt discrimination, even sometimes in the way of appreciation and preservation, but always in service of a political project beset by an originary contradiction: "What imperialists wanted was an expansion of political power without the foundation of a body politic."[43] The Nobel Prize-winning novelist V.S. Naipaul has quipped that they "wanted gold and slaves, like everybody else," but also "wanted statues put up to themselves as people who had done good things for the slaves."[44] Slaves are more of a metaphor already in the twentieth century and certainly also today, but Naipaul evokes the complex structures of feeling animating the imperialist enterprise quite well. Conformism and exceptionalism are contrasting but complementary solutions to the problem of an expansion of political power into the Muslim world without a parallel expansion of the political community. And this too, early on, in a both rapidly 'nationalizing' and 'individualizing' environment where self-determination and freedom were beginning to be seen as the primary modus operandi of politics in the West. To square the circle of imperial political power in this context required the interlocking discourses of 'not yet ready of freedom' that one encounters in Kipling's work, for example, and the unassailable difference of the native as in Conrad. Properly political relationships between the West and its many others such as Islam could therefore either be deferred indefinitely through the pedagogical model of development or the agonistic model of necessary if sometimes harsh domination. The end of overt colonialism has certainly led to modifications and adjustments in freedom talk but the underlying basis of its existence have nowhere been dismissed nor denied in the West. The recent neo-imperialist musings of folks such as Niall Ferguson and Michael Ignatieff are ample proof of freedom talk's persistence and its continuing utility. This is because the agnostic imperative of expansion continuously breathes new life into its companion structures of feeling, animating and reanimating the imperial enterprise even in the absence of empire. And "expansion as a permanent and supreme aim of politics," argued Hannah Arendt "is the central political idea of imperialism ... Since it implies neither temporary looting nor the more lasting assimilation of conquest, it is an entirely new concept in the long history of political thought and action."[45] Talk of freedom in the Muslim world is not always false or a pretense for some nefarious plan of resource extraction. Nor even inevitably a marker of Western condescension (although this is indeed often the case) and sometimes clearly animated by genuine concern. But to account for the novelty and necessity of expansion as a *political* idea, the tongue that speaks of such freedom has been forked since birth. And no decisive intervention has ever been made to fix this diabolical flaw. It is for this reason that while the logic of imperialism inevitably generates a single world, the rhetoric of imperialism necessarily turns this into "a compartmentalized world ... inhabited by different species." It depoliticizes the world, so to say, either through the construction of classrooms or in the spectacle of menageries.

Consider, for example, that vaguely defined expectations of democracy and secularism have only become salient as global talking points about Muslim societies in the last few decades, and for reasons of both historical contingency and political expediency. Talk of homosexuality is even more recent, and although talk of women has been around a long time, it has gone through many different registers over the years. Back in the day, Muslims were often accused of being depraved in their relaxed accommodations of homosexuality, and uncivilized for their excessive sexual appetites. Now they are judged deficient in precisely the opposite ways. Freedom remains the crimson interpretive thread of the West, but its content keeps shifting, and its deployment as a rhetoric of judgment on the Muslim world is as slippery as ever. Already, it appears that these talking points may soon shift decisively once again with the rising tide of right-wing politics in the West. Diminishing faith in democratic institutions in the West could well restore the 'whiskey and miniskirts' model of Muslim reform that gave us the White Revolution in Iran and served as the dominant model for evaluating Islam in the middle decades of the twentieth century. Or a resignation about the inherent difference of Islam and the desire for sufficiently pacified client states in the Middle East may turn the tide in favor of furious antagonisms toward Muslims in the homeland and abroad. More likely, and as always, some combination of these two responses will prevail. What remains redolent is the structure of freedom talk, the peculiar forking of the tongue that makes it so effective as the discursive instrument of pacification, the handmaiden of expansion.

It is for this reason that conflicting parties in these debates continue to conform as if to the two sides of the same sword as it cleaves through the organic mass of the Muslim body, rendering it into two inanimate objects, mere 'things': yes or no? It is these same 'things' that are fighting in the streets of Aleppo and attending an interfaith dialogue at a church near you. Is there no better way to talk? There are in fact roads less traveled that do not move in circles, and speech *sans* the forking of tongues. There always have been. Whether in Tahrir Square of 2011 or Delhi of 1857, Muslims on the ground have been animated throughout by complex and varied political views, actions and aspirations. And from the very beginning of their long tryst with modernity, they have articulated visions of their past, present and future that rarely conform easily to the binaries of yes or no answers. That these simple yeses and nos have come to dominate not just the global public imaginary but also the very vocabulary of Muslim political existence on the world stage is an unfortunate but remediable situation. Even denied their full humanity and made futile in representation, Muslims are after all as human and modern as anyone. The historian Cemil Aydin has argued that the ahistorical myth of an encounter between a modern West and an essentially supine Muslim world is in reality belied by the fact that:

> Before and during the colonial period Muslims' political views could be as imperial as Queen Victoria's, as nationalistic as Gandhi's, and as socialistic as Lenin's ... Individual Muslims were anarchists, feminists, and pacifists. They were as modern as their European counterparts.[46]

To this list I would add the innumerable ways in which Muslims continue to reconfigure their own traditions of political thought and practice to account for the newness of the modern context. It is certainly true – and as has been the thesis of this book – that a particular variety of Islamic thinking has indeed conformed to the either/or of absolute rejections or acceptances of the West. But this hardly exhausts the total discursive output of a distinctly Muslim experience of modernity, and it never has.

* * *

Consider, for example, the case of Muhammad Iqbal (1877–1938) in British colonial India. Iqbal was arguably the greatest Indian poet of the twentieth century and has the distinction of being one of the few figures revered equally in both India and Pakistan (although, of course, for very different reasons). He is credited by Pakistanis for coming up with the idea of a separate homeland for the Muslims of India and is cherished in India for his love of the homeland captured in India's national song, "Better Than All the World Is Our Hindustan" (*Sāre Jahāṉ se Acchā*). Eschewing the eithers and ors of these ostensibly conflicting subject positions, to say that Iqbal was a complicated man is perhaps something of an understatement! Equally complicated was his unconventional synthesis of Western philosophy and Islam in his uniquely Muslim exposition of freedom as a political idea. The Muslim body politic in early twentieth-century India was already bifurcated along conformist and exceptionalist lines, with the Muslim League of Muhammad Ali Jinnah (the founding father of Pakistan) committed to a conventional politics of nationalism and a procedurally 'secular' conception of the state, and the Jamat-e-Islami (Islamic Party) of Abu ala Maududi organized around a reactionary rejection of the West in whole. But Iqbal belonged to a different cast of characters (which included Mohandas Gandhi and Rabindranath Tagore, for example) in late colonial India for whom the parameters for independence had not yet settled into an acqiessence to a mere succession of the state to the locals. For these folks, the very nature of the future polity itself was still very much in question. Rejecting any conception of self-determination imagined along simple nationalist and statist lines conforming to either the nationalistic and procedurally secular Western model or excepting from it along Islamist lines, Iqbal wondered if freedom already captive to these pregiven political parameters could be called freedom at all. Iqbal filled this gap with two iconic poetic symbols – *khudi* (selfness/ego) and *bekhudi* (selflessness) – that could generate a peculiarly Muslim (and modern) conception of political freedom when imagined as either end of an ever-evolving historical dialectic.[47]

In an obvious response to the condition of Muslim servitude under colonial rule, Iqbal imagined *khudi* as the relentless explication of the self's freedom against any authoritarian attempts to control or subdue it. But *khudi* was also more generally a reflection of Iqbal's belief that "the ultimate fate of a people does not depend so much on organization as on the worth and power of individual men. In an over organized society the individual is altogether crushed out of existence."[48] Iqbal received his Bachelor of Arts from Trinity College at Cambridge and his doctorate in Philosophy from Ludwig Maximilian University in Munich, and was deeply influenced by Western philosophers such as Friedrich Nietzsche, Henri Bergson and Goethe. The concept of *khudi* therefore owes an obvious debt to Nietzsche's will to power, for example, and a dialectic understanding of the movement of history has clear affinities with Hegel's work. Iqbal was never shy about acknowledging these influences and was in fact openly critical of those insular and obscurantist tendencies among his co-religionists that led to a world-weary narrow-mindedness. But these Western influences were always folded back into the reconstruction of Islam itself as a potent ideological force in the modern world. The unyielding individualism of the modern Western conceptions of the self had to be accepted and internalized by Muslims if they were to rediscover "the inner impulse of Islam ... [and] the original verities of freedom, equality and solidarity with a view to rebuild [their] moral, social and political ideals out of their original simplicity and universality."[49] But an ego unleashed on the world as some variety of an *Übermensch* naturally led to the very condition of servitude for other egos that Muslims of India found themselves in. It is on this point, and in contradistinction to Nietzsche, that Iqbal offered a way out in *bekhudi*.

Bekhudi is the dialectical negation of a *khudi* already extant, for selflessnes as a condition of being has no meaning without a vigorous ego that willfully negates itself in service of some higher end. This negation produces a new ego and the process repeats ad infinitum in the self's continuous and relentless unfolding in freedom. Whereas *khudi* fortifies the self in its independence and freedom from constraint, the inverse negations of *bekhudi* are directed toward the higher ideals of Islam itself for it is "only as a member of society [does] the individual [become] conscious" of these ideals.[50] Iqbal walks a philosophical tightrope here much as the Muslims of India did, suspended as they were between either mimicry of the West, on one end, and a complete rejection of it, on the other. But Iqbal never wavered on the point that *khudi* is poetically, philosophically and politically *prior* to *bekhudi*. The parameters of collective self-determination are only a second-order explication of the self's freedom. For the self must determine itself freely first before it negates itself into place within a larger community. In practical terms, this meant that Muslims must will themselves to freely imagine what it means to speak and act as a Muslim in the modern world *sans* the constraining eithers and ors of freedom talk before any demand for a Muslim homeland in India could be reasonably construed as a demonstration of their political freedom. But Iqbal cautioned that much as a word finds its proper place within the constraints of rhyming couplet, and desires to be so constrained out of love, not fear, an individual self lacking a desire to find its proper station in the world is doomed to despair. Or as Annemarie Schimmel puts it in her analysis of Iqbal's *Javid-Nama* (1930):

> The complete development of the Ego does not lead to a cult of the "Ubermensch" or to exaggerated individualism and egotizm, but it is merely the initial stage; the final aim of life is the building up of something impersonal, i.e. the community of men, each of them loving, understanding, and tolerating the other – tolerance is respect for the Ego of the fellow-citizen, and it is better to go the way of God with the caravan.[51]

Iqbal's politics of desire are an odd combination of this and that, a bricolage of Western philosophy, flights of poetic fancy and Islamic theology. But his conception of freedom as a political idea bears the unmistakable marks of his absolute commitment to Islam as an ideology of life and not just another 'conventional' religion. Consider, for example, that Iqbal rarely compared Islam to other religions, but rather imagined it in contradistinction to other modern ways of organizing the polity, such as secularism, communism and liberalism. Yet he is no theocrat. And far from it, Iqbal criticized the "intellectual attitudes" of the *ulama* as having "reduced the Law of Islam practically to the state of immobility," and was the bane of many a Muslim mullah's existence back in the day and continues to be today.[52] This is because Iqbal's idiosyncratic and peculiarly Muslim exposition of self-determination has, over the years, provided succor and intellectual scaffolding to various 'modernist' constructions of the Muslim identity in India, Pakistan and elsewhere, and he continues to hold a special place in the beating hearts of all those Muslims still clamoring for "something new" to replace the tired old paradigms of either strident fundamentalism, on the one hand, or a soulless "Westoxification," on the other. Indeed, Pakistan's current prime minister, Imran Khan, has made Iqbal's poetry and ideology an explicit centerpiece of his plans for a "New Pakistan" (*naya Pakistan*) reborn not in the image of the West or a rejection of it, but rather through a politics of desire rooted in the Muslim experience of modernity. Writing for the *Arab News* in 2012 many years before he became prime minister, and in contradistinction to George W. Bush's ostensible love for "real" Islam, Khan intoned that:

> One of the problems facing Pakistan is the polarization of two reactionary groups. On the one side is the Westernized group that looks upon Islam through Western eyes and has inadequate knowledge about the subject. It reacts strongly to anyone trying to impose Islam in society and wants only a selective part of the religion. On the other extreme is the group that reacts to this Westernized elite and in trying to become a defender of the faith, takes up such intolerant and self-righteous attitudes that are repugnant to the spirit of Islam.

Khan is cognizant of the moral language of modernity and has stated elsewhere that, of course, Muslims in

Pakistan and elsewhere need "genuine democracy, freedom of speech that allows open debate, an evolution of our culture, and above all rule of law" to feel at home in the modern world. But "what [we do] not need is pseudo-westernization with Muslim westernized elites aping superficial aspects of the Western society, in reaction to which we have seen the growth of fundamentalism, which in turn stunts the growth of our culture."[53] Whatever one thinks of Khan as a politician (and there is plenty to be wary of on that front), his political theology is an explicit repudiation of both conformism and exceptionalism. And in this he is hardly alone. Iqbal has had a profound influence on a whole coterie of diverse Muslim thinkers, from Ali Shariati, Mehdi Bazargan and Dr. Abdulkarim Soroush in Iran, to the aforementioned Faiz Ahmad Faiz, Quaratulain Haider and Fazlur Rahman in India/Pakistan, to even non-Muslims such as B.R. Ambedkar and Annemarie Schimmel. The breadth of his influence is evidenced by the fact that fundamentalist and feminist Muslims, for example, can both quote his words with aplomb, and even Ayatollah Ali Khamenie (Iran's nominal leader) lauded him in saying that "we have a large number of non-Persian-speaking poets in the history of our literature, but I cannot point out any of them whose poetry possesses the qualities of Iqbal's Persian poetry."[54] This ubiquitous appreciation is a testament to the fact that Iqbal honestly spoke an unabashedly Muslim experience of being in the world into poetic existence at a time when the nature and meaning of this existence was depressingly obscure in the global public square. And times have hardly changed all that much in the ensuing hundred years or so.

To speak this experience into existence as a viable way of being in the world remains an urgent scholarly task, to be sure. But it may well be much more than that. Inasmuch as freedom talk is a corollary to a Schmittian concept of politics as rooted in a prior friend/enemy distinction, it necessarily inhibits an Arendtian politics of appearance where Muslims are accounted for in the full complex plurality of their existence.[55] Both the expansive inclusion of the Muslim as friend or the expansive obliteration of the Muslim as enemy rely on such inhibition to continuously clear the field, so to say, to siphon off the difference of Islam into piles of the familiar or unfamiliar. But the binary habits attendant to the practice of such politics are difficult to contain within the specifics of this or that context, relevant only for this or that subject. Already in the early 1990s, the West was euphoric about its absolute victory over all competitors, its rightful place at the very end of history assured by the provident collapse of Soviet communism. While the euphoria itself has worn off in the ensuing years, a certain attitude of having brought something to a close, of having completed something, if not history itself then at least some relevant portion of it, has persisted. This attitude is explicit in the neo-imperialism of Niall Ferguson, Michael Ignatieff and their ilk, but also implicit in the everyday common sense, natural familiarity and matter-of-factness of the West's moral lexicon for describing itself and the world. The cultures, values, virtues and institutions associated with this particular iteration of the West are beginning to harden in their already held meanings, their evolution sedimenting into completion, their meanings no longer as free to roam as they once were. And these sedimentations are themselves subject to either/or evaluations, the West as triumphant, superior and exceptional, or what could reasonably be called an 'empire of human rights'. Consider the following intriguing observation made back in 1994 by sociologist Jose Casanova:

> Western modernity is at a crossroads. If it does not enter into a creative dialogue with the other, with those traditions which are challenging its identity, modernity will most likely triumph. But it may end up being devoured by the inflexible, inhuman logic of its own creations. It would be profoundly ironic if, after all the beating it has received from modernity, religion could somehow unintentionally help modernity save itself.[56]

Although Islam was clearly not at the front of his mind – Casanova was commenting on the "conditions of possibility for public religion" in post-Christian, ostensibly secularized Western publics – it is nonetheless obvious that his core insight is relevant to this discussion. There is something terribly broken in Western modernity that may not be fixable within the parameters it has set for itself and the forms of knowledge it is capable of generating on its own. That the common problems now facing humanity – the searing inequalities of late capitalism and global finance, catastrophic climate change, a widening democratic deficit at home and abroad, the rapid and destabilizing movements of people from the global periphery to the metropoles of erstwhile empires, the rise of regressive populisms in the East and the West, and, yes, terrorism in all its state and non-state varieties – could well require notions of the self, community and the good life that are not available within the provincial moral lexicon of a West which is in fact complicit in causing these problems in the first place. In this provincial moral lexicon, Islam is merely the latest iteration of the post-Enlightenment notion of 'bad religion', a regressive and atavistic force that threatens to undermine the rule of reason and the utopian ends of universal progress. Now that these utopian ends appear permanently deferred by the frustrating contradictions of Western modernity itself, perhaps it is time to reconsider what role religion in general and Critical Islam in particular might play in bringing this common world back to a state of healthful vigor. And to question the regnant paradigms and normative "self-images of the age" before they devolve into ugly caricatures of themselves and destroy Western modernity from within – and the world with it.[57]

4

Reason Talk

In this chapter, I argue that public discourse on the problem of Islam is replete with references to reform and rationality because such discourse bends to the strictures of what I call reason talk about Muslims. This kind of talk is primarily concerned with identifying Islam as a religion that is then judged against the West's own peculiar historical experience as a normative ideal for evaluating all iterations of religion as such. The generic, fully privatized, and historically suspect ideals rooted in this experience have long served to highlight the deficiencies of Islam in its impartial ecclesiastic divestment from politics and in its inability to accept the public supremacy of reason. But particularly punitive tropes from the nineteenth century are enjoying a renaissance post-9/11. At least since Ernest Renan's famous lecture on "Islam and Science" (1883), the scientific, reasoned outlook of Westernized moderns has been contrasted with the Muslim's surfeit of religious enthusiasm that not only prevents material progress, but also boils over into zealotry and violence.[1] *These same themes have been picked up and developed further by the (so-called) New Atheists and critical ex-Muslims who demand that Muslims conjoin their faith to the established trajectory of the European Enlightenment. In this reading, Islam ceases to be an independent category of historical or intellectual analysis. It can either regurgitate an established role, acting out the necessary reformations and revolutions in a replaying of European history. Or it can decline the invitation to do so and remain unreasonable, irrational and obscure. In reason talk about Muslims, the only good Muslim is an ex-Muslim informant.*

* * *

The famed Christian realist Reinhold Niebuhr was fond of quoting Marx's oft-repeated dictum that the beginning of all criticism is the criticism of religion.[2] Niebuhr did this in print, and on multiple occasions and almost as often to highlight Marx's wisdom as his phobias. Considering Niebuhr's own rather complicated personal history with Marxism, his well-known distaste for Soviet communism and, of course, well, his Christianity, this seems an odd sort of thing for him to do. How to explain it, and what to make of it? Niebuhr himself offers us a clue when in an essay he wrote for *The Nation* in 1938, he notes that "one of the recurring motifs of Greek tragedy is the hero's deeper involvement in his own fate through his very efforts to extricate himself from it." Niebuhr called this "abundant proof of the profound insight [of the Greek dramatists] into human tragedy" and suggested that "they were [in fact] not writing melodrama but were interpreting history."[3] Marx belonged to that teeming cohort of nineteenth-century men who sought escape from the prison of belief and the tyranny of superstition in their rejection of religion as nowhere a veridic account of the nature of reality and everywhere a retardant on the full potential of the human condition. These men differed in their various renderings of reason and rationality, of the meanings and ends of the scientific enterprise, and even perhaps in their eschatological aspirations for the future of humanity. But living in the long historical shadow of the Inquisition(s) and wars of religion, and subject to persistent opposition from their contemporary religionists, they were united in their contempt for the religionist as an archaic order of being whose prior effacement was the necessary condition for salutary progress in this new age of science. Criticism of religion was therefore not a particular operation of reason, but foundational to the very existence of reason as the spirit of this new age. And the heroes of this age were to be the men of science and reason, the prophets "of the golden future time" and the harbingers of magnificent utopias.[4] Outgrowing the adolescence of religion was the necessary first step in humanity's evolution as a species into adulthood.

It is these sentiments – not only these outright rejections of religion and the eschatological hopes attendant thereof, but also the prior certainties about the essential nature and meaning of religion as such (i.e. what is this *religion* that is being overcome) – that Niebuhr identified as the beautiful hubris of these men and their "deeper involvement in [their] own fate through [their] very efforts to extricate [themselves] from it." In his sanctification of matter, for example, Marx had sought an existential escape from the chains of oppression through the dialectical rationality of the philosopher. He seized upon Hegel's brilliant and, some may argue, climactic synthesis of the entire Platonic tradition and Christianity with history itself as an opportunity to turn this tradition upside down. Or as Sidney Hook put it in his Marxist days, "right side up."[5] But upside-down, or right-side-up, inversions carry traces of that which they seek to invert. Even in Niebuhr's own lifetime, the expectations of beatific adulthood for a reasoned humanity were already being complicated by the realities on the ground. Marxist insights had gone from being inspiration to countless liberatory socialisms around the world to undergirding the horrors of the Stalinist regime in Russia. And the promise of reason to permanently assuage the ailments of the world that so inspired generations of liberal do-gooders was in turn just as manifest in scientifically sanctified racisms of empire and in the technological carnage of the two world wars. Niebuhr correctly intuited that these supposedly wayward tangents of reason were no tangents at all, but reason's "deeper involvement in [its] own fate" masquerading as an "[effort] to extricate [itself] from it." That the attempt to frame reason as an objective arbiter above the cacophony of religious particularities and excesses was always doomed – qua its heroic pedigree – to sediment into the same subjective chauvinisms it ostensibly sought to overcome. Even a cursory examination of the works of these pioneers of reason quickly reveals that their views of the world and their own place in it as European men of a certain vintage were shot through with the same certainties and hubris as the religion(s) they were ostensibly seeking to leave behind. And their universal reason was in essence an inverted tribal God made imminent in the rational actor's inerrant power over its various others at home and abroad. This much is obvious in Marx, for example, when he wondered why "the history of the East [appears] as a history of religion?"[6] Critique of religion was always already also criticism of inferior lifeworlds marked by corrupt beliefs and practices, and overcoming religion had an expansionist political valence. Scientific *noblesse oblige* and contempt for religion were cooked up in the same cauldron as the age of empire, and were in fact, from the beginning, part and parcel of an imperial state of mind.

For all of Niebuhr's warnings that the cult of reason is no more durable a panacea for the ills of the world than the supposed cults it seeks to replace, that the human condition is not susceptible on account of its humanity to permanent resolutions of utopias only provisional equilibria of politics, for all this and more from a wide variety of twentieth-century thinkers of various persuasions and backgrounds, the promise of reason as the one true universal language of paradise retains great sanction among large sections of the learned elite. Some version of the Marxist dictum – that the beginning of all criticism is the criticism of religion – is still a foundational mantra, a Magna Carta for enlightened secularists everywhere. Galileo looms large in their imagination, as does Bruno, Bacon, William of Ockham, Erasmus, Spinoza, Hume, Voltaire and, closer to our own time, Darwin, Freud and Nietzsche. The stories they tell of reason's origins, its oppressions and its eventual triumphs are just as mythic in their fabulism and poignancy as any ever told by the religions of the world. And the reversals of religion they espouse demand (and often receive) a pride of place in the scholarly enterprise. For as the story goes, the academic study of religion first emerged from an astonishing reversal of the Christian Church's power to name, to classify, evaluate and organize the world. It was in the regime of this normalized and absolute subjectivity that Galileo's science first became an object of scorn and Bruno was burned at the stake. But the Renaissance loosened the chains of the Church's authority, the Reformation decisively shattered its unreserved control over truth, and the Enlightenment consolidated this freedom in its disaggregation of reason from religion and science from faith. The public and political institution of secularism in modern Western societies was an aggregate corollary to these many reversals. It is for these reasons that whatever their particular normative stance on the value of religion, the nineteenth-century pioneers of a science of religion all shared a desire to turn the gaze around, to look at the looker, so to say, and to make the former subject par excellence an object of their scrutiny. It is in this sense that the study of religion is like nothing else in the academy. This objectification of 'religion', a deed disguised as discovery, marks a turning point in the millennial calendar and the coronation of a new World-Subject, the dawning of a new age.

This also explains why the science of religion is simultaneously the original humanistic science and the most despised science, like a science of abjection or of nightmares. Religion is a perennial source of anxiety because while its 'objectification' marks the triumph of science, its objectified presence is also a nagging reminder of an erstwhile abuser. But inasmuch as "the history of the East [appears] as a history of religion" to Marx and his ilk, anxieties about religion are also anxieties about the unreasoned other out there in the world, the unruly masses and the insufficiently evolved societies of the East and their contagion in Western metropoles. The science of religion has therefore served often not merely as a humanistic science, but as the science that grades humanity according to its distance from reason. And nowhere is this science's intertwined combination of condescension and contempt more evident today than in the furious condemnations of Islam by the so-called New Atheists and their (ex)Muslim allies. As the contemporary inheritors of nineteenth-century positivism – that bastard child of Cartesian skepticism and post-Enlightenment scientism – theirs is the most severe inversion of religion and therefore the most 'religious' of the scientific ways of looking at the world. This is why men such as Richard Dawkins and Sam Harris so easily replicate the zealotry of the medieval Church in their abject dismissal of heresies in the academy, and in their crude depictions of Islam, their unrelenting inquisition of Muslims. But positivism is only the deep end of the pool. To varying degrees of depth, anxieties such as these have informed nearly every critical appropriation of Islam as, in essence, a roadblock to the full flowering of reason and to the eschatological aspirations of the men of science. And the continuing viability of Islam in the modern world as a reservoir of meaning and identity has only exacerbated the anxiety that the 'objection' of this erstwhile subject is dangerously tentative, always in jeopardy of being done in by an outbreak. The devil lurks behind every instance of sentiment, and all appeals to meaning. *Reason talk* is that set of discourses that operationalizes this anxiety: too much of Islam still retains the power to name, too much subject remains in this object.

This idea of Islam as a kind of remainder that frustrates the balancing of modernity's equation is evident, for example, in Jacques Derrida's (far less disparaging) claim that unlike Christianity or Judaism:

[or] a mixed religious culture ... Islam, or a certain Islam, [is] the only religious or theocratic culture [worldwide] that can still, in fact or in principle, inspire and declare any resistance to democracy ... [and to the] process of secularization ... and thus, in the strict sense, of politicization.[7]

Notice that Derrida is making no claims here about Islam as such, nor even about Islam at large, but rather identifying "a certain Islam" – which he variously also calls "a certain Arab or Islamic world" and "an Arab and Islamic exception" – as the name for the only religious culture that, in principle, still retains the capacity to resist the "Greco-Christian and globalatinizing" processes of democratization and secularization.[8] Derrida was hardly the crude rebuker of Muslims that the New Atheists often appear to be; his underlying commitment to democracy as a universal practice of open-ended participatory politics *sans* any prior commitment to a universally applicable system of governance, what he called "a model without a model, that accepts its own historicity," tracks closely with both Arendt's and mine.[9] Still, the ease with which Derrida divides Islam into "a certain" this or that, and Muslims into "those who [fight] ... for secularization of the political ... [and] for the emergence of a laic subjectivity" and those who identify instead with "a certain Islam" that resists the "Greco-Christian and globalatinizing" West, echoes the myriad other voices that routinely (and much less charitably) cleave such Muslims into good and bad ones.[10] The New Atheists' positivist anxieties may seem brutish at times, hysterical in their many exaggerations and even dangerously ill-informed. But these are merely the pointed end of a long spear that extends back in time to the very origins of Western modernity and is reinforced in the present by common-sense conceptions of Islam as an exception, as a remainder to an unbalanced equation that the West must solve. This annexation of Islam to the origin myths of reason, and to the self-identity of a certain West itself, is one reason for the circular and interminable quality of contemporary debates about the future of the Muslim world. It also explains why when it comes to the Muslim Question, "the history of our era seems to move in tragic circles strangely analogous to those presented symbolically in Greek tragedy."[11] A certain Islam remains bad religion, the Great White Whale of reason.

* * *

There is very little new about New Atheism. Gary Wolf coined the term in an article for *Wired* back in 2006 for what he described as a post-secular turn in a group of militant non-believers who were no longer content with the accommodation attendant to the secular logic of Church–State separation.[12] The high priests of this new movement were the best-selling authors – Sam Harris, Richard Dawkins, Christopher Hitchens and Daniell

Dennett – who plainly rejected Stephen Jay Gould's influential thesis of science and religion as "non-overlapping magisteria"[13] and were instead committed to the notion that "religion is not only wrong; it's evil."[14] But writing in *Free Inquiry* back in 2010, Tom Flynn – the secular humanist editor of the journal – brushed off the supposed novelty of New Atheism as a function of new interest from big publishing houses, not of new ideas.[15] Post-9/11, publishers were responding to a surge in demand for polemical takes on Islam. The market was already saturated with the harrowing stories of ex-Muslim informants, political diatribes against Islamic fanaticism and faith-based books proclaiming the superiority of Christianity. The New Atheists' ostensibly ecumenical critiques of religion filled a gap in this market, the desire on the part of a certain kind of Western subject to conceptualize the danger of Islam not from the provincial angle of civilizational identity or the need for security, but from the universal vantage point of reason itself. In this reading, Islam and Muslims cannot be reliably subject to the regular secular logic of separation and fair accommodation because they inhabit the secular public imaginary not as any particular iteration of religion, but rather as religion as such in its primordial role as the nemesis of reason. The criticism and rejection of Islam is therefore a kind of prior, pre-political foundation for the viability of a political field marked by reason. It is for this reason that the mere presence of Muslims in public can elicit deep unease in the West, and coercive concern about ostensibly private matters such as their clothing, places of worship, food, speech and even physical appearance is often perceived as a legitimate exercise of political power over them. To argue that this kind of treatment is unreasonable is to fundamentally misconstrue the nature of the critique; such treatment is not an exercise of reason, but is prior to the fact of reason as a stable cornerstone of the regnant secular order. It is a criticism without which the reality of criticism itself is threatened. The sentimental veracity of the proposition that after 9/11 a certain Islam is what *remains* of religion, the undead subject demanding a stake through the heart, and not due process, is everywhere common sense. The New Atheists merely gave voice to this sentiment in their replaying of reason's origin myths with all its imperialist accoutrement intact, performed this time with Islam center stage.

Consider, for example, that whatever their equal opportunity opprobrium with religion itself, the penumbra of the New Atheists' rhetoric leaves little room for any doubt that Islam is a special case. Sam Harris unironically claims that while "Christianity and Judaism can be made to sound the same, intolerant note" as Islam, "it has been a few centuries since either has done so."[16] He then adds that "Islam, more than any other religion human beings have devised, has all the makings of a thoroughgoing cult of death," and that whatever Western politicians may say in public, in reality "we are at war with Islam."[17] Similar sentiments are evident in Christopher Hitchens' oddly anthropomorphized claim that while it has "been some time since Judaism and Christianity resorted openly to torture and censorship ... [Islam] still claims the right to do so in almost all of its dominions."[18] Elsewhere, Hitchens has also called Islam "the most depraved" of religions, and suggested that "at the moment ... the most toxic form that religion takes is the Islamic form."[19] Even Richard Dawkins recently admitted that he has "mixed feelings about the decline of Christianity, in so far as Christianity might be a bulwark against something worse." Echoing Hitchens, and making sure that this "something worse" is clear and unambiguous, Dawkins deadpanned that "there are no Christians, as far as I know, blowing up buildings. I am not aware of any Christian suicide bombers. I am not aware of any major Christian denomination that believes the penalty for apostasy is death."[20] Putting aside for the moment the empirical verity of these and other statements about Islam, Christianity and Judaism, the shared concern seems to be that while the latter have moved on from the most grievous lunacies of their past, Islam uniquely remains in a state of unreconstructed limbo. That with "many Muslims [still] standing eye deep in the red barbarity of the fourteenth century ... it is time to admit that not all cultures are at the same stage of moral development."[21] The very existence of a certain Islam is an abominable anachronism that corroborates the developmental logic of civilizational discourse with post-Christian societies at the pointed apex of progress. And it validates the paternalism and/or coercion attendant to any engagement with Muslims at home and abroad.

Sam Harris is somewhat unique even among the New Atheists for his unabashed and relentless recriminations of Islam, and for his often-boorish click-baiting statements not just about Muslims, but also about women and people of color in general. Hitchens was 'radicalized' by Ayatollah Khomeini's fatwa against his good friend Salman Rushdie. And Dawkins, for all his voluminous venom, often comes across as an out-of-his-depth old-timer, the kind of chauvinist dinosaur so common in the hallowed halls of Oxbridge. But Harris is *sui generis*. At various times in the last ten years, he has called for the racial profiling of Muslims, for keeping their numbers down in Western societies, for the use of torture against suspected Muslim radicals, for extra and perhaps unconstitutional scrutiny of their places of worship and community centers, and for myriad other special forms of attention merited by the exception of Islam.[22] He has decried the possibility of Muslim societies possessing advanced military technology and economic power symmetric with the West as *ipso facto* cause for alarm, and perhaps even for a reasonable nuclear first strike as "the only thing likely to ensure *our* survival."[23] And at all times and in all respects, Harris has been careful to give his proclamations the imprimatur of reason. But this is not reason as elaborated in the development and evolution of this or that human society through the use of science and rationality or even a regime of liberal political rights. No, it is rather reason as the elaboration *itself*, as the abstract fact of Western history and of secular, post-Christian societies. Islam is a contemporary external threat to this elaboration but it is also in one sense an internal threat from out of time, a moment in the early history of reason recurring centuries later in the inability of Muslims to move on from superstition. Criticism of Islam is therefore criticism of a certain "fourteenth-century" Christianity and criticism of religion itself, which is the beginning of all criticism. It is the ritual renewal of reason in the re-enactment of beginning times.

Underlying this trope of Islam as an exception, then, is the notion that reason is both universal *and* it has a specific history, and that this history is in some essential sense also the history of religion. When Harris claims that "many Muslims [are still] standing eye deep in the red barbarity of the fourteenth century," he gives explicit voice to the implicit notion that Islam as a religion lags behind Christianity and Judaism in its development along evolutionary axes grooved into history itself. The grooved path to the effulgence of reason is marked by signposts such as 'Renaissance', 'Reformation', 'Enlightenment' and 'Secularism' – there are heroes to lean on and villains to overcome along the way, and as in all good myths there are winners and losers. Reason unfolds, it flowers in historical time through the provident evolution of a particular potentiality into universal significance on this path alone. Inasmuch as a certain Islam remains *itself*, it remains behind.

In the discursive framework of this account of reason and religion, the Muslim Question, then, is a question about the status of this remainder: Must it forever remain itself or can it be blossomed into reason? Is it able to walk this well-trodden path out of the desert or must it always reject the nourishment? There are, of course, differing opinions on this matter. But in reason talk about Islam, if there is indeed a way out, it is only through conversion to 'a certain Christianity' as a precondition for any further progress; not usually in name, of course, but certainly in form. And in the ritual regurgitation of salvific techniques and miming the magnificent mantras of transformation: *Renaissance*, *Reformation*, *Enlightenment*, *Secularism*. If the history of reason is at once both the history of religion in the abstract and the history of Christianity in the particular, then it stands to reason that Muslims must abandon the history of Islam on the doorstep of modernity and wed themselves instead to this other history which is indeed universal. This is the crimson thread of reason talk, the true nature of the ask. And it is largely non-negotiable.

That the New Atheists comprehend reason through the lens of the history of Christianity is no failure of imagination on their part. Upside down or right side up, inversions carry traces of that which they seek to invert. And in any case, this sense that the triumph of reason is also the triumph of European civilization, and that the two are intertwined in a dialectical dance that continually synthesizes universal history for the world's consumption, is a common-sense notion in the West. It is part and parcel of the broader intellectual ecosphere the New Atheists inhabit, and has been for at least the last century or so. After all, the structures of feeling that ground an imperial state of mind are often contradictory and complementary all at once. Harris may be brazen, but he says little that is novel or new. As Talal Asad has pointed out, "the motive of 'European history' ... is the story of Europe's active power to reconstruct the world ... in its own Faustian image." It is a mistake, then, to imagine that "the epoch of overseas power [is] now decisively over" with the end of overt colonialism. This was in fact only "the beginning of an irreversible global transformation that remains an intrinsic part of 'European experience', and is part of the reason that Europe has become what it is today." Reason is one name for this elaboration, this 'motive of European history', this 'European experience' of world transformation. And Islam, or a certain Islam, is one name for the only 'religious' culture that resists this transformation. To critique Islam is to begin to undermine this resistance, to argue that:

> Muslims, as members of the abstract category of "humans" can be assimilated or (as some recent theorists have put it) "translated" into a global ("European") civilization once they have divested themselves of what many of them regard (mistakenly) as essential to themselves.

Namely a certain Islam, the remainder, *bad religion*. What Asad calls "this de-essentialization of Islam," this notion that "people's historical experience is inessential to them, that it can be shed at will, makes it possible to argue more strongly for the Enlightenment's claim to universality ... [and] to urge a Europeanization of the Islamic world."[24] The fall of communism and the events of 9/11 merely added urgency to this old, unfinished project and prompted renewed talk about it in tones of righteous, unguarded candor. And the New Atheists have hardly been alone in taking advantage of this new age of permissive talk about "religion-building" and the future of Islam.

* * *

One such non-New Atheist but vociferous critic of Islam is the ex-Muslim Ayaan Hirsi Ali. In a now infamous interview with *Reason* magazine back in 2007, she noted that "only if Islam is defeated ... [can it] mutate into something peaceful. It's very difficult to even talk about peace now," she added, "they're not interested in peace." When the interviewer sought clarification if she meant *radical* Islam, Ali retorted, "No. Islam, period ... There comes a moment," she continued, "when you crush your enemy ... in all forms, and if you *don't* do that, then you have to live with the consequence of being *crushed*." Later in the conversation, Ali adamantly defended her support for curtailing free speech rights of Muslims living in Western societies as:

an attempt to *save* civil liberties ... Western constitutions are products of the Enlightenment. They're products of reason, and reason dictates that you can only progress when you can analyze the circumstances and act accordingly. So now that we live under different conditions, the threat is different.

The interview ended with the obligatory identification of Islam with a political ideology that "hasn't been tamed like Christianity. See, the Christian powers have accepted the separation of the worldly and the divine. We don't interfere with their religion, and they don't interfere with the state. That hasn't happened in Islam."[25] Ali has been rumored as the informal replacement for Christopher Hitchens on the New Atheists' docket, the latest horse(wo)man of the non-apocalypse.[26] Whatever her status on this or any other august club of 'anti-establishment' rebels, it is safe to say that her credentials for belonging are unimpeachable.

Ali has received much flack over the years for this interview. Even Ian Baruma concluded a largely sympathetic review of her then recent book *Infidel* with the worry that she espoused "an absolutist view of a perfectly enlightened West at war with the demonic world of Islam."[27] And, of course, a bevy of progressive and Muslim voices have risen in the ensuing decade to denounce her for her supposed anti-Muslim bigotry. She has now also been placed on "A Field Guide to Anti-Muslim Extremists" by the Southern

Poverty Law Center.[28] Some of the vitriol directed at her is well-deserved. But most is misplaced handwringing rather than any serious analysis of her criticism of Islam. She is no third-rate bigot. Although critics have poked holes in her self-reported biography, her activism against the scourge of female genital mutilation (FGM) is undeniably informed by her own difficult experiences growing up in a strictly patriarchal Muslim milieu and her struggle to escape it. I will not belabor this biography; the reader is free to look it up. But suffice it to say that she is, in many ways, a remarkable woman, which makes some of her unnecessarily expansive proclamations against Islam that much more unfortunate. Polemicists are allowed a wider berth, but even still there are the limits of good sense. Baruma pointed out, for example, that if "enlightened reform of religious practices that clash with liberal democratic freedoms" is the task at hand, then Ali hardly "offer[ed] the best perspective from which to get this done."[29] Chastened perhaps by such criticism from a fellow liberal traveler such as Baruma, Ali's latest book is explicitly focused on the dynamics of reform in Muslim societies. In *Heretic*, Ali throws her lot behind "modifying Muslims" working to "modify, adapt, and reinterpret Islamic practice in order to make religious discourse more human." Bemoaning the 'fact' that Islam is "a religion that has resisted change for 1,400 years," she acknowledges that her "public intervention in the debate about the future of Islam" may seem "quixotic" to her Western audiences. Still, "it is plausible," she says, "that the internet will be for the Islamic world in the twenty-first century what the printing press was for Christendom in the sixteenth." Perhaps mutations and modifications can be had *sans* the crushing of enemies after all.

But how? In an instance of keen, creative and illuminating insight, Ali identifies the "new thinking" that emerged from the Protestant Reformation, the Enlightenment and the Scientific Revolution as a form of *blasphemy* against the regnant religious order, and that "in effect, it was *through* a process of repeated blasphemy that Christians and Jews evolved and grew into modernity." Herein lies the key for Muslims:

> The Muslim Reformation is not going to come from Al-Azhar. It is more likely to come from *a relentless campaign of blasphemy* ... Christians have been through this, Jews have been through it. It's now time for Muslims to go through it.[30]

I will address this strange, anomalous and yet ubiquitous mention of Jews alongside Christians later in this chapter. For now, let me just say that this Muslim comfort with and/or participation in blasphemy against their religion as a kind of test of their movement across the grooved axes of history explains much of the brouhaha surrounding debates about the free speech rights of Europeans to insult Islam. But even this is a sideshow. What is at stake here is the price of admission to the realm of reason.

Ali may have moved on from calling it defeat to calling it reform, but the mechanics of the anticipated change are not that different. The uncoupling of Islam from Muslim political identities must be consecrated with foundational acts of rejection. Islam must be shed not in the abstract, but in the public abandonments of those particular paths that trace out the peculiar histories of Muslim experience, and of wherever else these paths may lead. Blasphemy here is code for a new kind of inversion that carries no traces of that which it ostensibly seeks to invert, but instead mimics a different inversion already seared into the history of reason. It is criticism that is not constructive of anything except for an affirmation of a Western history that is already "right side up."

It is for this reason that even when New Atheists and ex-Muslim critics ostensibly vacillate between calling for the destruction of Islam as an essentially corrupt death cult and the "de-essentialization of Islam" through the process of reform, such vacillation hardly constitutes movement between distinct visions of the future of the Muslim world. The curious confusions and conflations of death with reform obscure a clearer insight: Islam cannot remain itself; it must pass away in either case. The only question is what to call it after it has passed. Burning the carcass to ashes has a kind of ritual appeal, but propping it up on stage with a name-tag attached would serve the mythology just as well. For only an inanimate discursive object can be made to act out not a reformation, but *the* Reformation, not an enlightenment, but *the* Enlightenment, not just any secularism, but Secularism in the *general universal*. In reason talk about Islam, no analysis is ever complete without the obligatory mention of Voltaire, and Locke, and Luther, and countless other figures from the history of reason in Europe. It is as if Islam has been in repose for the last thousand years and no Muslim has ever grappled with the theological and philosophical significance of changing circumstances. And if they did, then in any case, nothing they may have said is relevant to the task at hand. This is reform in reverse. We already know how this story ends.

Notice, for example, that many of the so-called "modifying Muslims" based in the West that Ali tasks with carrying out this Muslim Reformation hold political opinions that are indistinguishable from the fiercest critics of Islam. The journalist Asra Nomani has called for racial profiling of Muslims[31] and proudly voted for Donald Trump.[32] Maajid Nawaz is on board with limiting or ending Muslim immigration into Western societies.[33] Irshad Manji has been a darling of the neo-conservative right for her advocacy of military interventions in the Middle East. And Zuhdi Jasser has criticized nearly every instance of Muslim civil society advocacy in the United States as a front for radical Islamism. They all use their biographies as stories of ascent from the deep dungeons of a certain Islam to the light of reason.[34] They all hold anodyne liberal positions on secularism, human rights, democracy, and so on, with little reference in their spoken or written work to the histories of Muslim societies, the intellectual currents in the Muslim world, or the needs and desires of actually existing Muslims in the West. Their various ideas of reform appear to be versions of Jasser's so-called "Jefferson project" for Islam – thinly veiled threats to assimilate to the Western doxa, or else. The market for their ideas has great overlap with the New Atheists and ex-Muslims because the message is largely the same: Muslims need to grow up, Islam needs a Reformation, religion must be privatized, and most important of all, that Islam represents an existential danger that the West will do well to attenuate. This cropping of the distinctions of Islam to fit the mold of Western reason masquerades as salutary 'modification'. And the politics of such advocacy are almost always allied not with any reasonable project of reform, but with relentless criticism of Islam and Muslims.

* * *

Of course, such criticism of Islam among European peoples and their allies is nothing new. The Crusades were, after all, religiously sanctified conflicts against the enemies of Christianity. And Dante already put Muhammad in the eighth circle of Hell with his entrails hanging out, including "that disgusting tube which makes shit out of what goes down our throat."[35] Muslims were called Saracens back then and were often "depicted as frightening hordes that signaled the End of Days, as a monstrous race, dog-headed men," and the "Prophet Muhammad was at times cast as a heretic, at other times as a schismatic, or as the Antichrist, or a frightening monster."[36] Still, Islam was a malevolent force that occupied the hinterlands of the medieval Christian imagination, lurking on the far borders at the edges of the known world. This began to change with the incursions of the Ottomans into Bulgaria and Hungary. But it was not until the early modern expansion of Europe through trade and conquest that Muslims became proximate characters in the unfolding of Europe's now globalized self-imagination. This internalization of Muslims to the story of Europe is the critical context for the emergence of reason talk about Islam. For such talk is in one sense a variation on the medieval trope of the stubborn Jew who refuses to convert to Christianity despite the irrefutable reality of the incarnate Messiah. Reason replaces Christ in this new variation and Muslims are Semitized in their relationship to Europeans. No longer an unknown and mysterious nemesis, Islam is annexed to the inner working out of this revised eschatology.

The distinctive structure of reason talk has its origins, then, in the emergence of a lay messianism in the nineteenth century that nonetheless borrowed important tropes from its predecessor religious culture. And no single person embodied the inverted religiosity of this kind of talk about Islam more than the French philologist Ernest Renan. In fact, a straight line can be drawn without much deviation between the rhetoric associated with the romanticized positivism of Renan and the logic of the New Atheists and ex-Muslims regarding the status and future of Islam. Renan constitutes a fecund template which has nourished a century and a half of criticism and is still potent in its rhetorical efficacy and common-sense appeal in the West. But contrary to Edward Said's famous depiction of him, Renan was neither a particularly systemic thinker nor a reliably credulous resource for Orientalist scholarship in the late nineteenth century. Much like Sam Harris and Ayaan Hirsi Ali, his influence was mediated through seeding the popular imagination with ideas about the Orient and the Occident that cohered with the European zeitgeist. Indeed, "the importance of Renan lies not in his oriental scholarship but in his prominent function as a *public intellectual* and in the eclectic and broad character of his work, making him 'the complete mirror of his time'."[37] A lapsed Catholic who nonetheless preached the superiority of Christianity, Renan's many contradictions and dizzying transitions reflected the span of his life between the French Revolution and the Third Republic. And as perhaps the most widely read European of the latter half of the nineteenth century, the aggregated whole of his public interventions did much to shape the Western view not just of Islam, but of itself.

Renan grew into maturity within an intellectual milieu dominated by Auguste Comte. One could even reasonably go as far as to argue "that Comte's Positivist philosophy and its offshoots came closer to rivaling Aristotle's philosophy, not only in scope but also in intellectual and practical consequences, than the writings of any intervening thinker."[38] But the contemporary understanding of positivism as a kind of dry empiricism is belied by the fact that from the very beginning, "no less than Schlegel, Wordsworth and Chateaubriand, August Comte ... was the adherent and proponent of a secular post-Enlightenment myth whose outlines are unmistakably Christian."[39] A romanticist imprint was also evident in "the scientific regenerations of mankind envisioned by Comte" and in the harmonizing power of positive philosophy to reconcile the necessity of political order with the revolutionary imperative of social progress.[40] Like many of his European contemporaries, Comte believed that the rejection of clerical religion and its corrupt theologies must be complemented by the fashioning of a new secular and universal "Religion of Humanity" based on "insights into human behavior that only a complete science of society could provide." Though Comte did not believe in the inherent superiority of Europeans, he did proclaim that historical experience provides "a solid foundation of proof" that human societies "[go] through the same historical sequence of developments, though not at the same time or pace," from "the Theological, or fictitious; [to] the Metaphysical, or abstract ... [to] the Scientific, or positive," what he called the law of three stages. Now that Europeans were in possession of the insights attendant to positive philosophy/science, they "could show the way toward an accelerated progress for non-European societies."[41] This sequence of theology to philosophy to science has obvious, and perhaps even self-conscious, affinities with the Reformation to the Enlightenment to a reasoned secularism in Europe. And Comte's elevation of the human sciences to near the same level of law-like certainties as natural sciences in the final stage of intellectual development would do much to augur in the various forms of scientism that dominated Europe in the latter half of the nineteenth century.

Renan inherited from Comte both a view of the world as populated by cultures and societies at different levels of civilizational development and a confidence that science could elucidate the nature and meaning of these distinctions. He believed that in philology, he had discovered the *uber* science of humanity itself, and the ability to systematically organize and categorize the human condition. In his magnum opus *The Future of Science* (1848), Renan exults in "being there at the center, inhaling the perfume of everything, judging, comparing, combining, inducing – and in this way I shall arrive at *the very system of things*." For "philology is the exact science of mental objects. It is to the science of humanity what physics and chemistry are to the philosophic sciences of bodies." What made Europe *modern* in relation to its own past, namely "rationalism, criticism, liberalism," was the same variety of overcoming, and indicative of the same 'subjective' control that it exhibited over the Orient in the present.[42] Or as Said put it, "philology [for Renan] ... is both a comparative discipline possessed only by moderns and a symbol of modern (and European) superiority."[43] It enables the European to see the world from the vantage point of a generalized, universal subject and authorizes his mastery over it.

Renan's great philological contribution to the public imaginary was the concept of 'the Semitic' as the primary and apposite counterpart to 'Indo-European' not merely as a linguistic category, but as a marker of something more profoundly basic and essential about the character of the peoples that these language groups represented. Renan imagined language as "a mold" that once generated by the human mind, "shapes the spirit of the people that uses it ... [and that] there is a necessary link between the structure of a language ... and the soul of a people." It is in this sense that "language for Renan was first of all a question of *race*, a mold as decisive in its influence as was the shape of the cranium for adepts of physical anthropology."[44] His theory of language was therefore nothing as simple as the study of grammar or conjugations; it was a theory of religion, culture and society, even a theory of history and geography, all rolled into one. 'Semitic' was a category of *linguistic racialization* that was a far more potent indicator of the essence of a people than mere phenotypic information about them. Forged in the barren uniformity of the desert, the 'Semitic mind' reflected the desolate expanse and featureless terrain in its suspicion of multiplicity. Although this explains the Semitic discovery of monotheism, it renders the "languages in which monotheism was first formulated ... carved in impervious, hence unalterable 'bedrock'." Christianity offered a way out of this arrested development and provincial stagnation of the Semitic mind by combining the spirit of monotheism with the pluralistic fecundity on offer with the rival Indo-European or Aryan peoples. Where the Semitic languages, in their sparse grammar and invisible vowels, were "stuck in an infantile stage of development ... trapped in an expanse of time without an exit," much like the desert that gave birth to them, the Indo-European languages were a cacophony of proliferating and differentiated dialects "implicated in the movement of history" and hence destined to spawn the abstractions of philosophy and science.[45] Renan postulated the grand arc of human history as constituted by a constant struggle between these two rival ideal-type genera, with "the organic, biologically generative process represented by Indo-European ... [and] an inorganic, essentially un-regenerative process, ossified into Semitic."[46] The Christian peoples of the Occident were the inheritors of the Aryan spirit whereas the peoples of the Orient were stagnant, in repose, yoked by the constraints of the Semitic mind. This a priori thesis that "bestowed the polytheistic culture of Indo-Europeans with a progressing character, whilst declaring the monotheistic Semites to be immobile in time and space, hardly able to contribute to universal historical progress," was already a truism among the learned European public in the nineteenth century.[47] Renan did much to both popularize it and render it common sense among an even broader swath of the population.

By the nineteenth-century elevation of science in Occidental societies, Comte's third and final stage of intellectual development, Christianity in its orthodox, religious form was no longer necessary as an incubator for the Aryan spirit. Renan therefore rejected and criticized it, and fought for the laicization of politics and the public sphere in France. But the danger Islam posed to Europe and to the world at large was of a whole different order. Whereas Christianity had seeded history with the reformations and revolutions of its own overcoming by the age of reason, Islam was a reiteration of the Semitic spirit with ambitions of global domination. Renan's disdain for Islam is strewn throughout his corpus. Already in his inaugural lecture delivered in 1862 at the *Collège de France* on assuming the chair of Hebrew, Chaldaic and Syriac Studies, Renan contends that "the Mussulman (the Shemitic mind is everywhere represented in our times by Islamism) and the European, in the presence of one another, are like beings of a different species, having no one habit of thought and feeling in common." So much so in fact – and in an uncanny prefiguring of Ali and Harris – that "the one essential condition for the expansion of European civilization is the destruction of the principle of Shemitic action – the destruction of the theocratic power of Islamism, and consequently the destruction of Islamism itself." Elsewhere in the same lecture, he continues with this torrent:

Islamism is the perfect negative of Europe; Islamism is fanaticism ... Islamism is contempt of science, suppression of civil society; it is the frightful weakness of the Shemitic spirit, narrowing the mind of man; closing it against every delicate conception, every fine feeling, every rational research, to place it immovably in front of one unceasing tautology: *God is God*.[48]

Criticism of Islam is the indispensable disposition of European enlightenment itself and the key to its progressive expansion. It is criticism of religion as such in its static, immobile and regressive form.

Renan was hardly alone, or even the first European to paint an essentialized portrait of Islam with respect to its place of origin and its antagonistic role vis-à-vis the expansion of Europe. Already in the late eighteenth century, the German philosopher John Gottfried Herder had imagined Islam as an expression of the Arab spirit, of "the sublime conceptions ... fostered [by] ... solitary, romantic men ... from the remotest time."[49] A few decades later, Hegel contended that the Arabs constituted "the human society in which the Spirit was embodied in one of the phases of its development," on "the principle of pure unity: nothing else exists – nothing can become fixed – the worship of the One remains the only bond by which the whole is capable of unity."[50] Muhammad was often portrayed as the antagonist of Christ, but some also argued that in the grand arc of history "his life nevertheless had a providential purpose: by fighting against idolatry, Judaism and Christian heresies, Islam could 'shape the course of things' towards Christianity, and so was 'essential to the recovery and ultimate perfection of pure belief'."[51] These and other treatments prefigured Renan's own, and provided much of the flesh he fashioned into a semitized body for Islam. And as more of the Islamic world increasingly came under imperial domination in the later years of the nineteenth century, these kinds of sentiments became one bedrock principle of the European colonial encounter with Muslim natives and their 'decadent' cultures. Treatments of the Orient as essentially supine and 'asleep in history' competed with anxieties about the regressive Semitic gene and the dangers it posed to the full flowering of Europe's rationalized control over the world. This mix of sentiments remain the lifeblood of reason talk even today as both critics and reformers argue the risks and opportunities on offer in debates about the future of Islam.

* * *

Whenever critics of Islam who single out Muslims for exceptional scrutiny have been accused of racism, they have responded that Islam is not a race. But this is a cop-out. As is obvious from Renan's ruminations on the essence of the Semitic mind, the racialization of Muslims was always, from the beginning, more complicated than mere identification with certain phenotypic markers, and the Orient was always more an idea than a place. Reason talk *is* race talk layered under a whole host of other markers, the most prominent of which is, of course, religion. In fact, there is no simple way to fully separate race from religion when it comes to such treatments of Islam either in the nineteenth century or in the contemporary West. Just as the Jew is in one sense a racial other but also represents a moment arrested in the history of Christianity and reason, the Muslim exhibits a liminal alterity in the European imagination. The imperative to 'internalize' and ensoul the Semite is built into the expansive messianic mission of universal reason and leads to talk of reform. But the stubborn persistence of a seemingly irreducible and essential difference that *remains* rooted in the Semitic mind itself, in the very contours of its construction and its representations in the world, invites talk of destruction. Reason talk vacillates between death and reform in the same manner that the *Reconquista* vacillated between expulsion and conversion. But as the experience of the *conversos* in fifteenth-century Spain indicates, even the ex/modified Muslim (and the Jewish part of the *Judaeo*-Christian) cannot just go about her business. The transition has to be marked by elaborate refutations and criticisms so as not to invite inquisition. And even then, there are no guarantees.

It is this vacillation of reason talk, for example, that Said noticed in Renan's conception of philology itself:

> For what was philology on the one hand if not a science of all humanity, a science premised on the unity of the human species ... and yet what was

the philologist on the other hand if not ... a harsh divider of men into superior and inferior races, a liberal critic whose work harbored the most esoteric notions of temporality, origins, development, relationship, and human worth?[52]

And it is this same vacillation that marks the works of New Atheists and ex/modifying Muslims in general as they debate the future of Islam. Reason vacillates because, as Niebuhr correctly intuited, it is implicated in originary contradictions that are part and parcel of its construction. It is the universalization of a provincial inversion. Moreover, it is simultaneously a break from religion as such and the apotheosis of the grooved history of a particular religion. This vacillation in the structure of reason talk presents as an 'open' space of discursive flexibility inhabited by the back and forth between outright rejections of Islam by 'its cultured despisers' and talk of its modification by so-called reformers. But such presentation serves only to shroud the contradictions of reason talk, to cover them over with the spectacle of debate. That all these conversations follow the same well-worn blueprint, that they regurgitate the same clichés time after time, their cyclical futility is not a failure, but a reflection of their essential function – to render the histories and particularities of Muslims 'unessential' to their future and to cloak the constitutive paradoxes attendant to the Christian origins of Western reason with vociferous claims to its universality. And "to respond with reason," argued Arendt, "when reason is used as a trap is not 'rational'; just as to use a gun in self-defense is not 'irrational'."[53] To break the cyclical futility of reason talk requires something different, something new which is not on offer with mere participation in it.

Consider, for example, two such 'debates' separated in time by a century and a half and yet in exact alignment with each other on how they plug the space opened up by the vacillations of reason talk. The first took place between Ernest Renan and Jamal al-din al-Afghani in 1883, and the second between Sam Harris and Maajid Nawaz in 2015. Renan's views on Islam as a genus did not extend to all Muslims, some of whom he actually considered worthy intellectual interlocutors and perhaps even capable of squeezing the 'Semitic' out of their own religion. One such Muslim was the peripatetic reformer al-Afghani, about whom Renan gushed that:

> The liberty of his thought, his noble and loyal character made me believe while I was talking to him that I had before me, restored to life, one of my old acquaintances – Avicenna, Averroes, or another of those great infidels who represented during [the first] five centuries [of Islam] the tradition of the human mind.[54]

In a lecture delivered in 1883 at *La Sorbonne* titled "Islamism and Science," Renan argued that the flourishing of science and philosophy under Muslim rule during these first five centuries reflected not some genius of the religion, but in fact the forces arrayed against it: "do not let us honor [Islam] then for what it has been unable to suppress."[55] These insufficiently Islamized societies were a hodgepodge of Greek and Sassanian influences that temporarily elevated the conquered Persian (Aryan) culture over the Arab core of Islam. In time, this core asserted itself over its conquered peoples and the supposed golden age of reason in Muslim lands was brought to an end. True to their Semitic nature, contemporary Muslims have "the most profound disdain for instruction, for science, for everything that constitutes the European spirit ... Western theology has not persecuted less than Islamism," he continues, "only it has not been successful, it has not crushed out the modern spirit, as Islamism has trodden out the spirit of the lands it has conquered."[56] Addressing himself to his detractors in the audience and elsewhere, Renan warned that "liberals who defend Islam do not know ... [that Islam] is the heaviest chain humankind has ever borne."[57]

Al-Afghani published his "Answer to Renan" in the *Journal des Débats* a few weeks later. Far from being a refutation of any sort, al-Afghani's response capitulates on nearly all points except that Muslims cannot also walk the tightrope out of the darkness just as Christians already have: "Muslim society has not yet freed itself from the tutelage of religion [because] ... the Christian religion preceded the Muslim religion in the world by many centuries." Al-Afghani then hopes "that Muhammadan society will succeed some day in breaking its bonds and marching resolutely in the path of civilization after the manner of Western civilization."[58] Nikki R. Keddie, the great modern biographer of al-Afghani, has pointed out that this answer to Renan was clearly "directed at … an elite Western audience … [and] shows the work of an advanced mind in its evolutionary view of history."[59] Elsewhere, al-Afghani had also spoken favorably of the founders of Protestantism and, according to Keddie and others, fancied himself a Muslim Martin Luther.[60] This makes sense. In a global public sphere increasingly marked by European power, "non-European intellectuals had to conform to a high degree to the discursive patterns that had been established by Europeans … to participate in [these] debates."[61] This is not to argue any bad faith on al-Afghani's part, only to suggest that the rules of engagement are not independent of the content of reason talk. Al-Afghani's corpus of ideas is indeed far too significant and complex to be rendered as entirely derivative of European intellectual currents. But this particular exchange is a textbook instance of reason talk, and al-Afghani's participation in it is a paradigmatic early example followed by a whole bevy of Muslim reformers in the years since. Back then, Renan brought this faux debate to a close by agreeing with al-Afghani that "Galileo was no better treated by Catholicism than Averroes by Islam" and that "one point on which [he] may have been unjust to the Sheikh is that [he] did not develop enough the idea that all revealed religions manifest themselves as hostile to positive science."[62] They were both agreed on the developmental lag of Islam vis-à-vis Christian Europe and on the already grooved path forward, although the reason for this lag continued to be in some dispute. But with Islam criticized, reason's universality established and Western superiority affirmed, nearly all the boxes had been checked. Everyone could go home happy.

The same manner of exchange has been ubiquitous in the West over the last century or so, and certainly in the days since 9/11 it has become a requisite feature of much vacuous dialogue on the nature and place of religion in modern societies. The reasoned atheist critic takes on religion in general, and then singles out Islam for special opprobrium as the contemporary embodiment par excellence of all obscurantist evils associated with religious faith. The liberal Muslim apologist affirms the critic's concerns about Islam but notes that reform is a viable possibility. The critic is skeptical but agrees to 'dialogue'. They talk about the possible sources of reformation and enlightenment in the Muslim world. The critic begrudgingly agrees that perhaps Christians are not so great either, but, you know, it's been a while since they were really terrible. The obligatory mentions include terrorism, free speech and tolerance. They both agree on the need for science, reason and secularism in Muslim societies, and for human rights (and women's rights and gay rights, depending on the decade) and eventually perhaps even democracy and liberal political institutions. The dialogue ends with a still skeptical critic wishing the apologist good luck, who in turn thanks his interlocutor for the benefit of this engagement. For "it is not easy to reach across divides – real or imagined – and try to hold a sensible dialogue amid so much background noise and confusion."[63] I have, of course, just described a 'debate' between Sam Harris and Maajid Nawaz in 2015, published in book form as *Islam and the Future of Tolerance*. But this could just as well be a description of a thousand other such engagements that follow the basic structure of the Renan/al-Afghani debate from over a century ago in all important respects. Nawaz has perhaps the added benefit of being a former member of the pan-Islamist (non-violent) international group *Hizb ut-Tahrir* who had already documented his own personal reformation from a radical Islamic extremist to a defender of liberal values.[64] But nearly all ex/modifying Muslims have some kind of story to tell of an ascent out of the darkness that informs their criticism of 'a certain Islam' they have decisively left behind. Traveling their different roads to Damascus, they all naturally still end up in the same place.

All this is, of course, a reflection of the fact that Islam as an exception, as the remainder, as bad religion, is in all cases fabricated against the rule to which it is an exception, the whole to which it is the remainder, the good religion to which it is bad. As Arendt said about the Jews of Europe:

Reason Talk

> Whether [they] are a religion or a nation, a people or a race, a state or a tribe, depends on the special opinion non-Jews – in whose midst Jews live – have about themselves, but it certainly has no connection whatever with any germinal knowledge about the Jews.[65]

Notice that she does not say *no* knowledge, but rather no knowledge germinal to the particular status that is ascribed to the other as an exception, as the remainder, as bad religion. This status depends entirely, as Arendt puts it, "on the special opinion non-Jews have about *themselves*." The eithers and ors of reason talk are different from the ones we encountered in the last chapter. But the structure of the trope remains the same. On offer is either incorporation into the logic and ongoing history of a pre-existing elaboration staged as universal and human or banishment as an abject particularity that has no salutary relevance to the future of a common world. In these discourses, words such as 'freedom' and 'reason' exist in a liminal quantum state; they can both connote something universal and mark particular tribal affiliation all at the same time. It is in this sense that reason and science need to be examined not merely as representing a method or an epistemology, but rather also, and perhaps more importantly for our purposes, as markers of an elastic identity that emerged in post-Enlightenment Europe. Even as it congealed out of a reversal and objectification of religion, this identity made *knowing* the world and the people in it a sacred mission with eschatological significance. And it is this identity which is, and has been, the dark mirror to its own exceptions and remainders throughout these many years. It is for this reason that the positivist anxieties and aspirations of the New Atheists and their ilk reverberate with the messianic echoes of Comte's "Religion of Humanity" and Marx's communist utopia. And also of Renan's inverted religiosity, of making science:

> the object of [his] life ... Immortality means to labor at a lasting work. According to the primitive Christian idea, the true one, only those shall rise again who have contributed to the divine work; furthering God's kingdom on earth. The punishment for the wicked and frivolous will be utter annihilation.[66]

These are the antecedent sentiments that explain criticism of Islam by New Atheists and ex-Muslims, and the salvation offered to other Muslims by modifying reformers. Renan sought confirmation of Islam's infernal status in the linguistic racialization of its adherents. Harris and others blame the propositional architecture of belief in the Quran itself for all manner of violence in lieu of making a proper "political analysis of our time." But in either case, there is the sense that the rot runs so deep and that the Muslim is so in grip of her ideological or linguistic DNA that coercive and even violent intervention may well be the only way out of this mess. This is why debates among these various different protagonists are in truth better understood as sanctified displays of conversion. They are choreographed and formulaic because their design is not to advance a conversation, but to affirm a creed: criticism of Islam is the beginning of all criticism. In the regime of reason talk, the answer to the Muslim Question is plainly the Marxist one.

* * *

But does it have to be? Some years before Afghani's tête-à-tête with Renan in the pages of the *Journal des Débats*, he had a rather more interesting exchange with the Indian Muslim reformer Sayyid Ahmad Khan on the nature and meaning of Islam, and on the proper relationship between religion and reason. Like Muhammad Iqbal (who we encountered in Chapter 3), Khan's place in Indian colonial historiography is a mess of clichés, caricatures and contradictions. Best known for founding the Muhammadan Anglo-Oriental College in 1875 (Aligarh Muslim University since 1920), where young Muslim men could be educated in Islamic theology and Western philosophical and natural sciences as part of a single and unified curriculum, Khan spent much of his life railing against the obscurantism of traditional *ulama* and many of his other co-religionists. Knighted by the British for services rendered to the empire, he is also often depicted as a simple 'modernist' who sought to reform his community to account for the superiority of the West in science, technology and philosophy. This simple story is true as far as it goes.

But a deeper reading of Khan's work reveals a set of far more complex aspirations for Indian Islam. I have dealt extensively with his oeuvre elsewhere and will not belabor a full accounting of it here.[67] But this particular argument with al-Afghani nicely illustrates in brief his broader concern with rendering reason neither in opposition (or inversion) with religion nor as the teleological end of religion in the grand systematic way that both al-Afghani and Renan clearly imagined it. Instead, Khan offered an account of reason that identified it as an aspect of religion (and vice versa) rooted in the full acknowledgment of human finitude and fallibility in the regime of divine infinity.

Al-Afghani's main issue with Khan was the latter's ostensible "naturalism" in matters of faith. In a tract titled *Khutubāt-i Ahmadīyah*, for example, Khan had laid out the following position on the relationship between what he called "the work of God" and "the word of God":

> A true principle [is that] with which man must bring all his powers of will, body, soul and spirit into harmony as long as he is in control of his physical and mental powers ... If we want, therefore, from among different religions to establish critically the true religion, we should see whether it is in harmony with this true principle or not ... As far as man can know by his rational powers (*quwat-i 'aqli*), [this true principle] is nothing but nature (*qudrat*) or the law of nature (*qanun-i qudrat*) ...

Thus this [nature] alone is true and those principles alone which are in harmony with it are true principles, not those which depend entirely on the belief of a passing being capable of error and sin – the belief of man.[68]

Referring obliquely to Khan as a *niechiri* (a bastardization of 'naturalist'), al-Afghani railed against what he saw as this enfolding of Islam (the true religion) into the bosom of nature itself, and entirely subsumed within the rubric of man's rational powers (*quwat-i 'aqli*).[69] While at first glance this manner of thinking about religion in general and Islam in particular may strike the reader as subordinating religion to reason, al-Afghani correctly recognized that the true implication of Khan's reconstructed naturalist theology (*ilm al-kalam*) was to render religion and reason near synonyms by thoroughly transforming the meaning of each of these terms.

Hearkening forward to Niebuhr's warning about conceiving of reason as rooted fundamentally in the criticism of religion, Khan was intuitively aware that pitting religion against reason or setting up a telelological framework between the two invites a cascade of inversions whereby religion either becomes entirely defanged of its distinctions in its complete conformity to Western accounts of reason or it becomes a font of resistance and rejection of all that is new in the modern world. Even in his own day, he saw many of his co-religionists falling into this either/or trap.

Anticipating therefore the abysmal backs and forths of conformist and exceptionalist thinking that continue to plague treatments of Islam in the global public sphere, and also the fear of Islam as "a remainder" that must be eliminated for the equation of modernity to make sense, Khan redefined both faith and reason not with reference to what they overcome (evil, uncertainty, etc.), but rather by the limits they impose on the finite human animal:

> Then I asked myself how reason can with certainty remain free from error. *I admitted that such certainty is not really obtainable.* Only if reason is used constantly can the error of the reason of one person be corrected by the reason of a second person, and the reasonings of one period by the reasonings of a second. Whereas as long as knowledge or certainty or faith are kept outside the reach of reason, certainty cannot be obtained at any period of time whatsoever. At that point a doubt arose in my heart. I held reason to be the paramount guide. Why did I not count on the possibility that there could be a greater guide than reason, a guide that could subdue even reason? The fact that we are not acquainted with it surely does not constitute a proof of its non-existence. But then I thought that to presume the existence of such a guide *would not lead us any further.* What we need is knowledge and certainty about it. Since this is lacking there is no other guide but reason alone.[70]

Reason Talk

This particular account of reason is reminiscent of Frederick Buechner's wistful soliloquy about faith, that "without somehow destroying me in the process, how could God reveal himself in a way that would leave no room for doubt? If there was no room for doubt, there would be no room for me."[71] Uncertainty is the nature of reason, just as doubt is the nature of faith. And both reason and faith for Khan are mere representations of a singular reality, *tauhid*, the unicity and unity of God, the "true principle ... with which man must bring all his powers of will, body, soul and spirit into *harmony*."

Al-Afghani's alarm at Khan's naturalism now begins to make sense. In classical Islamic theology, *tauhid* is an ontological concept concerning the nature and reality of God. But in Khan's treatment, as the true principle underlying reality *as such*, *tauhid* is now also an epistemological concept pertaining to reason and a moral one pertaining to the dynamics of salvation. Notice, for example, how Khan reframes the traditional legalistic doctrine of *taklif*, or the condition of being put under binding burden/obligation by God to do good rather than evil, as an exercise in moral psychology:

> Since man is made for worship, that is for religion, or religion for man, it follows that there should be something in man – *as distinct from other living things* – which can perceive the content and binding character of this obligation (*taklif*). This

special thing or faculty in man is intellect (*'aql*). Whatever religion is given to man, therefore, cannot lie beyond the grasp of intellect (*'aql-i insān kē māfauq nah hō*).⁷²

Reason and religion here are both but an aspect of every person's, every people's and every age's burden of uncertainty and doubt which naturally reflect man's creaturliness and the vicissitudes of history. In Khan's own time, he imagined the doubt and uncertainty attendant to being colonized not as cause for Muslim cynicism in the face of their weakness and inferiority, but rather an opportunity to develop their faith and reason anew. A new regime of restraint, of being obligated (*taklif*) to the powers that be, is just the latest, context-specific instantiation of the general condition of human existence. As such, it is neither cause for alarm nor for any handwringing. The parameters of the modern age offer novel openings for the development of both faith and reason as an aspect of religiosity itself. There are to be no rejections here, no inversions, and certainly no millenarian hopes of "a golden future time" as the fruit of *an* age of Reason. Man is made for worship, yes, but worship is reason. And man is made for reason, yes, but reason is worship. There are no remainders because unlike the New Atheists and ex-Muslims, Khan's Islam does not offer any equations out of the uncertainties of existence, no paths out of the desert into the full effulgence of a terminal Enlightenment, and no final solutions such as Comte's

"Religion of Humanity" and Marx's communist utopia. There are only ever-changing paradigms of constraint, uncertainty and doubt (in short, *taklif*) constantly generating new adventures of faith and new paradigms of reason.

Khan's corpus runs into thousands of pages, and certainly these few pages do it no justice. But as far as the particular strictures of reason talk are concerned, these short paragraphs are ample indication that Khan skillfully sidesteps them without denying their reality. Plenty in his own time and plenty since have not been so successful. Even al-Afghani, an otherwise towering figure in early Islamic 'modernism', failed to acknowledge the dangers of either strict separation between religion and reason, or the wedding of religion to the grooved paths of European history, specifically to Islam itself. In our time, these dangers have now fully congealed into the dueling utopias and dystopias of men of science and of faith as they play their complementary parts in the narrative construction of antagonistic identities framed around the eithers and ors of religion and reason. It is against precisely these kinds of dueling self-images in mirroring resonance with each other and seared onto the body of modernity itself that folks such as Reinhold Niebuhr and Sayyid Ahmad Khan counseled circumspection. And in questioning the regnant paradigms of their respective place and age, they also model for us a way of talking about religion, and about Islam, *sans* the binaries and grooved histories of reason talk.

5

Culture Talk

Fed in equal parts by theories of biological evolution, Comtian positivism and eugenics, social Darwinism had its heyday in the late nineteenth and early twentieth centuries. But the idea that cultural norms associated with Euro-American societies are an ever-evolving apotheosis of human social development has been a consistent feature of Western thinking right up to the present. This idea is the basis of what I call culture talk about Islam, a way of cognizing and articulating the proximate presence of Muslims that I examine in this chapter. This kind of talk is primarily concerned with identifying Islam as a culture that is then judged against the vanishing contemporary, the cultural consensus of the West that is constantly on the move and hence difficult to pin down as a theoretical ideal. Unlike freedom and reason talk, this kind of talk is animated by "structures of feeling" and impressions of unease, a sense of being wronged by the presence of difference.[1] Its effects are evident in an abiding repugnance of Muslim cultural symbols and in attempts to coercively re-engineer ostensibly private spheres of Muslim life such as clothing, speech, dietary codes and physical appearance on the European continent. Such punitive tendencies have historically been weaker in the United States, but suspicion still runs deep that any unmonitored private Muslim spaces are ipso facto cauldrons of radicalization. Culture talk imagines the historical, and ongoing, development of Western cultural norms as co-produced with its material and political supremacy and as therefore so many signs of its superiority. The Islamic equivalents of these norms (variously imagined and immediately essentialized), of food and drink, of clothing and personal hygiene, and sometimes even music and literature, are therefore inextricably tied with lagging development, regression, disorder and violence. On the left, culture talk is a principal feature of benevolent cultural and political paternalism. On the right, it often takes the form of nationalistic chauvinism. In either case, some version of a cultural conversion is a prerequisite to an adequate integration of Muslims into Western societies and the expedient evolution of the Islamic world along Euro-American lines. But since the evaluative standard is a moving target, there is also an asymptotic quality to culture talk in that it can never meaningfully reach a resolution unless the historical development of Islam as culture is directly pegged to some

Culture Talk

generic Western counterpart and Muslims become master mimics. Once again, then, with culture talk, we find ourselves in the realm of farce, not politics.

* * *

The final chapter of David Mitchell's novel *Cloud Atlas* contains a most instructive exchange between the preacher Giles Horrox, a representative of the London Mission Society on the Pacific island of Raiatea, and Dr. Henry Goose, a passenger on the *Prophetess* then docked on the island's Bethlehem Bay. The year is 1850 and aside from saving the souls of the island's inhabitants, Horrox also runs a plantation where these same natives toil to extract arrowroot starch and coconut oil to fund the missionary school, and as payment for their bible study and church services. A dinner time conversation between Horrox and some of the *Prophetess*' crew and passengers (including Goose) turns to a "fundamental mystery" so obviously in need of explanation, especially in a place such as Raiatea: "Why do White races hold dominion over the world?" Flush with the triumph of his mission's forces over the initially recalcitrant natives, Horrox offers the following explanation:

> I have unswervingly held, that God, in our Civilizing World, manifests himself not in the Miracles of the Biblical Age, but in Progress. It is Progress that leads Humanity up the ladder

towards the Godhead. No Jacob's Ladder this, but rather 'Civilization's Ladder', if you will. Highest of all the races on this ladder stands the Anglo-Saxon.

Speaking of the Asiatics – who he places below the Latins but above the Negros – Horrox mocks the "sinologists [who] insist they once aspired to greatness, but where is your yellow-hued Shakespeare, eh, or your almond-eyed da Vinci?"

But as an alternative to Horrox's evolutionary musings, Goose proposes a much simpler theorem: "The weak are meat the strong do eat." The White races dominate:

> because, Preacher, of all the world's races, our love – or rather our *rapacity* – for treasure, gold, spices & dominion, oh, most of all sweet domination is the keenest, the hungriest, the most unscrupulous! This rapacity, yes, powers our Progress; for ends infernal or divine I know not. Nor do you know, sir. Nor do I overly care. I feel only gratitude … that my Maker cast me on the winning side.

Later in the evening, the dinner conversation having been unceremoniously cut short by his incivility toward the host, Goose explains himself to the narrator of the novel, Adam Ewing:

Why tinker with the plain truth that we hurry the darker races to their graves in order to take their land & its riches? Wolves don't sit in their caves, concocting crapulous theories of race to justify devouring a flock of sheep![2]

Almost as if to prove the veracity of his own theorem, Goose later poisons Ewing and steals his effects. The weak are meat the strong do eat, indeed!

Of all the contemporary purveyors of "crapulous theories" that explain or justify the global dominion of the West (and there are many), Stanford historian Niall Ferguson is perhaps the truest heir to both the nineteenth-century progenitors of a civilizing mission and the early twentieth-century hawkers of race panic. Also, in one sense, heir to that transformation of race talk into the more respectable (and amorphous) claims of Western cultural superiority as the Christ of the coming millennium. He is Rhodes, Toynbee and Stoddard all rolled into one, and with such effective measure of each that he can parry the accusation of being like one of them by the deft deployment of the others.[3] Ferguson has been, at one time or another, a nostalgist of the British Empire, a champion of an America-driven 'Anglobalization', an enthusiast for the complementary amalgamation of Chinese and American power – what he called "Chimerica" – and, in his latest incarnation, both the cheering chronicler of Western civilization and the lamenting raconteur of its imminent demise. A self-exile from

Oxbridge to the hallowed halls of Harvard and Stanford, and a trusted adviser in the corridors of American power as it attempted to remake the Muslim world after 9/11, Ferguson has been openly peddling the benefits of political and cultural neo-imperialism at home and abroad for quite some time now. In a searing back and forth with him in the pages of the *London Review of Books* back in 2011, Pankaj Mishra lamented that "it says something about the political culture of our age that Ferguson has got away with [his] disgraced worldview for as long as he has."[4] As one of Ernest Renan's biographers also said of him, Ferguson is the twenty-first-century equivalent, "the complete mirror of his time."[5]

What Ferguson mirrors is a curious melange of sentiments, a "gallimaufry" of ostensibly retro ideas (to use Mishra's terminology) that made a furious comeback into intellectual propriety in the years following the end of the Cold War. Seemingly more suited to "the intellectual certainties of the summer of 1914" than the end of the twentieth century, talk of clashing civilizations with their rival cultural genii, of imperial missions and the West's burdens, of the ends of history and the beginnings of millennia, was everywhere.[6] In reality, such talk had never actually gone away, but lingered throughout in the interstices of the rival discourses of East and West that animated the ideological conflict between capitalism and communism. Now freed of the dialectic constraint placed on its expansive meaning by its ideological rival, capitalism's history-making entanglements

Culture Talk

with the other imperial sentiments of *noblesse oblige* and race talk could once again ensue openly in the Western public imaginary. But as I showed in Chapter 2, 'race' had long ago been replaced by 'culture' in the imperial lexicon, just as 'white' had given way to 'the West'. These were not distinctions without a difference, of course, but certainly the structure and mood of old was hardly done away with as a whole. And now it could be evoked with a flourish that had been absent for some time. The urtexts of this revival were Samuel Huntington's *The Clash of Civilizations and the Remaking of World Order* and Francis Fukuyama's *The End of History and the Last Man*, the latter being a vastly more measured argument than the former, but both equally consequential in their own ways. These books are too well known for me to belabor a precis here, but needless to say where Huntington's Darwinist culturalism was reminiscent of Benjamin Kidd's from the early part of the twentieth century, Fukuyama's albeit understated proclamation of a conclusive victory of liberal democracy as the new global consensus evoked Toynbee's eschatological aspirations for the West. Ferguson and a whole host of neo-imperialists came to their intellectual maturity at a time when talk of empire was no longer taboo and even, by some measure, elicited swagger and chest-thumping by the new rulers of a unipolar world. "The tendency to consider the whole world as one country's *imperium*," Edward Said intoned in one of his later books, "is very much in the ascendancy in today's United States, the last remaining superpower."[7]

Islam was always going to be a special case in this new world order, if for no other reason than the fact of oil in the Middle East. But from the beginning of the end of the Soviet Union, there was more at play. There was Iran. There was Israel. There were the large numbers of Muslims now living in European metropoles. Unlike Hinduism and Buddhism, which had been tamed to the culture of spiritualist consumption, and Judaism, which had been hyphenated into community with its erstwhile Christian tormentor, Islam remained the one great world religion that could neither be healthfully consumed nor the fact of its difference elided with ease. There were Muslim women who needed saving and Muslim men who needed to be controlled. There was the religious imperative of unfinished business and the cultural imperative of conversion. And, of course, as Huntington put it, Islam had "bloody borders." To quote Derrida again:

> Islam, or a certain Islam, [is] the only religious or theocratic culture [worldwide] that can still, in fact or in principle, inspire and declare any resistance to democracy ... [and to the] process of secularization ... and thus, in the strict sense, of politicization.[8]

All of this came to a head with 9/11, of course. But with the regnant paradigms of the post-Cold War *mondialisme* in the West as they were, conflict was inevitable. So was the manner in which this conflict has often been framed, as a competition between civilizations, as the Islamic resistance to a salutary 'Anglobalization', as a consequence of the cultural defects of the Muslim peoples, be they out there in the world or right here at home. In these debates, Ferguson has consistently served the function of a respectable superego to the unvarnished chauvinism of the Western id, pruning the hedges, so to speak, while leaving the substance of the undergrowth largely intact.

This undergrowth is composed of best-selling alarmist authors such as Ann Coulter, Pamela Geller and Paula Ingraham, 'scholars' such as Robert Spencer, Daniel Pipes and Frank Gaffney Jr., literally hundreds of anti-Muslim think tanks and activist organizations such as ACT for America, Middle East Forum and the David Horowitz Freedom Center, and the various foundations and wealthy benefactors that fund these individuals and groups. The Center for American Progress put out a detailed analysis of this networked hydra of actors and activists back in 2011 called *Fear, Inc.*, which also included politicians and media, and was updated in 2015.[9] These bottom feeders are not my concern in this book, so I will not dwell on their writings and activities. Suffice it to say that while their many prejudiced proclamations are often disparaged in the more respectable corners of the Western intellectual ecosphere, the crux of their treatment of Islam and Muslims can still be found in the rarefied air occupied by highly reputable scholars such as Huntington, Ferguson and Bernard

Lewis, noted journalists such as Christopher Caldwell and Douglas Murray, and in the foreign policy establishments of the various Western metropoles.

In his excellent monograph *Good Muslim, Bad Muslim*, Mahmood Mamdani calls these kinds of treatments of Islam examples of *culture talk* about Muslims. Unable to improve on Mamdani's terminology, I have therefore adopted it. And I mean much the same by it. Mamdani identifies two discrete discursive moments in "the rapid politicizing of a single term: culture" in the post-Cold War public imaginary. Instead of making a historically grounded "political analysis of our time," culture talk in the first instance "assumes that every culture has a tangible essence that defines it, and it then explains politics as a consequence of that essence."[10] In this version, culture talk represents the Huntington and Lewis end of the imperialist revival. The cultural theorist Etienne Balibar has argued that culture in these kinds of discourses can come to "function like a nature ... [and] as a way of locking individuals and groups *a priori* into a genealogy, into a determination that is immutable and intangible in origin."[11] When applied to Islam, such talk suggests that Muslims "presumably made culture only at the beginning of creation, as some extraordinary, prophetic act. After that, it seems Muslims just conformed to culture." Hence the abiding fascination in certain segments of the West (and of the Muslim world) with finding the source of a distinctively Muslim genus "inscribed in early founding texts, usually religious, and mummified in early artefacts." But in addition, culture talk also divides the world "between those who are modern and those who are premodern. The moderns *make* culture and are masters of it; the premoderns are said to be but conduits." À la Fukuyama, it is this culture of the moderns that has now brought history to its proper ends. In this second sense, culture talk carves out a special exception for the West, a unique role as the kind of culture that frees its subjects from the constraints of culture identified in the first sense. This is in fact precisely what it means to be modern. And it is for this reason that in culture talk "it is no longer the market (capitalism), nor the state (democracy), but culture (modernity) that is said to be the dividing line between those in favor of a peaceful, civic existence and those inclined to terror."[12] Culture talk is therefore a two-step rigmarole where a variegated map of clashing civilizations is then overlaid with the dueling colors representing a binary conflict: the West vs. the rest. Islam obviously does not constitute the entirety of this 'rest'. But as an exceptional case, it demands special scrutiny.

* * *

Consider, for example, that Ferguson made his reputation as a public intellectual with rollicking histories of empire and war that rightly credit European imperia's central role in creating a vastly more integrated world but that contain nothing but the faintest acknowledgment of non-Western peoples in the making of this modern world other than as imitators of the West or as resistors to this new world's fabrication.[13] His books are perhaps the finest examples of the West as the world, and as World-Subject, where the entirety of this world's common recent history is exhausted in the intramural intrigues of European powers and their ascents and descents on the world stage. Ferguson applauds the Victorian imperialists who "'undeniably pioneered free trade, free capital movements and, with the abolition of slavery, free labour. [They] invested immense sums in developing a global network of modern communications. [They] spread and enforced the rule of law over vast areas."[14] And (according to Mishra) "in a typical counterfactual manoeuvre," he repeats the same argument over and over that without British imperial rule, "colonised peoples, such as Indians, would not have what are now their most valuable ideas and institutions – parliamentary democracy, individual freedom and the English language."[15] Completely glossing over the burgeoning anti-colonial movements well in advance of the two world wars, Ferguson laments that this empire was ultimately "dismantled not because it had oppressed subject peoples for centuries, but because it took up arms for just a few years against far more oppressive empires."[16] His syrupy treatises on the British Empire are so thick with nostalgia and virtue-signaling that mere reading out loud requires washing the sugar out of one's ears.

Inasmuch as Muslims make an appearance in these books, it is almost always as the peril they represented (and still represent) to this newly constituted globalism, and to which they appear as perpetual outsiders. From the pan-Islamic threats of the Ottoman Sultan, to the Mahdi's rebellion in the Sudan, to the "three mutinies by Muslim soldiers in Iraq who refused to fight their co-religionists" during the First World War, and on and on, Muslims erupt sporadically in Ferguson's histories as irritants to the orderly government of empires and the salutary march of cultural progress.[17] Only in the near contemporary does Islam begin to take shape as an existential threat to Western civilization and, naturally as such, a threat to the world itself. But the mold in which this new threat has been cast is an ancient one. For what else was bin Laden but the latest offspring of what Ferguson calls "the Middle East's distinctive civilization of clashes, a retarded political culture in which terrorism has long been a substitute for both peaceful politics and conventional warfare"?[18] As the Sudanese Mahdi for a time frustrated British designs in the region, so al-Qaeda, ISIS and al-Shabab aggravate the salutary playing out of American interests. The notes may change, but the song remains the same. A certain Islam – Ferguson prefers the moniker Islamo-Bolshevism over Islamofascism – constantly exasperates the *pax imperia* of Western power. Writing for the *Financial Times* in 2015, Ferguson muses that "war is back and much of it is holy war." Failing to mention that Western powers have waged multiple wars in Muslim-majority lands over this intervening decade and a half, Ferguson claims that "in 2000, according to my own calculations, 35% of the fatalities in armed conflicts were in wars involving Muslims. In 2014 it was 79%." In deference to his scholarly reputation (and differentiating himself from the undergrowth), Ferguson then predictably walks back the most blunt implication of this data by pointing out that clearly Islam "is not the *sole* cause of increasing conflict." But he cautions against passivity in the face of this threat, for "it is more than a co-incidence that global warfare is so concentrated in the Islamic world."[19] In the discursive logic of neo-imperialism, one can decry both the rise of violence in the Muslim world and champion enhanced military interventions against it all at the same time. For it is their culture that breeds this violence and only our modern culture that can rescue Muslims from the grasp of their premodern one through the use of 'reasonable' violence against them.

But whereas "Britain in its heyday was able to draw on a culture of unabashed imperialism which dated back to the Elizabethan period," Ferguson ruefully notes that "the US … will always be a reluctant ruler of other peoples."[20] Already some months before 9/11, he was arguing that "the United States should be devoting a larger percentage of its vast resources to making the world safe for capitalism and democracy," if need be through military interventions primarily in the Muslim world.[21] After 9/11, of course, the gloves came entirely off. Now a full-fledged formal 'empire' on the Victorian model, which would drive the US to "export its capital, its people and its culture to those backward regions" (read: the Middle East) "which need them most urgently," was the utmost necessity for the global "dissemination of Western civilization" and to stave off "the greatest threats to its security." This important task could no longer be "safely entrusted to Messrs Disney and McDonald."[22] With the Cold War over and a new age of conflict emergent, "the world needs an effective liberal empire," implores Ferguson, "and the United States is the best candidate for the job."[23] The British Empire faded too soon before the millenarian task of 'Anglobalization' could be culturally sedimented and baked into the new world order. Ferguson explicitly references Kipling as he implores Americans to take on this burden, to serve their captives' need, their new-caught, sullen peoples on their path to modernity.[24]

There is something quaint and alluring about Ferguson's honest (if woefully incomplete) reckoning with the history of *pax Brittania* and its lessons for global power in the present. There is also the fact that he is a gifted writer, with metaphors and lyrical turns of phrase always at the ready to delight and inspire the reluctant imperialist that dare not speak his own name. Even more scrupulous (if you are into that sort of thing) is his unequivocal identification of the civilizing mission as at core a cultural one that requires a rigorous and sustained application of imperial effort at cultural conversion, and not flash-in-the-pan military victories and the holding of elections. America is faltering in its global mission because whereas "the British regarded long-term occupation as an inherent part of their self-appointed civilizing mission" and proceeded on the assumption "that British rule would end once a country had been sufficiently 'civilized' – read: anglicized – to ensure the continued rule of law and operation of free markets," Americans lack the "stamina" for this sort of thing.[25] Oxbridge imperialists spent decades in Britain's foreign dominions, painstakingly nudging the natives along this path of anglicization. In contrast, "as far as America's Ivy League nation-builders are concerned, you can set up an independent central bank, reform the tax code, liberalize prices and privatize the major utilities – and be home in time for the first reunion."[26] Ferguson is thus wary of fellow travelers such as Robert Kaplan who nonetheless only defend an idea of the American Empire that roams:

> the world with its ships and planes, but is wary of where it gets involved on the ground ... [for empire] by no means obliges the American military to repair complex and populous Islamic countries that lack critical components of civil society.[27]

But for Ferguson, such obligation and commitment is not ancillary to imperial rule, but the very substance of it. Iraq and Afghanistan are failures, for example, not of imperial overreach, but of too little empire, too cautiously implemented and too reluctantly imposed. In his entreaties to the Americans, Ferguson therefore often appears to be channeling something akin to David Ben-Gurion's aspirations of "a Galilee free from Arab population," that "we must uproot from our hearts the assumption that the thing is not possible. It can be done."[28]

Ferguson is hardly alone in his imperial musings. Writing in the *Weekly Standard* only a month or so after 9/11, Max Boot already made "The Case for American Empire" by declaring that "Afghanistan and other troubled lands today cry out for the sort of enlightened foreign administration once provided by self-confident Englishmen in jodhpurs and pith helmets."[29] One finds similar though more measured reflections in Michael Ignatieff's "empire lite," which "reveals how American military power, European money and humanitarian motive have combined to produce a form of imperial rule [in Bosnia, Kosovo and Afghanistan] for a post-imperial age."[30] Long thought to be dead and buried, modernization theory is making something of a comeback in this guise of liberal humanitarianism and aid politics. The Iraq War was supported by a wide variety of public intellectuals and political philosophers on precisely these grounds. And an entire generation of neo-conservatives and 'liberal hawks' has grown up since the fall of the Berlin Wall with aspirations of a liberal American empire bringing democracy and human rights to the Muslim world. Some of this is born of circumstance. With China ascendant, India largely on board, and Russia still too powerful to be summarily ensouled by the West, the Muslim world remains the ideal theater on which to stage imperial fantasies of 'global' transformation. The battles currently brewing in Eastern Europe may one day rise to the same level of world-historical importance, but for now terrorism and war are the cultural burden of Muslims and of the "retarded political culture" of the Middle East. Even many former supporters of the Iraq War now amend their erstwhile enthusiasm only insofar as they may have underestimated the *culture* of sectarian hatreds in the Iraqi population or the incompetence of the Bush administration. The project of liberal interventionism is itself inoculated from critique, to be tried bigger and better the next time around.

* * *

This form of talk is nothing new, of course. It hearkens back to the intense race consciousness and escalating white panic of the age of imperialism (dated roughly from the scramble for Africa in 1881 to the beginning of the First World War). Back then, as more of the world came under direct European rule, the natives and their strange customs and rituals, their *difference*, became an object of immediate and unmediated concern for the imperialists. In the books of Conrad and Kipling and of countless others, Europeans were also exposed to the vastness of this world and of the myriad exotic peoples that inhabited it. While this exoticism sometimes ignited yearnings for a re-enchantment of the Western soul by the spiritualism of the East – both Hinduism and Buddhism were 'constructed' in the late nineteenth century as repositories of this kind of esoteric knowledge – it more often than not also produced a deep sense of anxiety and danger, of contamination, of being resisted and run over by the hordes in the far-flung dominions that were the source of so much of Europe's wealth and of its new self-image as the World-Subject. That this sense of white superiority would immediately become entangled with notions of white fragility makes perfect sense. Inasmuch as this superiority was rooted in constitutive difference, it was always going to be susceptible to biological and cultural miscegenation in the colonies – the sheer numbers were never in the colonists' favor. Also, the very fact of the colonized 'brute' was itself an affront and danger to the civilizing mission. And the mere expression of his identity, the manners and customs of his ordinary existence, were in one sense always already acts of aggression against white supremacy. But while the danger to white world supremacy was real enough, the European continent itself was thought to be largely immune from any direct impregnation by the East. The white race may well become "swamped in certain parts of the world by the black and yellow races," but this would at worst mean being "driven from every neutral market and forced to confine [itself] within [its] own."[31] At issue was not the existence of the white race itself, but, as Lothrop Stoddard put it, rather "the legend of white invincibility" and "the veil of prestige that draped white civilization."[32]

The providential expansion of European power and culture was under dire threat in white panic literature. Still, whiteness itself was thought to be more resilient.

Inasmuch as 'the West' is a successor concept to racialized imperial whiteness, it does much of the same work that whiteness did to structure the feelings that animated the old imperial sense of identity and mission. And it is prone to the same crisis of confidence and lamentations of decline that whiteness once suffered from. Ferguson's valorizations of the West and his elegiac warnings of its imminent collapse on the world stage are but mere reiterations of this old admixture of destiny and dread. But there is one important difference. America always had its blacks, but the European continent was an island of whiteness surrounded by colored lands that it dominated. This is no longer the case. Color is now very much on the continent. And the shade that overshadows all others in the Euro-American imagination is green. The 'brutes' are firmly in-house, and the danger they pose is very real. The burgeoning right-wing movements across the European continent, and increasingly also in the United States, have Muslims in their crosshairs as they wage an existential conflict aimed at saving Western civilization itself from extinction. In this, they replicate much of the mood of white panic and deploy alarmist tropes and rhetoric that hearken back to the beginning years of the last century. But they do so now with an amplified sense of anxiety provoked by the proximity of cultural difference and the fear of cultural annihilation.

Ferguson and his neo-imperialist coterie are naturally at the intellectual forefront of disseminating these kinds of sentiments as well, although as per their respectable status they do maintain a safe distance from the very worst elements of the chauvinist right. From the outside looking in, Ferguson ruefully imagines Spain's tiny North African enclave of Ceuta as "no longer an outpost of an aggressively expansionist European empire, but a defensive bulwark maintained by a continent under siege." Where "a hundred years ago ... Europe's surplus population was still flocking across the oceans to populate America and Australasia," now "a youthful society to the south and east of the Mediterranean is quietly colonizing ... a senescent and secularized continent to the north and west of it."[33] This sense that Europe is 'senescent' recalls Marx's descriptions of Asia as 'asleep in history' and hence somehow deserving of Europe's rousing interventions. The alarms being raised now are therefore designed to wake the West up before it's too late. Books such as Bruce Bawer's *While Europe Slept* (2006) and *Surrender* (2009), Christopher Caldwell's 'seminal' *Reflections on the Revolutions in Europe* (2009), and Douglas Murray's *The Strange Death of Europe* (2017) are published by reputable presses and receive starred reviews. The Muslim 'demographic threat' is a source of endless speculation and heightening unease. Caldwell, for example, insists that Islam is "in no sense Europe's religion and it is in no sense Europe's culture," but "when an insecure, malleable, relativistic culture meets a culture that is anchored, confident and strengthened by common doctrines, it is generally the former that changes to suit the latter."[34] Bawer paints the dire picture of an escalating contagion, for Muslim "neighborhoods [in European cities] aren't temporary ghettos that will fade with integration; they're *embryonic colonies* that will continue to grow as the result of immigration and reproduction."[35] Unsaid but underlying these sentiments is, of course, the presumption that there are such discrete things as 'European' culture and 'Muslim' culture, that cultures are 'creatures' that naturally colonize each other, and that lack of confidence and pride in one's own culture invites domination. It is as if Western "culture is creative, heterogeneous, and constantly evolving, while Muslim culture … [is] empty habit, monolithic, mindless conformity to lifeless customs … [and] Muslims [are] a destructive and 'museumized peoples'."[36]

The muscle memory from Europe's own colonizations is perhaps one source of this rising discomfort with Muslims. Another that recalls America's experience with its blacks is that having first ghettoized these populations and segregated them out of any role in the political and social evolution of societies in which they reside, Muslims are now only recognizable as monsters lurking at the edge of town, itching to terrorize their erstwhile oppressors. It is in this sense that any public displays of Muslim difference are *ipso facto* a provocation and any affirmative expressions of identity are intentional acts of aggression against the host culture. In an excellent investigation of Islam talk in

Europe, Samuel M. Behloul makes the intriguing point that Muslims are often subject to a form of "post-racial racism" which "is no longer linked to a particular physiognomy or skin type, but interprets the visual appearance of a religion and its members (minaret, *burqa*, hijab, beard) as a threat."[37] In the same anthology, David Llewelyn Tryer explains:

> 'Muslim' offers an interesting counterpoint to 'white'. Like all other racialized identities, it has no positive ontic racial status. Yet like white, Muslim appears racially invisible. We can thus ask: are Muslims white? The answer, of course, is that the contemporary discourse that problematizes Muslim minorities categorizes them *in opposition* to white.[38]

Muslims are therefore experienced not as just another religious minority, but as the mirrored antithesis of the cultural essence of the West. In being insufficiently racialized, they complicate and frustrate the racial hierarchies that undergird the Western project and sow confusion and constraint on the civilizing mission. As Mamdani points out, whereas the unreserved *blackness* of Africa means that it can be legitimately portrayed as "*incapable* of modernity, hard-core Islam is seen as not only incapable of but *resistant* to modernity."[39] And modernity here is gaged not per some objective measure of civilizational development (as if one could be reasonably construed absent the workings of power), but rather as the ever-evolving cultural repository of the West that underpins its proprietary institutions and norms, and its justifiable domination of the 'rest' as the appropriate archetype for civilization. The self-identified, self-expressing 'Western' Muslim throws a wrench in the salutary exposition of this civilization and by definition threatens the progress of modernity as such.

The myriad controversies and crises surrounding Muslim presence in Europe and America over the last two decades or so must be understood with these kinds of concerns in mind. Every time the building of a new mosque or an Islamic center becomes embroiled in long drawn-out battles over zoning, security or 'propriety', there is of course much more at play. The visible presence of Islam as a feature of the shared public landscape is in itself a reminder that there is something foreign and insidious in our midst that does not conform to the graphic cues of cultural modernity. Depending on the level of secularity in this or that Western society, the arguments against mosque construction modulate between a defense of religion–state distinction and a defense of Christianity. But the underlying premises remain much the same. The ubiquity of church spires is a 'natural' visual marker of the historical evolution of Euro-American culture in a way that mosque minerats can, and should, never be. Accommodating Muslim dietary needs in schools or other public institutions often becomes an issue of national cultural sovereignty, and their clothing and habits a source of consternation and disgust that recall Kurtz's famous concluding exclamation to his report for the International Society for the Suppression of Savage Customs in *Heart of Darkness* (1899): "Exterminate all the brutes!"[40] The viability of far-right parties that extol the virtues of this or that ethnicity in Europe is explicitly buttressed by broader claims of the cultural unity of a Christian West against the moral contagion of Islam. In the United States, these kinds of claims are most evident in the various anti-sharia legislations being debated and passed across the country, and especially in the American South, where the presence of actual Muslims remains negligible. It is not my intention to inundate the reader with the countless examples of this sort – this book is rather more concerned with the discursive architecture of these debates and controversies than with an enumeration of them. And in any case, some excellent work has already been done in analyzing the specifics of these matters. Suffice it to say that from the furious debates surrounding the veiling (or unveiling) of Muslim women in Europe, to the surveillance of mosques and MSAs (Muslim Student Associations) in the United States, to the arguments for and against immigration from Muslim countries, it is now evident that Islam has become a *permanent* feature of the political culture of Western societies, which are profoundly reliant on the fact of Islam's cultural alterity for their own internal expositions.

Reinhard Schulze has argued, for example, that in many of these cases, "as Islam is debated within the *autopoiesis* of society, [it] is not communicated as a 'religion', but as a 'societal other'." In effect, this means that "Islam is conceived as a new environment of society and as a disturbance ... [not] with respect to its 'religious' frame of reference, but related to worldly affairs. That is why Islam has often been termed a 'political religion'."[41] To this I would add that 'worldly affairs' here can also mean the mundane facts of Muslim life, the banal choices they make regarding what to eat, what to wear and where to pray perceived as acts of cultural and political resistance. When 'burkinis', headscarves and beards are experienced as existential threats to the French Republic and halal food is seen as a sign of a hostile Muslim takeover of its public institutions, clearly there is more at play than simply a concern about public safety. Talk of values and culture is at least more honest even if it has the potential to (and oftentimes does) slide down into the gutter of explicitly nativist sentiments. As the number of Muslims living in the West continues to increase, we may yet only be at the beginning point of a long and drawn-out reckoning with the cultural legacy of imperialism now playing out at home.

* * *

Neo-imperialism and resurgent nativism are two sides of the same coin. They are fueled by the same intermingling desires and anxieties. And they rely on the same culturalist assumptions about the West and about Islam. Whether these assumptions are 'racist' or not is a useless debate, a sideshow that often overshadows the reality of how they

Culture Talk

actually function to structure the relationship between the West and Muslims. Consider, for example, that Ferguson's *Civilization* ostensibly tells the *longue durée* story of how the West came to dominate the world in material terms but is actually a thinly veiled triumphalist account of the normative superiority of Western culture. What else would it mean in any case to title the book 'civilization' in the singular? And to lump the rest into, well, the Rest? Still, there are useful indicators here of culture talk at play. Ferguson identifies six "killer apps" (his terminology) as setting the West apart from the Rest and as together constituting the advanced (and proprietary) cultural software of Western societies. These include such Western 'inventions' as property, science, medicine, competition, consumption and work ethic. They can be willfully downloaded by others (Ferguson is obsessed with China) or they can be forcefully hacked into resistant cultures such as "the civilization of Islam – of the cult of submission – [which] is still built on the Koran."[42] Of course, the idea that one can reasonably tell the story of the modern world as meaningfully divided into closed systems with patented cultural DNA no longer holds much water for serious historians. And the astonishing annexation of the historically complex evolution of panoramic phenomena such as 'science', 'property' and 'work ethic' exclusively to an amorphous entity called 'the West' would be cringeworthy for any sincere student of them. In his groundbreaking *The Birth of the Modern World, 1780– 1914* – which Ferguson inexplicably called "a masterpiece" but apparently took none of its most germane lessons to heart – C.A. Bayly argued effectively that "it is no longer really possible to write 'European' or 'American' history in a narrow sense ... [because] *all* local, national, or regional histories, must, in important ways ... be global histories."[43] Regardless, Ferguson soldiers on: the "Western package still seems to offer human societies the best available set of economic, social and political institutions ... [but] the big question is whether or not we are still able to recognize the superiority of [this] package."[44] All innuendo about the *package* aside, this operating software is clearly a viral impregnator of other people's hardware that modernizes their software and brings them up to date. But the integrity of the West's operating software is compromised if too many alien programs are circulating in its homeware. This explains the intertwined desires and anxieties associated with empire abroad and immigrants at home. The world needs the West to be the West, and not some hybrid such as 'Eurabia' or 'Londonistan'. In Ferguson's Hegelian fantasies, history itself would grind to a halt without the culture-*making* facility of the Western moderns, and nothing new could enter the world.

The West as this coherent unity separated from the rest is therefore an ideological construct with tenuous basis in sociological reality. And Islam, or a certain Islam, is the name for the principal contemporary adversary of this ideology. It appears that 'Islam' has now become "practically useful as a political boundary term, both to outsiders and to insiders who [wish] to draw lines around themselves."[45] Looked at from this Western perspective, 'extremism' is the resting bitch face of Islam out there in the world, and 'radicalization' its natural cultural excrement at home. These insolences, extremism and radicalization, are the twin attributes of 'Islam as a culture' sieved through the two essential assumptions of culture talk. First, that the cultural burden of Islam binds Muslims to an almost genetic predisposition toward motivations, desires and actions rooted in the essential experience of their religion. This is the sense in which it makes no sense to talk about a Muslim woman actively *choosing* to wear the hijab, for example, in that the hijab is already a visual indication of her enslavement by her culture, and of false consciousness if not also false modesty. It is for this reason that the Muslim subject is often simultaneously infantilized and made menacing in culture talk, both a candidate for tutelage in the Western creed but also a dire threat to the West in any extreme exposition of her native culture. Second, that Islam is the foremost repository of the pre-modern spirit in this modern world and is by definition aligned ideologically against modernity understood as an artifact of Western history and culture. This artifact is the engine of Progress which leads humanity up not "Jacob's Ladder ... but rather 'Civilization's Ladder', if you will" and that powers the motor of history. Freedom, the crimson interpretive thread of the West, is precisely this capacity to continuously *make* culture rather than be subject to it.

In this reading, Islam is an enervating load weighing down movement up "Civilization's Ladder." Its cultural symbols are like so many signs of a Satanic anti-modernity waging its endless war on human progress. And these symbols now overflow their given meaning as pointing to an identity and congeal instead as an *anti-identity*. If the modern is civic, tolerant, peaceful and progressive, then the mosque, the hijab, the beard and the halal are cyphers for the uncivic, the intolerant, the violent and the regressive. Whatever the banality of their content, their utility or their actively expressed meaning, cultural markers of Islam are constitutively radical in their *orientation* toward the West; Muslims are therefore always only a short step or two from being further radicalized into violence.

When "the definition of radicalization has been widened so far as to include any kind of opposition to the status quo" and extremism attends to any strong deviations from the cues of Western cultural modernity, then the global public sphere is of necessity enfeebled as a context for collaborative evolution of the common world.[46] This explains why the prospects of a properly political relationship between the West and Muslims (right here or out there) are as dim as they are. Inasmuch as culture is a naturalized carceral inheritance, then 'Muslim' is an ascriptive identity already molded before its habitation by this or that person. In his analysis of contemporary Islamophobia, for example, the media scholar and journalist Arun Kundnani points out to a great extent "Muslims are everywhere the same" and similarly predisposed to rebellion. "Protests against Danish cartoons, urban unrest in French *banlieues*, or young Muslims volunteering to leave the West to fight foreign occupations in the Middle East, Africa, or Asia," Kundnani continues, "all these different actions are not made sense of by culturalists in terms of the specific social and political histories involved but explained as symptoms of an inevitable, underlying conflict between Islam's regressive cultural identity and Western values."[47] Once the different political valences and contexts of these and other acts by Muslims are strained through the culturalist thesis, they sublimate into a singular substance called 'Islam'. They are revealed therefore as not political acts at all, but rather the corrupt predispositions programmed into premodern software now operating in a modern world. Depoliticized in the very fact of their existence, there is ultimately "only one political act that Muslim fellow citizens can perform without suspicion: rejection of their Muslim identity."[48] All else is sham and masquerade.

Notice that even ostensibly humanizing treatments of Muslims in contemporary Western media usually rely on some version of such rejection for their narrative efficacy. Both Aziz Ansari's excellent Netflix series *Master of None* (2015–) and Kumail Nanjiani's Oscar-nominated *The Big Sick* (2017) are biographical sketches whose recent mainstream success suggests that there is a market for comforting portrayals of 'normalized' Muslims to go along with the radicalized and extremist ones. But there is little appetite for complex or critical characters 'in between'. If Ansari and Nanjiani are rebelling against anything in these stories, it is the constraints imposed by their inherited religious culture. Such rebellion is typified in the former's obsession with pork and pasta and the latter's pursuit of a career in stand-up comedy and of a white woman against his Muslim parents' objections. One reflection of the decades-long evolution of a politicized black identity has been the discursive transition from movies such as *Guess Who's Coming to Dinner?* (1967) to *Get Out* (2017), from *To Sir with Love* (1967) to *Django Unchained* (2012). No such transition is yet on offer for Muslims. Instead, we have the anodyne perennialism of everyone's favorite 'Muslim' scholar Reza Aslan, whose Islam appears so bereft of distinction as to lack any substance at all.[49] News media Muslims are similarly non-threatening and, like Fareed Zakaria of CNN, have often spent long years prefacing their careers with loyal and public enculturation in the West before 'coming out' as Muslim.[50] Islam is worn very lightly, if it is worn at all. For there is great danger that attaches to any vigorous proclamations of an identity that provokes such *ex ante* anxiety.

But there is more. 'Muslimness' now also attaches to any interpretive strategies for *explaining* the modern world that are not entirely exhausted in the various expositions of Western sensibilities and concerns. One need sport no explicit cultural markers of Islam or have a particularly well-honed sense of one's own Muslim identity to nevertheless experience the world in a manner that sets one apart from the Western mainstream. To come of age in the countless peripheries of modernity engenders a natural suspicion of triumphalist accounts of Progress and of any uncomplicated acceptance of Western norms and values. But any reluctance 'to go along to get along' on the part of even such nominally Muslim (and even non-Muslim) actors generates culturalist arguments that discredit their critiques as provincial, anti-modern or entirely in thrall of Islam. This means that vast swaths of human experience have been ghettoized out of any constructive involvement in the task of theorizing the human condition as a whole and in general. This task, this philosophical burden, falls only on the resilient shoulders of properly constituted World-Subjects in conversations with each other. This intellectual depoliticization goes hand in hand with the neo-imperialist and nativist attempts to clear the political field of any Muslim debris so the task of making and remaking the modern world in the image of the West (while simultaneously keeping the West safe from the world) can continue unhindered. And such refusals of other people's reflections on the modern world are hardly only a feature of right-wing thinking, but rather remain a principal attribute of Western philosophy as such.[51] It is these same sentiments that attend to the spirited defense of "Western Civ" courses on university campuses and which prompted Ferguson to bemoan that "maybe the real threat is posed not by the rise of China, Islam or CO_2 emissions, but by our own loss of faith in the civilization we inherited from our ancestors."[52] To keep the faith in Western civilization means to keep it politically, culturally and intellectually separated from the Rest until the civilizing mission is complete. It's a tall order, but "it can be done."

Now it is clearly the case that escalating violence in Muslim societies and by Muslims in the West is a real problem that requires serious analysis as to its historical and sociopolitical causes and the proper ways of responding to it. Culturalist arguments appear uninterested in doing the former and hence generate ham-fisted answers to the latter. The long history of colonial and postcolonial politics in the Muslim world and the intellectual currents that ebbed and flowed around the embankments of the Cold War are good places to start. The marginalization of immigrant Muslims from the cultural and political mainstream in the West through either a depoliticizing and ghettoized 'multiculturalism' or the bad faith rhetoric of 'take it or leave it' assimilation should also draw our attention. But this would require abandoning earnestly held beliefs about constitutive difference and cultural superiority as the core engines of modernity, and the problem of Islam as essentially a conflict between moderns and premoderns. And again, the historical dynamics that led to the economic, political and indeed cultural domination of the world by certain societies located on the far western edges of the Eurasian continent merit consideration. But as Pankaj Mishra points out in a scathing review of Ferguson's *Civilization*, "to explain the contingent, short-lived factors that gave a few countries in Western Europe their advantage over the rest of the world requires a sustained and complex analysis, not one hell-bent on establishing that the West was, and is, best," and contending "that it resulted basically from the wonderfulness of the West, not to mention the hopelessness of the East."[53] These kinds of unreconstructed sentiments naturally (and rightly) recall the imperialist justifications for world domination of folks such as the preacher Giles Horrox, just as Ferguson himself personally evokes Horrox's creed that the "highest of all the races on [Civilization's] ladder stands the Anglo-Saxon." It is hardly surprising, then, that culture talk meanders around issues of race, religion and civilization in a manner so reminiscent of its nineteenth-century antecedents.

* * *

As these kinds of conversations about Muslims proliferate in the global public mainstream, there are now definite indications of their increasing impact on what counts as Western culture itself and on the self-identity of Western peoples. These effects are most obvious in the ubiquitous lurch to the political right in the United States and many countries in Europe. But more alarming perhaps is the intellectual drift of left-leaning thinkers such as Michael Walzer, Mark Lilla and, of course, Christopher Hitchens toward an almost nativist disdain for the difference of Islam as so culturally sedimented as to elicit weariness, apprehension and even outright dread.[54] Paul Berman's unwillingness to countenance even a conversation with Tariq Ramadan is just one such example. Another is Linda Sarsour, the hijab-wearing Palestinian-American firebrand co-founder of *Woman's March* and a longtime advocate for civil rights in New York City, whose 'Islam' gets dragged into all that she says or does, as a cudgel to demean and diminish her contributions as mere fronts for some nefarious theocratic agenda. Speaking of the War on Terror, for example, Kundnani noted that "in [this] campaign to transform Islamic identity, liberalism itself underwent a transformation: it became an ideology of total war that led its advocates into what Italian theorist Domenico Lustrodo calls 'a tragic performative contradiction'." This obsessive focus on Muslim culture as an existential problem means that many so-called liberals have now permanently "turned the values they once fought for into icons of Western identity. What was once a call to fight for freedom in Western societies [has] degenerated into a call to defend a liberal way of life from foreign enemies." And in many corners of the Western intellectual ecosphere, these 'liberal' values are being "held up as the cultural basis for Western identity and the universal standard for civilization ... [and] taken to imply an identitarian politics of national security rather than an egalitarian politics of social security."[55] What this means on the flip side, of course, is that liberal notions of democratic citizenship, participatory politics, reason-giving and even secularism are instead gradually giving way to more sinister conceptions of 'modern' and 'liberal' as "fully arrived" cultural identities – to use Wendy Brown's formulation – that are not amenable to any 'outside' intervention.[56] And that this "tragic performative contradiction" of carving Muslims out of the conversation is now having significant effects on the nature and meaning of the conversation itself.

Recent books by Nadia Marzouki and Peter O'Brien make precisely this point as they examine how the concept of 'Islam' has evolved in the domestic political *imaginaire* of both America and Europe post-9/11. Marzouki argues that on both sides of the Atlantic, liberal arguments for fairness and equal rights are being increasingly undermined by an "affective disposition characterized by the visceral feeling of having been offended, betrayed [and] dispossessed" by the proximate presence of Muslims and their cultural symbols, and "by a need to have this wound recognized." These kinds of claims "can be mobilized for both reactionary or progressive agendas," but in either case, "to invoke affective feelings is to propose a ritualist vision of the community, one founded on a mimicry of feelings and ways of life."[57] In effect, to be a 'liberal' can then come to mean "to laugh at a caricature of Mohamed, to feel worried about a mosque at Ground Zero, and to be disgusted at the sight of a burka" irrespective of the normative ideals insinuated by the moniker. This drift toward "collective feelings" and "affective norms" in the meaning of liberal secularism and democracy reflects pre-existing anxieties now being framed in opposition to and exacerbated by the fact of Islam. In this variant of culture talk, "the slightest attempt to suggest that adhering to Islam is a way of proposing an alternative conception of the world or way of life is immediately inflated into proof of anti-Americanism."[58] And in being circumscribed for the purposes of constraining Muslims, the bedrock principle of pluralism is also more broadly diminished portending "the ever-increasing fragility of the liberal argument" itself.[59] Similarly, Peter O'Brien uses the notion of a *Kulturkampf* (culture struggle) to describe an ideological war currently underway where forms of "liberal assimilationism, nativism and Hobbesian postmodernism" appear to be converging into a "normative alliance" against both Islam and more pluralist, open-ended conceptions of the political community. O'Brien maintains that "mutual fragilization" between the public philosophies of liberalism, nationalism and postmodernism does theoretically leave enough room for hospitality and mutual recognition, what he calls "conviviality without consensus." But he is hardly optimistic. Weary from the "self-adulation about the resilience and greatness of French and European civilization" that predictably followed the Bataclan theatre massacre, O'Brien suggests that if Europe "truly wishes to incorporate Muslims into the very essence of its identity, [it] will have to enable an open and likely unsettling and uncertain dialog about why so much of its foreign policy seems to place lesser value on Muslim lives."[60] The intimate connection between an imperialist foreign policy and the problems 'Islam' generates at home is as clear as can be. Even so, culture talk persists.

Perhaps all this is only a reflection of the fact that the institutions and values that the West has wrapped itself in as its 'core identity' in recent years were never more than skin-deep to begin with. Tony Blair's incessant harping on "British values" during the early oughts provoked eye-rolls in much of the formerly colonized world, just as George W. Bush's confidence in the West's mission to bring peace and prosperity to 'the Rest' induced only anxious slumber on the part of his non-Western audiences. The idea that the West has been a bastion of freedom, human rights and democracy for all even at home, much less abroad, is Cold War propaganda discursively projected into deep history as some inborn and inherent feature of a rolling Enlightenment. But whatever rights were won, whatever freedoms were gained, whatever laws were changed reflected not some natural enfolding of the West's proprietary DNA, but furious social movements and political agitations that spanned decades and were frantically resisted all the way. The same is true today. It is hardly surprising, then, that culturalist arguments are once again on the ascendancy just as the world is getting smaller and more complicated by the minute and the ideological seals that maintain distinction and separation between the West and the Rest are beginning to come undone. Whatever their respective liberal or conservative political credentials, Ferguson's rueful fantasies of a re-Christianized Europe ready to stand up to Islam and Donald Trump's aspirations for a literal wall on America's southern border to keep the 'brutes' out are the same species of resistance to making a proper "political analysis of our time" in lieu of talk of culture and civilization. As far as "crapulous theories" go, these are not particularly bad ones. And they are hardly peculiar to the West alone. While this book is primarily concerned with the Muslim Question in the West, many Muslims themselves subscribe to strongly culturalist accounts of both their own identities and those of their Western counterparts. The roles are reversed, of course, but the messianic passion for bringing salvation to a broken world is unfortunately often just as strident on the other side. And the fruits of this passion are on spectacular display every day in conversations, newsreels and body counts around the world. For there are 'Horroxes' aplenty on all sides and no dirth of crapulous theories to justify their dominions.

* * *

Notice, for example, that Edward Said was wary of precisely these kinds of discursive moves by the peripherally positioned peoples of the world when he complained that:

> In [their] wish to make [themselves] heard ... [they] tend very often to forget that the world is a crowded place, and that if everyone were to insist on the radical purity or priority of one's own

voice, all we would have would be the awful din of unending strife, and a bloody political mess, the true horror of which is beginning to be perceptible here and there in the re-emergence of racist politics in Europe, the cacophony of debates over political correctness and identity politics in the United States, and – to speak about my own part of the world – the intolerance and illusory promises of Bismarckian despotism, à la Saddam Hussein and his numerous Arab epigones and counterparts.

Said was writing this in the early 1990s, and the situation he described then has only become more strident since. This expanding cacophony, this din of strife, this incessant back and forth between claims of Western superiority and what Said calls the "culture of complaint" by the peripheral peoples of the world, is itself a corollary of "the one idea that has scarcely varied ... throughout the exchange between Europeans and their 'others' [that] began systematically half a millennium ago ... that there is an 'us' and a 'them' each quite settled, clear, unassailably self-evident."[61] But even acknowledging the importance of rooted belonging to the construction of modern identities, most serious scholarship in humanistic disciplines now clearly rejects the simplistic idea of human cultures as entirely independent units of sociological analysis. In her work on modern global cultures, for example, the political philosopher

The Muslim Speaks

Seyla Benhabib decries how a "great deal of contemporary debate [is] bogged down by [such] false epistemological assumptions" about the nature of cultural and religious difference. Inasmuch as 'cultures' can be identified as useful categories for a scholarly investigation of the human condition, they are and always have been "formed through complex dialogues and interactions with other cultures [because] ... the boundaries of cultures are fluid, porous and contested." Only when exceptionalist assumptions about cultures as objective things out there in the world with differentiated essences and disparate evolutions are decisively rejected can "new modalities of pluralist cultural coexistence be re-imagined."[62] And this is as true for an essentialized (ostensibly beleaguered) Muslim 'culture' as it is for an essentialized (supposedly overbearing) Western one. What Said calls this "fundamentally static notion of identity that has been the core of cultural thought during the era of imperialism" is in fact a discursive obfuscation of the reality on the ground, the fact that "partly because of empire [itself], all cultures are involved in one another, none is single and pure, all are hybrid, heterogeneous, extraordinarily differentiated, and unmonolithic." That even accounting for the fundamentally unjust and asymmetrical relationships attendant to European colonialism, "most of us should now regard the historical experience of empire as a common one."[63] A politics of identity and recognition is the necessary corrective to provincial universalisms that fail to properly account for difference, to what

Arendt calls the human condition of *plurality*. But *sans* an underlying humanistic impulse toward the shared creation of better futures and a common world worth living in, such politics is always in danger of devolving into just another zero-sum competition between variously humanized or dehumanized contestants.

Said's own life history reflected both the din and cacophony of modernity and the humanistic possibilities it nonetheless still offered to its denizens. As a Palestinian Christian struggling to make sense of his place in the world, and dispossessed of his homeland by another dispossessed people struggling to make sense of their place in the world, Said had a front-row seat to modernity's perplexing realities and its many contradictions. He was not Muslim by religion, but firmly maintained his connection to an *Islamicate Weltanschauung* that was coming undone under the relentless squeeze of modern imperialism and its aftermaths. And yet as a cosmopolitan New Yorker for most of his life, Said also belonged nowhere and everywhere at one and the same time. He critiqued the West, sure, but also had an enormous love for Western literature and Western peoples and the West as such that belies any easy characterization of his work as simple polemics. The cultural reality attendant to both his work and his existence belies the simple prevarications of folks such as Ferguson whose own stated love of the West is more a form of magical thinking than a desire for recognition. Said the humanist knew that the desire to belong, to be at home in this world, required a solemn recognition of this world's complex realities, and not crapulous theories of cultural superiority.

It is for this reason that Said wanted it:

> to be remembered [that] narratives of emancipation and enlightenment [among the colonized] in their strongest form were also narratives of *integration* not separation, the stories of people who had been excluded from the main group but who were fighting for a place in it.[64]

Such narratives often did turn sour under stress from an intensifying imperialism. But the core of their concern has always been finding a sense of belonging in this new world and a way to feel at home in it. This prompted Said to wonder, "are there ways we can reconceive the imperial experience in other than compartmentalized terms, so as to transform our understanding of both the past and the present and our attitude toward the future?"[65] Said was deeply troubled that:

> Generations later, the conflict [between colonial powers and formerly colonized societies] continues in an impoverished and for that reason all the more dangerous form, thanks to an uncritical alignment between intellectuals and institutions of power which *reproduces* the pattern of an earlier imperialist history.[66]

His foreboding that history appeared stuck in a time-loop mirrored Fanon's. But Said was worried that "the entire legacy of what can metaphorically be called the tension between Kipling, who finally saw only the politics of empire, and Fanon, who tried to look past the nationalist assertions succeeding classical imperialism, has been disastrous."[67] The continuing back and forth attendant to this discursive tension between Kipling and Fanon has only generated hardened horizons that don't fuse in encounter, but bang into each other with the force of bombs and the hollow sound of clichés. And even if this Sisyphusian exercise in futility may have had a literary sort of charm the first time around, it has made for terrible sequels.

Said offered a way out with what he called a "contrapuntal" approach to modernity. Although most fully explicated by Said as a form of doing literary analysis, this approach tries to juxtapose into concurrence "those views and experiences that are ideologically and culturally closed to each other and that attempt to suppress other views and experiences."[68] "To read Austen," for example, "without also reading Fanon and Cabral – and so on and on – is to disaffiliate modern culture from its engagements and attachments."[69] Depending on the particular object of inquiry, to contrapuntally approach the archive of modernity is to take Western cultural forms "out of the autonomous enclosures in which they have been protected, and [place them] instead in the dynamic global environment created by imperialism, itself revised as an ongoing contest between north and south, metropolis and periphery, white and native."[70] In making these pronouncements, Said was asking us to imagine what it would mean for "Beethoven [to belong] as much to West Indians as he does to Germans, since his music is now part of human heritage."[71] But in their desire to preserve 'the West' and keep it secure against 'the Rest' by condescendingly benign domination, folks such as Ferguson are fundamentally incapable of such imagination. And their crapulous theories about cultures and civilizations are nowhere less secure than when exposed to the full, complex humanity of their subjects. For it is with this humanity in mind that the "polyphonic accompaniment to the expansion of Europe" prompts Said to focus instead on a different kind of desire, "to preserve what is unique about each [of us] so long as we also preserve some sense of the human community and the actual contests that contribute to its formation, and of which they are all a part."[72] The desire to love the world, that is, without getting lost in it.

Conclusion
Amor Mundi

In a letter to her longtime mentor Karl Jaspers back in 1955, Hannah Arendt intimated that "I've begun so late, really only in recent years, to truly love the world," and that "out of gratitude, I want to call my book on political theory *Amor Mundi*."[1] With Americans notoriously dubious about foreign languages, of course, this preferred title did not survive the publication process. Nevertheless, *The Human Condition* is still a book about learning to love the world as a way of practicing one's humanity. For *Amor Mundi* is not the flattening love of *eros* or *agape*, nor even the comforting love of empathy and community, but rather the challenging political love of plurality, of "the fact that men, not Man, live on the earth and inhabit the world."[2] It is also the affective response to an acknowledgment of the humanity of others and to reconciling oneself with the world as it actually is, and not as we wish it was. It is a way of being in the world, then, where "we humanize what is going on in the world and in ourselves only by speaking of it, and in the course of speaking of it we learn to be human."³ The opposite of *Amor Mundi* is not hate, but a kind of lazy indifference toward the facts of the world as mere irritants, as largely irrelevant to the smooth elaboration of this or that theory about this world rather than engagement with its lived history and with its continuously differentiating reality. It is this manner of anti-political indifference that Arendt noticed in postwar Germany back in 1950, what she called "this apparent heartlessness, sometimes covered over with cheap sentimentality, [that] is only the most conspicuous outward symptom of a deep-rooted, stubborn, at times vicious refusal to face and come to terms with what really happened."⁴ A defeated people, the Germans have done much in the intervening decades to face the horrors of their past and to acknowledge the humanity of those that many in their own ranks sought to exterminate. In speaking of such horrors and in the solemn recognition of their reality, Germans humanize themselves and the world around them. To love the world is nothing other than this.

Such love of the world has been notably absent in many corners of what we now call the West. And in other places too – and especially perhaps in what some call the Muslim world – but nowhere other than the West with as much significance for all of us who inhabit this world. For the "vicious refusals to face and come to terms with what really happened," these failures "to make a political analysis

Conclusion

of our time,"⁵ the choosing of "comforting pieties over curiosity, complexity, and humility"⁶ have been consistent features of the Western mainstream's view of the world, and of those who inhabit it, for quite some time. And it persists now even as the world itself appears to be coming apart at the very seams fabricated to safely cocoon it in what Arnold Toynbee called the "progressive erection, by Western hands, of a scaffolding within which all the once separate societies have built themselves into one."⁷ In all the various ways it is asked by all the various participants in the debate, the Muslim Question is but one indication of this unraveling. Of this lack of love of the world. To desire the world, to desire to be the world, to desire to see oneself everywhere in the world, is not love of the world. It is love of desire itself, of the expansion of this desire to all corners of the world (and beyond), and of a self-referential feedback loop fueled by anti-political abstractions such as 'Progress' and 'Civilization'. It is this profoundly dehumanizing form of love that Pavel Kohout had in mind perhaps when he warned that *sans* "a new example" to organize it better, this world that Europeans had created could well augur a millennium not of human beings, but "an era of supercivilized monkeys."⁸ And Fanon as well, when he called for the synthesis of a "new man" in the agonistic encounter between the colonized and the colonizer "if [the colonized] want humanity to take one step forward ... to another level than the one where Europe has placed it."⁹ This is what Arendt meant when she said:

> What makes man a political being is his faculty to act. It enables him to get together with his peers, to act in concert, and to reach out for goals and enterprises which would never enter his mind, let alone the desires of his heart, had he not been given this gift – to embark upon *something new*.[10]

Neither the teaching of children nor the fear of monsters makes for a properly political relationship with the world. Nor, for that matter, does *Amor Mundi* conceived as the provident transformation of others in the *imago occidens*. Such is the divine love gods may have for their creatures, not the political love citizens should have for each other in the *polis*.

A clear interpretive thread holding this book together is the notion that at least for the purpose of talking about it, of speaking it continuously into existence, the world itself is now akin to a *polis*. It is one place, inhabited by one humanity that is nonetheless also constitutively plural in its worldly elaborations. It is this one world that is being made, remade and often unmade in the babble of talk about Islam. And in the myriad conversations about Muslims that pursue nothing new, but only repeated confirmations of something already lodged deep in the discursive crevices of a 'West' that has yet to fully come to terms with the facts of its own history and the lived realities attendant to its contemporary existence. Such talk strives for an either/or answer to the Muslim Question, and from the Muslim herself it demands either a comforting confirmation of the

Conclusion

West's own self-images or an outright rejection of them. Yes/no? No essays. No maybes. This is not the political talk of a *polis*. This is rather talk of an *oikia*, talk fit for masters, children and slaves, not human beings.

But the slave's fantasies of a retributive reversal, whether actualized as violence, theorized as absolute negation or experienced in the abstract joy of seeing the erstwhile master suffer, are also symptoms of futility. Arendt was deeply suspicious on precisely these grounds of the manner in which Fanon's brand of creative agonism had been received in left-revolutionary circles. This reception was predisposed toward a spectacular inversion of the regnant order rather than any serious engagement with it. And inversions always carry traces of that which they seek to invert; they do not set "a new example," nor produce a "new man." Such depoliticization is evident in Fanon's frequent (and unfortunate) biologization of the human condition, for example, in his welding of Hegel's historicism and Nietzsche's will to power with the unfolding imperative of life itself. And again in his claim that "the practice of violence binds men together as a whole, since each individual forms a violent link in the great chain, a part of the great organism of violence which has surged upward."[11] Fanon was more nuanced elsewhere, of course, but the point remains. As Arendt put it:

> No body politic I know of was ever founded on the equality before death and its actualization in violence, but it is undeniably true that the strong

fraternal sentiments, engendered by collective violence, have misled many good people into the hope that a new community together with a "new man" will arise out of it.[12]

The resort to violence among certain groups of Muslims as a life-affirming negation of the West is therefore a futile response to an already futile situation. Worse perhaps is not the violence itself, but the more generalized attitude of rejection toward the West that mirrors the West's own rejections of 'Muslimness' as a viable way of being in the world. These mutually reinforcing negations are like a perpetual motion machine of futility, endlessly inscribing and reinscribing this futility in the biological rhythms of organismic conflict between cultures, religions and civilizations.

It has been the argument of this book that the doublespeak and forked tongues of freedom talk, the grooved histories and provincial universalisms of reason talk, and the imperialist *noblesse oblige* and civilizational panic of culture talk represent ways of conducting conversations about Islam and Muslims that are dehumanizing for *all* involved. This manner of talking about Muslims and about the various others of the West has its origins in those dramatic historical developments of the nineteenth century which also gave birth to the world as we know it today. This "compartmentalized world" was first born in European discourse as both one and many. It was the universal context for provincial Europe's providential

Conclusion

expansion as the World-Subject to fill the world, so to say, in the very process of this world's 'discovery'. But once discovered, this world immediately resisted ensoulment by the West. In the countless instances of explicit and implicit defiance, in the alternative cartographies for this world and counter-theorizations of it in the minds and acts of 'brutes' that were in fact never "asleep in history," these 'objects' of Europe's discovery proclaimed their aspiration to subjectivity. Not all certainly, perhaps not even most, but more than enough to make this modern world from the very beginning a common context for plural "horizons of expectation" and for competing visions of the good life.[13] While some of these competing visions were inverted negations of the West that fed back into the vortex of futile backs and forth, many others were complex engagements with the newness of modernity cognized and experienced from its discursive peripheries. Muslims have been a rich repository for these alternative views of the world, and they still are today. But in being taxonomized and tamed through monikers such as 'modernist', 'liberal' or 'fundamentalist' in the global public mainstream, the novelty of these visions has been obscured and their meaning exhausted in their mere reference to the West.

Even within the West itself, the aspiration "to become subjects as well as objects of modernization, to get a grip on the modern world" has generated innumerable political agitations and social movements with varying degrees of success. But through world wars and cold wars, a true reckoning with the past, "to face and come to terms with what really happened," has been assiduously avoided. And the "apparent heartlessness" of endless foreign wars, of drone strikes and Muslim bans, has only been "covered over with the cheap sentimentality" of empty talk about freedom, and rights, and democracy. The rot at the core has lingered even as the self-image grew ever-more effulgent in its presentation and reached its apotheosis with the fall of the Berlin Wall. But with the election of Donald Trump, Britain's impending exit from Europe, and the rise of various right-wing parties and movements on the continent itself, even this euphemistic age of cheap sentimentality appears to be coming to an end. And with much of the liberal left now also almost entirely on board with the rest on the problem of Islam, Muslims find themselves squarely in the bullseye of this latest iteration of the West. The question of their existence is very much on the international agenda. And it is being spoken in a manner that offers no answers, only solutions.

* * *

So, what is to be done? This is not a question to which theoretical answers are desirable or even possible. For such answers "are matters of practical politics, subject to the agreement of many; they can never lie in theoretical considerations or the opinion of one person."[14] The promise of such politics is the pragmatic and always provisional goal of speaking the kinds of tomorrows into existence where

Conclusion

more people can feel at home in this world; not just better fed and clothed, or privy to the latest technology and the most excellent freedoms, but "to become subjects as well as objects of modernization, to get a grip on the modern world" and to speak it in a language that is meaningful to them.[15] This, then, is the elementary challenge: To stop and "think what we are doing" in this world and to speak it better. To speak those who inhabit it better. To speak its pasts and presents better so as to make better futures available for it. To speak its hopes and aspirations better. And to learn to let Muslims in on these conversations, and the courage to listen. And all of this out of love of the world, not mere desire for it. As a structure of feeling, *Amor Mundi* is an alternative to both imperialist sentiments and to postcolonial rage. It is a way of speaking the world to reflect the lived experience of the many, not the ideological programs of the few, or the one. It is becoming increasingly clear that the sedimenting of provincial notions of freedom, reason and civilization into an identity in the West does not augur well for the future of an ever-evolving world. As one remedy to this sorry state of affairs, what would it mean to imagine Critical Islam as an immanent critique of the West? Not a minority report or an antagonistic rejection from the outside, but as internal to the unfolding of a common modernity that has always been plural in the horizons of expectations it generates at any given point in time?

Talk of horizons brings us to the German philosopher Hans-Georg Gadamer, who identified dialogue as not some vacuous exercise in mutual affirmation, but rather as a challenging, often uncomfortable but ultimately productive experience of difference. For Gadamer, a person can be said to have acquired a "horizon of experience" if she "learns to look beyond what is close at hand – not in order to look away from it but to see it better, within a larger whole and in truer proportion."[16] This horizon of experience "is not a rigid boundary but something that moves with one and invites one to advance further."[17] But as plural "horizons of experience" jostle in the global marketplace of ideas, they often interpolate in agonistic encounters that generate winners and losers based on the discursive power of the contestants. Gadamer's hermeneutical approach counters this agonism with an ethos of humility, and with the sublimation of a desire to dominate into a desire to expand one's horizons. A "fusion of horizons" allows us "to experience the Thou truly as a Thou – i.e., not to overlook his claim but to let him really say something to us,"[18] and in turn "makes it possible to venture into the alien, the lifting up of something out of the alien, and thus the broadening and enrichment of our own experience of the world."[19] It is important to note here that for Gadamer, such fusion of our own horizons with those of others entails "neither neutrality with respect to content nor the extinction of one's self."[20] And again, it "consists neither in the empathy of one individual for another nor in subordinating another person to our own standards."[21] It is neither cultural relativism

Conclusion

nor a terminal universalist synthesis. Instead, it is an ever-evolving conversation in which the participants constantly seek elevation to "a higher universality that overcomes not only our own particularity, but also that of the other."[22] In foregrounding the constitutive limitedness and finitude, the temporality and historicity of our horizons, "hermeneutics thus entails a to-and-fro movement between the whole and the part where we never truly escape our prejudices, nor are we fully constrained by them."[23]

Gadamer equated this hermeneutical ethos with *Bildung*, self-cultivation or self-transcendence, a never fully resolved "striving for understanding from the perspective of universality through consciousness-elevating dialogue."[24] His hermeneutical approach can therefore be applied not just to the writing of Muslims past and present, but to political encounters with Muslims themselves in their historical and contemporary biographies and in the myriad stories they tell of their experience of the emergent world and their place in it. Both Jürgen Habermas and Charles Taylor have expanded on Gadamer's insights, and some would even argue improved on them. But their writings often lack the pathos of Gadamer's vision, and the lyrical simplicity of an ongoing conversation as the "only way that the word becomes binding, as it were: it binds one human being with another. This occurs whenever we speak to one another and really enter into genuine dialogue with another."[25] Gadamer was in this sense closer in his intellectual bearing to other mid-century thinkers such as Arendt and Fanon, who had come out of the carnage of world wars and the horrors of racist imperialism with great suspicion of grand narratives but who were not yet jaded into a rejection of an avant-garde for the world. Their modernism was perhaps reluctant (as Seyla Benhabib said of Arendt's) but it was still animated by a humanism that is in short supply these days.[26]

Many critical Muslims we have encountered in this book have been similarly engaged in widening their horizons, enlarging their mentality and searching for something new to make themselves feel at home in the modern world. Unlike some of their co-religionists who have opted to play the either/or game on one side or another, these Muslims continue to hover over the slanted abyss, in person or in retrospect, in defiance of the regnant 'common sense' on Islam. But this defiance is never, nor has it ever been, a case of simple anger. No, it is a critical engagement with the world around them out of love for it, and out of a desire to belong to it in the full complexity of their humanity. When Tariq Ramadan complains, for example, about the treatment of Muslims in the West, he does so out of love not just for his particular community, but also for the place to which he belongs and the land he calls home – Europe. Yet when his peculiar horizon, marked as it is by his Muslim identity, rubs up against the horizons of other Europeans such as Paul Berman, instead of fusion there are the hard clanking sounds of summary rejection and deepseated suspicion. But Ramadan soldiers

Conclusion

on. In striving for the universality of belonging as a human being to the community of other human beings within which he is embedded without giving up on the particularity of his Muslim existence, Ramadan has over the years been the very personification of *Bildung*.

Both in his practice of *Bildung* and in being caricatured as this or that within the restrictive architecture of the either/or, Ramadan belongs to a long tradition of Muslims who have similarly sought reform and reconstruction of their lifeworlds. But their complex engagements with the escalating transformations of modernity remain obscure in the global public square. Even though this book is not primarily focused on their work, but rather on the discursive dynamics of what creates and sustains their obscurity, I have nonetheless lightly peppered these pages with little pearls from their oeuvres. As an invitation and as a challenge, dear reader. Look them up. And read them true, not seeking yes/no answers to the Muslim Question, but rather as Muslims questioning the nature of their reality in the modern world and contributing to knowledge about 'the human condition' as such in the process. Novelists such as Tayeb Salih, Qurratulain Hyder and Mohsin Hamid, poets such as Muhammad Iqbal and Faiz Ahmad Faiz, politicians such as Imran Khan, and reformers such as Sayyid Ahmad Khan, Muhammad Abduh and even Jamal al-Din al-Afghani, these and many others require recognition therefore not merely as intriguing specimens of the genus 'Muslim', but rather also as a humanist complement to the dehumanizing tendencies within Western accounts of Islam. To love the world as it is and has been, and those in it as they are, and not as we wish them to be, demands nothing less.

And then there is also the sense in which the marginalization of Islam could very well be a kind of test case for the status of difference and plurality itself in the coming millennium. As the West continues its endless battles with phantasmic ghosts from its own past now projected onto the bodies of 'Islamofascists' and 'Islamo-Bolsheviks', there is every indication that these battles will not long remain confined to the Muslim Question. That they will impoverish the global public sphere and render it ever-more hostile to plurality and novelty of any sort that is not thought up by an ever-diminishing number of World-Subjects. What kind of world does this augur? And what manner of humanity will inhabit it? It is instructive in this regard that *The Human Condition* does not begin with any conventional treatise on political thought, but rather with the launching of *Sputnik* (the first man-made satellite) into space by the Soviet Union in 1957. Arendt was concerned about the world-weariness implied by this launch, symbolizing the collective ascendancy of *Evadere Mundi* rather than *Amor Mundi*. But there is another, unstated but equally germane meaning that applies to this event. It marked the first time that the world could literally be *seen* as one thing from the vantage point of space. That its interconnected unity could be established by the proof of our electronically enhanced eyes in addition to the reality

Conclusion

of our experience of it. This launch was, of course, also simultaneously a triumph of science and a down payment on possible world destruction in the escalating conflicts of a supposedly 'Cold' War. That the same event could be emblematic of both *wordlessness* and *worldliness* in equal measure is just one among the many ironies of modernity that this book has sought to illuminate. The problem of Islam is similarly both about Muslims and about everyone other than Muslims. The Muslim Question, then, is ultimately and always has been a political question, which is to say a question about the humanity of others. But it is also in this sense always already a question about what kind of world we imagine this world to be and what manner of futures we make available for it in speaking it continuously into existence.

Notes

Preface

1 Quoted in Adam Gopnik, "Finest Hour: The Making of Winston Churchill," *New Yorker*, August 30, 2010.
2 "Poll Says Muslims Angry at US," February 27, 2002, http://news.bbc.co.uk/2/hi/americas/1843838.stm#map
3 Mohsin Hamid, *The Reluctant Fundamentalist* (New Delhi: Penguin Books India, 2007), 72–73.

Introduction

1 W.E. Dubois, *The Soul of Black Folk* (New York: Dover Publications, 1903), 2–3.
2 Betty Friedan, *The Feminine Mystique* (New York: W.W. Norton & Company, 1963), 15.
3 See also Qaiser Nazir, *Iqbal and the Western Philosophers* (Lahore: Iqbal Academy, 2001).
4 See also Andrew March, "Taking People as They Are: Islam as a 'Realistic Utopia' in the Political Theory of Sayyid Qutb," *American Political Science Review*, vol. 104, no. 1, February 2010, pp. 189–207.
5 See also Tariq Ramadan, "Free Speech and Civic Responsibility," *New York Times*, February 5, 2006,

www.nytimes.com/2006/02/05/opinion/free-speech-and-civic-responsibility.html

6 Sylvia Chan-Malik, *Being Muslim: A Cultural History of Women of Color in American Islam* (New York: New York University Press, 2019); Sylvester Johnson, *African American Religions, 1500–2000: Colonialism, Democracy and Freedom* (Cambridge: Cambridge University Press, 2016).

7 Khurram Hussain, *Islam as Critique: Sayyid Ahmad Khan and the Challenge of Modernity* (London: Bloomsbury Academic, 2019), 2–3.

8 Edward W. Said, *Culture and Imperialism* (New York: Vintage Books, 1993), xxv–xxvi, xxii.

9 Hannah Arendt, *The Human Condition* (Chicago, IL: University of Chicago Press, 1998), 198–199.

10 Here, 1798 refers to Napoleon's invasion (and brief occupation) of Egypt and 1857 refers to the Sepoy Mutiny against British East India Company rule in India. In support of my overall argument, let me just say that the events in France and America mentioned need no further explication on my part to be obvious references.

11 Cf. Joseph A. Massad, *Islam in Liberalism* (Chicago, IL: University of Chicago Press, 2015).

12 Ibid., 7.

13 Cf. Charles Taylor, *A Secular Age* (Cambridge, MA: Belknap Press, 2007).

14 Cf. Muhammad Iqbal, *The Reconstruction of Religious Thought in Islam* (Stanford, CA: Stanford University Press, 2012).

15 Ernest Renan, Sally P. Ragep (trans.), "Islam and Science: A Lecture," www.mcgill.ca/islamicstudies/files/islamicstudies/renan_islamism_cversion.pdf

16 Raymond Williams, *Marxism and Literature* (Oxford: Oxford University Press, 1977), 128–135.

17 Frantz Fanon, Richard Philcox (trans.), *Wretched of the Earth* (New York: Grove Press, 2004), xx.
18 Edward W. Said, *Humanism and Democratic Criticism* (New York: Columbia University Press, 2004), x. This saying is usually attributed to the second-century BCE Roman playwright Publius Terentius Afer (better known as Terence). The complete quote from the play *Heauton Timorumenos* reads: "*Homo sum, humani nihil a me alienum puto,*" or "I am human, and I think that nothing of that which is human is alien to me."
19 Edward W. Said, *Culture and Imperialism* (New York: Vintage Books, 1993), 18–19.
20 Ibid., 33.
21 Ibid., 60.
22 Arendt, *The Human Condition*, 7.
23 Hans-Georg Gadamer, *Truth and Method* (New York: Bloomsbury Academic, 2013), 246.
24 Ibid., 403.
25 Richard Palmer, *Hermeneutics: Interpretation Theory in Schleiermacher, Dilthey, Heidegger, and Gadamer* (Evanston, IL: Northwestern University Press, 1969), 209.
26 Jürgen Habermas, *The Postnational Constellation: Political Essays* (Cambridge, MA: MIT Press, 2001), 58.
27 Aaron W. Hughes, *Muslim Identities: An Introduction to Islam* (New York: Columbia University Press, 2013), 230–231.
28 Christopher de Bellaigue, *The Islamic Enlightenment: The Struggle between Faith and Reason, 1798 to Modern Times* (New York: Liveright, 2017), xvi.
29 Ibid.
30 Cf. Walter Mignolo, *The Darker Side of Western Modernity: Global Futures, Decolonial Options* (Durham, NC: Duke University Press, 2011).

31 Cf. Seyla Benhabib, *The Reluctant Modernism of Hannah Arendt* (New York: Rowman & Littlefield, 2000).
32 John J. Donohue and John L. Esposito (Eds.), *Islam in Transition: Muslim Perspectives* (Oxford: Oxford University Press, 1982), 152.
33 Marshall Berman, *All That Is Solid Melts into Air: The Experience of Modernity* (New York: Penguin Books, 1982), 5.

Chapter 1
1 Hannah Arendt, *Men in Dark Times* (New York: Harvest Books, 1970), 83.
2 Pankaj Mishra, *Age of Anger: A History of the Present* (New York: Farrar, Strauss & Giroux, 2017), 13.
3 Frantz Fanon, Richard Philcox (trans.), *Wretched of the Earth* (New York: Grove Press, 2004), 5.
4 Arendt, *Men in Dark Times*, 24–25.
5 Mahmood Mamdani, *Good Muslim, Bad Muslim: America, the Cold War and the Roots of Terror* (New York: Three Leaves Press Doubleday, 2004), 15–16.
6 "George W. Bush: Address to the Joint Session of Congress following 9/11 Attacks, Delivered 20 September 2001," www.americanrhetoric.com/speeches/gwbush911joint sessionspeech.htm
7 See also John Esposito, *Who Speaks for Islam?* (New York: Oxford University Press, 2009).
8 Jacob Poushter, "In Nations with Significant Muslim Populations, Much Disdain for ISIS," *Pew Research Center*, November 17, 2015, www.pewresearch.org/fact-tank/2015/11/17/in-nations-with-significant-muslim-populations-much-disdain-for-isis/
9 There is some confusion in the record about al-Baghdadi's educational background. Biographies circulated by his

followers and the Islamic State claim that he has a BA, MA and PhD in Islamic Studies from the Islamic University of Baghdad. Iraqi and American intelligence officials say that he has a doctorate in Quranic Studies from Saddam University in Baghdad. Still others suggest that he has a PhD in Education from the University of Baghdad. Suffice it to say that this confusion is itself a sign of his lack of visibility as a scholar of Islam before his rise as the leader of ISIS and relative prior anonymity.

10 "George W. Bush: Address to the Joint Session of Congress following 9/11 Attacks, Delivered 20 September 2001," ibid.
11 See also Richard S. Dunn, *The Age of Religious Wars, 1559–1715* (New York: W.W. Norton & Company, 1979).
12 Richard Rorty, "Religion in the Public Sphere: A Reconsideration," *Journal of Religious Ethics*, vol. 31, no. 1, 2003, 141.
13 Carl Schmitt, *The Nomos of the Earth in the International Law of the Jus Publicum Europaeum* (New York: Telos Press 2003), 59–62.
14 Ibid.
15 See also Brad S. Gregory, *The Unintended Reformation: How a Religious Reformation Secularized Society* (Cambridge, MA: Belknap Press 2015).
16 See also Max Weber, *The Protestant Ethic and the Spirit of Capitalism* (New York: Pearson 1 Edition, 1977); Kenneth Pomeranz and Steven Topik, *The World That Trade Created: Society, Culture and the World Economy, 1400 to the Present* (New York: Routledge, 2012).
17 See also James M. Byrne, *Religion and the Enlightenment: From Descartes to Kant* (Louisville, KY: Westminster John Knox Press, 1997); Ian G. Barbour, *Religion and Science: Historical and Contemporary Issues* (New York: HarperOne, 1997).

18 Some scholars have argued persuasively that the very concept of 'religion' itself is a modern creation emerging from within a soup of myriad competing discourses animating modern epsitemes and sustaining assorted political projects. See also Russell T. McCutcheon, *Manufacturing Religion: The Discourse on Sui Generis Religion and the Politics of Nostalgia* (New York: Oxford University Press, 2003); Talal Asad, *Genealogies of Religion: Discipline and Reasons of Power in Christianity and Islam* (Baltimore, MD: Johns Hopkins University Press, 1993); Tomoko Masuzawa, *In Search of Dreamtime: The Quest for the Origin of Religion* (Chicago, IL: University of Chicago Press, 1993).

19 See also Mark Lilla, *The Stillborn God: Religion, Politics and the Modern West* (New York: Vintage Books, 2008).

20 Andrew March, "Who's Afraid of Tariq Ramadan?" *The American Prospect*, vol. 21, no. 5, 2010, https://prospect.org/culture/afraid-tariq-ramadan/

21 Paul Berman, *The Flight of the Intellectuals: The Controversry over Islamism and the Press* (New York: Melville House, 2010).

22 March, "Who's Afraid of Tariq Ramadan?" ibid.

23 See also Tariq Ramadan, *To Be a European Muslim* (Markfield: The Islamic Foundation, 2003); *Islam, the West, and Modernity* (Markfield: The Islamic Foundation, 2009); *Western Muslims and the Future of Islam* (Oxford: Oxford University Press, 2003).

24 Ian Baruma, "Tariq Ramadan Has an Identity Issue," *New York Times Magazine*, February 4, 2007.

25 Marshall Berman, *All That Is Solid Melts into Air: The Experience of Modernity* (New York: Penguin Books, 1982), 16.

26 Andrew March, *Islam and Liberal Citizenship: The Search for an Overlapping Consensus* (New York: Oxford University Press, 2009).

27 March, "Who's Afraid of Tariq Ramadan?" ibid.
28 Tariq Ramadan was famously denied a visa by the United States Department of State to teach at Notre Dame University.
29 Andrew March, "Arguments: *The Flight of the Intellectuals* and Tariq Ramadan," *Dissent UpFront: Online Argument and Commentary*, May 25, 2010, www.dissentmagazine.org/online_articles/arguments-the-flight-of-the-intellectuals-and-tariq-ramadan
30 Ibid.
31 Ira M. Lapidus, *A History of Islamic Societies* (Cambridge: Cambridge University Press, 2002), 453.
32 Muhammad Qasim Zaman, *The Ulama in Contemporary Islam* (Princeton, NJ: Princeton University Press, 2002), 7.
33 Mishra, *Age of Anger*, 19.
34 March, "Who's Afraid of Tariq Ramadan?" ibid.
35 Wendy Brown, "Sovereign Hesitations," in Cheah Pheng and Suzanne Guerlac (Eds.), *Derrida and the Time of the Political* (Durham, NC: Duke University Press, 2009), 130.
36 Nadia Marzouki, *Islam: An American Religion* (New York: Columbia University Press, 2017), xx–xxii.
37 Ibid., 4–6.
38 Tayeb Salih, Dennis Johnson-Davies (trans.), *Season of Migration to the North* (New York: New York Review of Books, 1969), 139.
39 Qurratulain Hyder, Qurratulain Hyder (trans.), *River of Fire* (New York: New Directions Press, 1989).
40 Faiz Ahmad Faiz, Agha Shahid (trans.), "The Dawn of Freedom (August 1947)," *Annual of Urdu Studies*, vol. 11, 1996, https://mronline.org/2010/07/17/the-dawn-of-freedom-august-1947/
41 Hannah Arendt, *The Human Condition* (Chicago, IL: University of Chicago Press, 1998), 5.

Notes

Chapter 2

1. G.W.F. Hegel, V.A. Miller (trans.), *Phenomenology of Spirit* (New York: Oxford University Press, 1977), 111–119.
2. Robert Brandom, "Interview, Summer 2008," www.youtube.com/watch?v=WdIPuERVjk0
3. Only 'provisionally' since for Hegel, any synthesis is only the beginning of a new, as yet unknown (and unknowable) dialectic that will require its own synthesis.
4. Frantz Fanon, Richard Philcox (trans.), *Black Skin, White Masks* (New York: Grove Press, 2007), xiii. Fanon's reading (misreading, interpretation, critique, inversion, etc.) of Hegel's master–slave dialectic has generated its own set of controversies and debates that are not my concern here. If any deep readers of Fanon are uncomfortable with this juxtaposition with Hegel, you have my sympathies. Regardless, please read on.
5. Ibid., 14.
6. Judith Rollins, "'And the Last Shall Be First': The Master–Slave Dialectic in Hegel, Nietzsche and Fanon," *Human Architecture: Journal of the Sociology of Self-Knowledge*, vol. 5, no. 3, 2007, p. 175.
7. Frantz Fanon, Richard Philcox (trans.), *Wretched of the Earth* (New York: Grove Press, 2004), 239.
8. Ibid., 50. Hegel's own position on the salutary value of violence is more obscure than Fanon's. But considering his great admiration for Napoleon, ("the world soul ... an individual, who, concentrated here at a single point, astride a horse, reaches out over the world and masters it"), Hegel clearly did not abhor the use of violence for revolutionary transformation.
9. Lewis R. Gordon, *What Fanon Said: A Philosophical Introduction to His Life and Thought* (New York: Fordham University Press, 2015), xi.

Notes

10 See also Hamid Dabashi, *Can Non-Europeans Think?* (London: Zed Books, 2015).
11 Gordon, *What Fanon Said*, 2.
12 Fanon, *Black Skin, White Masks*, 10.
13 Zareena Grewal, "The Muslim World Does Not Exist," *The Atlantic*, May 21, 2017, www.theatlantic.com/international/archive/2017/05/the-muslim-world-is-a-place-that-does-not-exist/527550/?utm_source=twb
14 Zareena Grewal, *Islam Is a Foreign Country: American Muslims and the Global Crisis of Authority* (New York: New York University Press, 2014), 5.
15 Fanon, *Wretched of the Earth*, 5.
16 Grewal, *Islam Is a Foreign Country*, 5.
17 Faisal Devji, "Against Muslim Unity," *Aeon*, July 12, 2016, https://aeon.co/essays/the-idea-of-unifying-islam-is-a-recent-invention-and-a-bad-one
18 Cemil Aydin, *The Idea of the Muslim World: A Global Intellectual History* (Cambridge, MA: Harvard University Press, 2017), 30.
19 Tamim Ansary, *Destiny Interrupted: A History of the World through Muslim Eyes* (New York: PublicAffairs, 2009), 218.
20 Aydin, *The Idea of the Muslim World*, 28.
21 Albert Hourani, *Islam in European Thought* (Cambridge: Cambridge University Press, 1991), 9.
22 Aydin, *The Idea of the Muslim World*, 43, 46–48.
23 Christopher de Bellaigue, *The Islamic Enlightenment: The Struggle between Faith and Reason, 1798 to Modern Times* (New York: Liveright, 2017), 155.
24 Ibid., 10
25 Aydin, *The Idea of the Muslim World*, 33.
26 For a wonderful, sympathetic account of these lives, refer to William Dalrymple, *White Mughals: Love and Betrayal in Late 18th Century India* (New York: Penguin Books, 2004).

27 Hourani, *Islam in European Thought*, 15.
28 Joseph A. Massad, *Islam in Liberalism* (Chicago, IL: University of Chicago Press, 2015), 15. The 'Eastern Question' refers to debates in Europe about how to handle a weakening Ottoman Empire and the instability this produced on Europe's eastern frontiers.
29 Aydin, *The Idea of the Muslim World*, 50.
30 Ibid., 17.
31 Hannah Arendt, *The Origins of Totalitarianism* (New York: Harcourt, 1968), 172.
32 Ibid., 12.
33 Prasenjit Duara, "The Discourse of Civilization and Decolonization," *Journal of World History*, vol. 15, no. 1, 2004, p. 2.
34 See also Voltaire, M. Nugent (trans.), *Essay on Universal History, the Manners, and Spirit of the Nations: From the Reign of Charlemagne to the Age of Lewis XIV* (Farmington Hills, MI: Gale Ecco Print Editions, 2010).
35 Although the formulation 'survival of the fittest' is often attributed to Charles Darwin, it was actually coined by Herbert Spencer in his *Principles of Biology* (1864) as an alternative to Darwin's use of 'natural selection' in *The Origin of Species* (1859).
36 Aydin, *The Idea of the Muslim World*, 65.
37 Catherine LeGouis, *Positivism and Imagination: Scientism and Its Limits in Emile Hennequin, Wilhelm Scherer, and Dimitri Pisarev* (Cranbury, NJ: Associated University Press, 1997), 28.
38 Ibid., 4.
39 Dietrich Jung, *Orientalists, Islamists and the Global Public Sphere* (Sheffield: Equinox Publishing, 2011), 106.
40 Ernest Renan, *The Life of Jesus* (New York: Prometheus Books, 1991), 37.

41 Aydin, *The Idea of the Muslim World*, 61–64.
42 Ibid., 56. All dispassionate modern histories of the events clearly suggest that to describe the rebellion as a Muslim affair is to grossly misrepresent what actually happened. In fact, the rebellion was the last robust example of political and organizational unity between India's Muslim and Hindu populations, and the presumably Muslim Ottoman Empire sided with the British in the conflict.
43 David Motadel (Ed.), *Islam and the European Empires* (New York: Oxford University Press, 2016), 263.
44 See also Talal Asad, *Genealogies of Religion: Discipline and Reasons of Power in Christianity and Islam* (Baltimore, MD: Johns Hopkins University Press, 1993); *Formations of the Secular: Christianity, Islam, Modernity* (Stanford, CA: Stanford University Press, 2003).
45 Aydin, *The Idea of the Muslim World*, 57.
46 Edward W. Said, *Orientalism* (New York: Vintage Books, 1979), 3.
47 Aydin, *The Idea of the Muslim World*, 75. E.M. Forster evokes this newfound totalizing importance of Islam wonderfully in this revealing quote from *A Passage to India* (1924): "Here was Islam, his own country, more than a Faith, more than a battle cry, more, much more ... Islam, an attitude towards life both exquisite and durable, where his body and his thoughts found their home." E.M. Forster, *A Passage to India* (New York: Harvest Books, 1984), 16.
48 Jung, *Orientalists, Islamists and the Global Public Sphere*, 28.
49 Said, *Orientalism*, 6.
50 Arendt, *The Origins of Totalitarianism*, 5.
51 Although Edward W. Said did remedy this problem to a great extent with *Culture and Imperialism* (New York: Vintage Books, 1993).

52 Samira Haj, *Reconfiguring Islamic Tradition: Reform, Rationality, and Modernity* (Stanford, CA: Stanford University Press, 2009), 7.
53 Aydin, *The Idea of the Muslim World*, 37.
54 Charles Kurzman (Ed.), *Modernist Islam: 1840–1940* (New York: Oxford University Press, 2002), 273.
55 Ibid., 150.
56 Ibid., 104.
57 Ibid., 106.
58 Mansoor Moaddel and Kamran Talattof (Eds.), *Modernist and Fundamentalist Debates in Islam* (New York: Palgrave Macmillan, 2002), 47–48.
59 Seema Alavi, *Muslim Cosmopolitanism in the Age of Empire* (Cambridge, MA: Harvard University Press, 2015), 34, 45.
60 Aydin, *The Idea of the Muslim World*, 67.
61 Moaddel and Talattof, *Modernist and Fundamentalist Debates in Islam*, 263.
62 Ibid., 343.
63 De Bellaigue, *The Islamic Enlightenment*, 320.
64 Ernest Barker, *Ideas and Ideals of the British Empire* (Cambridge: Cambridge University Press, 1941), 4.
65 From "Another Brick in the Wall, Part 2" by Pink Floyd.
66 Alastair Bonnett, *The Idea of the West: Culture, Politics and History* (New York: Palgrave Macmillan, 2004), 22.
67 Julian S. Huxley and Alfred C. Haddon, *We Europeans: A Survey of Racial Problems* (London: Jonathan Cape, 1939), 220–221.
68 Bonnett, *The Idea of the West*, 26.
69 Peter Berger, "What is the West? And Where Is It?" *The American Interest*, April 20, 2011, www.the-american-interest.com/2011/04/20/what-is-the-west-and-where-is-it/
70 G.W.F. Hegel, *The Philosophy of History* (Amherst, NY: Prometheus Books, 1991), 103.

Notes

71 Karl Marx, *Surveys from Exile: Political Writings, Volume 2* (London: Penguin Books, 1992), 319.
72 See also Karl Marx, *Capital, Vol. I* (London: Pelican Books, 1976), Chapter 14: "The Division of Labor and Manufacture." The idea of an Asiatic mode of production (AMP) was developed by Marx over many years in the 1850s, mainly in his writings for the popular press. The first book treatment of AMP is probably Karl Marx, *A Contribution to the Critique of Political Economy* (New York: International Publishers, 1970), 21.
73 Quoted in Bonnett, *The Idea of the West*, 25.
74 Arendt, *The Origins of Totalitarianism*, 123–126.
75 Said, *Culture and Imperialism*, 53–55.
76 Raymond Williams, *Marxism and Literature* (Oxford: Oxford University Press, 1977), 128–135.
77 Rudyard Kipling, "The White Man's Burden" (1899). The following exchange in E.M. Forster's *A Passage to India* between a newly arrived Mrs. Moore and her colonial administrator son Mr. Heaslop is very instructive of this particular structure of feeling. Mrs. Moore has just indicated that Heaslop's wife Adela, also recently arrived in India, is irritated that the English colonial officers do not behave pleasantly toward the natives. H: "We're not here for the purpose of behaving pleasantly!" M: "What do you mean?" H: "What I say. We're out here to do justice and keep the peace. Them's my sentiments. India is not a drawing room." M: "Your sentiments are those of a god," she said quietly *but it was the manner rather than his sentiments that annoyed her.* Trying to recover his temper, he said, "India likes gods." M: "And Englishman like posing as gods." ... H: "We're not pleasant in India, and we don't intend to be pleasant. We've something more important to do." Forster, *A Passage to India*, 51–52.

78 Said, *Culture and Imperialism*, xxi.
79 J.G. Herder, *Reflections on the Philosophy of the History of Mankind* (Chicago, IL: University of Chicago Press, 1968).
80 Arendt, *The Origins of Totalitarianism*, 166.
81 Joseph Conrad, *Heart of Darkness and Other Tales* (Oxford: Oxford University Press, 2008), 155.
82 Herbert Spencer, *The Study of Sociology* (New York: Appleton, 1874), 85.
83 Arendt, *The Origins of Totalitarianism*, 159.
84 Joel Mokyr, *A Culture of Growth: The Origins of the Modern Economy* (Princeton, NJ: Princeton University Press, 2017), 6.
85 Ibid., 265.
86 Arendt, *The Origins of Totalitarianism*, 125.
87 Gertrude Millin, *Rhodes* (London: Harper & Brothers, 1933), 138.
88 Christopher GoGwilt, *The Invention of the West: Joseph Conrad and the Double-Mapping of Europe and Empire* (Stanford, CA: Stanford University Press, 1995), 15.
89 Bonnett, *The Idea of the West*, 15.
90 Arnold J. Toynbee, *Civilization on Trial* (Oxford: Oxford University Press, 1948), 90–91.
91 Bonnett, *The Idea of the West*, 33.
92 Toynbee, *Civilization on Trial*, 90–91.
93 Benjamin Kidd, *The Principles of Western Civilization: Being the First Volume of a System of Evolutionary Philosophy* (London: Macmillan, 1902), 458, 289, 309, 340.

Chapter 3

1 Richard C. Auxier, "Egypt, Democracy and Islam," *Pew Research Center: Global Attitudes and Trends*, January 31, 2011, www.pewglobal.org/2011/01/31/egypt-democracy-and-islam/

Notes

2 Portions of this introduction have appeared before online in Khurram Hussain, "A Muslim Revolution in Egypt," *The Immanent Frame*, http://blogs.ssrc.org/tif/2011/02/24/a-muslim-revolution-in-egypt/
3 Bret Stephens, "Understanding the Muslim Brotherhood," *Wall Street Journal*, February 15, 2011.
4 H.G. Wells, *The Island of Dr. Moreau* (Oxford: Oxford University Press, 2017).
5 Edward W. Said, *Orientalism* (New York: Vintage Books, 1979), 6.
6 See also Michael Walzer, *Thick and Thin: Moral Argument at Home and Abroad* (Notre Dame, IN: University of Notre Dame Press, 1994).
7 George W. Bush, Speech at Whitehall, November 19, 2003, www.presidentialrhetoric.com/speeches/11.19.03.html
8 Timothy J. Lynch, "Kristol Balls: NeoConservative Visions of Islam and the Middle East," *International Politics*, vol. 45, no. 2, pp. 182–211.
9 Michael Novak, *The Universal Hunger for Liberty: Why a Clash of Civilizations Is Not Inevitable* (New York: Basic Books, 2004), xiii, 203.
10 Irshad Manji, *The Trouble with Islam Today: A Muslim's Call for Reform of Her Faith* (New York: MacMillan, 2003), 2.
11 David Frum and Richard S. Perle, *An End to Evil: How to Win the War on Terror* (New York: Random House, 2003), 43.
12 Joseph A. Massad, *Islam in Liberalism* (Chicago, IL: University of Chicago Press, 2015), 73.
13 Leonard Binder, *Islamic Liberalism: A Critique of Development Ideologies* (Chicago, IL: University of Chicago Press, 1988), 1.
14 Daniel Lerner, *The Passing of Traditional Society: Modernizing the Middle East* (New York: Free Press, 1958), 45.

Notes

15 Khaled Abou el Fadl, *The Great Theft: Wresting Islam from the Extremists* (New York: HarperCollins, 2007), 2. Abou el Fadl was awarded the University of Oslo Human Rights Award, the Leo and Lisl Eitinger Prize in 2007, and named a Carnegie Scholar in Islamic Law in 2005. He was also appointed by President George W. Bush to serve on the United States Commission on International Religious Freedom and served as a member of the board of directors of Human Rights Watch.
16 Khaled Abou el Fadl, "Islam and the Challenge of Democracy," *Boston Review*, April/May 2003.
17 Abou el Fadl, *The Great Theft*, 5–6.
18 Abou el Fadl does not seem aware of the irony of calling the 'bad guys' in this reformation the 'puritans'.
19 John L. Esposito and John Obert Voll, *Islam and Democracy* (Oxford: Oxford University Press, 1996), 7.
20 John Esposito, *Who Speaks for Islam?* (New York: Oxford University Press, 2009), 4.
21 It should be noted that all these calls for a Muslim Reformation or a Muslim Martin Luther are based on a fundamentally flawed reading of history and an unforgivable perversion of the facts of the Protestant Reformation in sixteenth- and seventeenth-century Europe. It was a bloodbath. And the so-called reformers most closely resembled not folks like Abou el Fadl, but the very puritans he decries. This particular rhetorical deployment of European history as any kind of normative model is so fraught with problems that its very appearance should put the right thinking on immediate alert for the intellectually facile arguments that usually follow.
22 Joseph A. Massad, *Islam in Liberalism* (Chicago, IL: University of Chicago Press, 2015).

23 Cheryl Benard, "Five Pillars of Democracy: How the West Can Promote an Islamic Reformation," *RAND Review*, Spring 2004, www.rand.org/pubs/periodicals/rand-review/issues/spring2004/pillars.html

24 Saied Reza Ameli, *Bibliographical Discourse Analysis: The Western Academic Perspective on Islam, Muslims and Islamic Countries 1949–2009* (London: Islamic Human Rights Commission, 2012), 49.

25 Samuel P. Huntington, "The Clash of Civilizations?" *Foreign Affairs*, vol. 72, no. 3, Summer 1993, pp. 22–25, 35.

26 Samuel P. Huntington, "The West: Unique Not Universal," *Foreign Affairs*, vol. 75, no. 6, Winter 1996, p. 28.

27 Bernard Lewis, *Islam and the West* (Oxford: Oxford University Press, 1993), 5–6.

28 Of course, these aspirations were pursued somewhat differently in the early centuries. While Christianity initially 'expanded' mainly through the activities of the Church (especially in Western and Northern Europe), Islam's expansion consistently took a military course.

29 Lewis, *Islam and the West*, 182.

30 Ibid., 13. See also Bernard Lewis, *The Muslim Discovery of Europe* (New York: W.W. Norton & Company, 2001).

31 The Mongols did invade and conquer the heart of the Arab Empire in the thirteenth century. But they came out of nowhere and quickly converted to Islam within a generation or two. They did not loom as a danger for centuries, like the Muslims did for Western Christianity.

32 See also Bernard Lewis, *The Political Language of Islam* (Chicago, IL: University of Chicago Press, 1991).

33 Lewis, *Islam and the West*, 186.

34 See also Shadi Hamid, *Islamic Exceptionalism: How the Struggle over Islam Is Reshaping the World* (New York:

St. Martin's Press, 2016); Wael Hallaq, *The Impossible State: Islam, Politics and Modernity's Moral Predicament* (New York: Columbia University Press, 2014).
35 Samuel P. Huntington, *Who Are We? The Challenges to American National Identity* (New York: Simon & Shuster, 2005).
36 Sayyid Qutb, *Milestones* (Chicago, IL: Kazi Publications, 2007), 7–8.
37 Albert J. Bergesen (Ed.), *The Sayyid Qutb Reader: Selected Writings on Politics, Religion, and Society* (New York: Routledge, 2008), 37.
38 Sayyid Qutb, "The America I Have Seen: In the Scale of Human Values" (1951), reprinted in Kamal Abdel-Malek (Ed.), *America in an Arab Mirror: Images of America in Arabic Travel Literature: An Anthology* (New York: St. Martin's Press, 2000), 9–28.
39 Bergesen, *The Sayyid Qutb Reader*, 37, 40.
40 Homi K. Bhabha, *The Location of Culture* (London: Routledge, 1995), 85.
41 Editorial Staff, "The Olympics: Black Complaint," *Time Magazine*, October 25, 1968.
42 See also Jasbir Puar, *Terrorist Assemblages: Homonationalism in Queer Times* (Durham, NC: Duke University Press, 2007).
43 Hannah Arendt, *The Origins of Totalitarianism* (New York: Harcourt, 1968), 135.
44 V.S Naipaul, *A Bend in the River* (New York: Vintage, 1989).
45 Arendt, *The Origins of Totalitarianism*, 125.
46 Cemil Aydin, *The Idea of the Muslim World: A Global Intellectual History* (Cambridge, MA: Harvard University Press, 2017), 12.
47 Cf. Muhammad Iqbal, R.A. Nicholson (trans.), *The Secrets of the Self (Asrar-I Khudi)* (New York: Cosimo Classics, 2010);

Muhammad Iqbal, A.J. Arberry (trans.), *The Mysteries of Selflessness (Rumuz-I Bekhudi)* (Lahore: Kazi Publications, 2001).
48 Muhammad Iqbal, *The Reconstruction of Religious Thought in Islam* (Stanford, CA: Stanford University Press, 2012), 120.
49 Muhammad Iqbal, A.J. Arberry (trans.), *Javid-Nama* (London: George Allen & Unwin, 1966), 138.
50 Iqbal Singh Sevea, *The Political Philosophy of Muhammad Iqbal* (Cambridge: Cambridge University Press, 2012), 141.
51 Annemarie Schimmel, "Muhammad Iqbal 1873–1938: The Ascension of the Poet," *Die Welt des Islams*, vol. 3, no. 3/4, 1954, pp. 155–156.
52 Iqbal, *The Reconstruction of Religious Thought in Islam*, 131.
53 Imran Khan, "Why the West Craves Materialism and Why the East Sticks to Religion," *Arab News*, January 14, 2012.
54 Ali Khamenie, quoted in Fateh Mohammad Malik, *Iqbal's Reconstruction of Political Thought in Islam* (New Delhi: MediaHouse, 2004), 119.
55 See also Carl Schmitt, *The Concept of the Political* (Chicago, IL: University of Chicago Press, 1996); Hannah Arendt, *The Promise of Politics* (New York: Schocken Books, 2005).
56 Jose Casanova, *Public Religions in the Modern World* (Chicago, IL: University of Chicago Press, 1994), 234.
57 This is Alasdair MacIntyre's polemical formulation from *Against the Self-Images of the Age: Essays on Ideology and Philosophy* (Notre Dame, IN: University of Notre Dame Press, 1989).

Chapter 4

1 Ernest Renan, Sally P. Ragep (trans.), "Islam and Science: A Lecture," www.mcgill.ca/islamicstudies/files/islamic studies/renan_islamism_cversion.pdf

Notes

2 Karl Marx and Frederick Engels, *On Religion* (New York: Dover Publications, 2008), 41.
3 Reinhold Niebuhr, "Greek Tragedy and Modern Politics," *The Nation*, vol. 146, January 1938, p. 740.
4 George Orwell, *Animal Farm* (New York: Brawtley Press, 2012), 12.
5 Sidney Hook, quoted in Hannah Arendt, *Between Past and Future* (New York: Penguin Books, 2006), 35.
6 Marx and Engels, *On Religion*, 121.
7 Jacques Derrida, *Rogues: Two Essays on Reason* (Stanford, CA: Stanford University Press, 2005), 29–31.
8 Ibid., 28, 31, 41.
9 Mustafa Chérif, *Islam & the West: A Conversation with Jacques Derrida* (Chicago: University of Chicago Press, 2008), 42
10 Derrida, *Rogues*, 28.
11 Niebuhr, "Greek Tragedy and Modern Politics," ibid.
12 Gary Wolf, "The Church of the Non-Believers," *Wired*, November 1, 2006, www.wired.com/2006/11/atheism/?pg=1&topic=atheism&topic_set=
13 S.J. Gould, "Nonoverlapping Magisteria," *Natural History*, vol. 106, March 1997, pp. 16–22.
14 Wolf, "The Church of the Non-Believers," ibid.
15 Tom Flynn, "Why I Don't Believe in the New Atheism," *Free Inquiry*, vol. 30, no. 3, April/May 2010, https://secularhumanism.org/volume/no-3-vol-30/
16 Sam Harris, *The End of Faith: Religion, Terrorism and the Future of Reason* (New York: W.W. Norton & Company, 2004), 116.
17 Ibid., 123, 109.
18 Christopher Hitchens, *God Is Not Great: How Religion Poisons Everything* (New York: Twelve, 2007), 125.
19 Christopher Hitchens, "Don't Waste My Time with Islam," https://youtu.be/5sEcBzxoMB8

Notes

20 Richard Dawkins, quoted in Ruth Gledhill, "Scandal and Schism Leave Christians Praying for a 'New Reformation'," *The Times*, 6 April 2010, www.thetimes.co.uk/article/scandal-and-schism-leave-christians-praying-for-a-new-reformation-lflgv79r7js

21 Harris, *The End of Faith*, 143–145.

22 Glenn Greenwald, "Sam Harris, the New Atheists, and Anti-Muslim Animus," *The Guardian*, April 3, 2013, www.theguardian.com/commentisfree/2013/apr/03/sam-harris-muslim-animus

23 Harris, *The End of Faith*, 129.

24 Talal Asad, *Formations of the Secular: Christianity, Islam, Modernity* (Stanford, CA: Stanford University Press, 2003), 169–170.

25 Ayaan Hirsi Ali interview with Rogier van Bakel, "The Trouble Is the West," *Reason*, November 2007, http://reason.com/archives/2007/10/10/the-trouble-is-the-west

26 For an interesting discussion of the gender dynamics of New Atheism, see also Anja Finger, "Four Horsemen (and a Horsewoman): What Gender is New Atheism?" in Christopher R. Cotter, Philip Andrew Quadrio and Jonathan Tuckett (Eds.), *New Atheism: Critical Perspectives and Contemporary Debates* (London: Springer International Publishing, 2017), 155–169.

27 Ian Baruma, "Against Submission," *New York Times*, March 4, 2007, www.nytimes.com/2007/03/04/books/review/04buruma.html

28 "A Journalist's Manual: A Field Guide to Anti-Muslim Extremists," *Southern Poverty Law Center*, www.splcenter.org/20161025/journalists-manual-field-guide-anti-muslim-extremists

29 Baruma, "Against Submission," ibid.

30 Ayaan Hirsi Ali, *Heretic: Why Islam Needs a Reformation Now* (New York: Harper, 2015), 18, 25, 224–234.
31 Asra Nomani, "Airport Security: Let's Profile Muslims," *The Daily Beast*, November 28, 2010, www.thedailybeast.com/airport-security-lets-profile-muslims
32 Asra Nomani, "I'm a Muslim, a Woman and an Immigrant. I Voted for Trump," *Washington Post*, November 10, 2016, www.washingtonpost.com/news/global-opinions/wp/2016/11/10/im-a-muslim-a-woman-and-an-immigrant-i-voted-for-trump/?utm_term=.5d11efc7a666
33 Nathan Lean, "What Does Maajid Nawaz Really Believe?" *The New Republic*, January 27, 2016, https://newrepublic.com/article/128436/maajid-nawaz-really-believe
34 See also Maajid Nawaz, *Radical: My Journey out of Islamic Extremism* (Guilford, CT: Lyons Press, 2013); Asra Nomani, *Standing Alone: An American Woman's Struggle for the Soul of Islam* (New York: HarperOne, 2006); Irshad Manji, *Allah, Liberty and Love: The Courage to Reconcile Faith and Freedom* (New York: Free Press, 2011).
35 Dante Alighieri, C.H. Sisson (trans.), *The Divine Comedy* (New York: Oxford University Press, 1981), 164.
36 Sophia Rose Arjana, *Muslims in Western Imagination* (New York: Oxford University Press, 2015), 23–24.
37 Dietrich Jung, *Orientalists, Islamists and the Global Public Sphere* (Sheffield: Equinox Publishing, 2011), 111.
38 Richard G. Olson, *Science and Scientism in Nineteenth-Century Europe* (Urbana, IL: University of Illinois Press, 2008), 62.
39 Edward W. Said, *Orientalism* (New York: Vintage Books, 1979), 115.
40 Ibid., 114.
41 Olson, *Science and Scientism in Nineteenth-Century Europe*, 63–67.

42 Ernest Renan, quoted in Said, *Orientalism*, 132–133.
43 Said, *Orientalism*, 132.
44 Ibid., 57.
45 Maurice Oleander, Arthur Goldhammer (trans.), *The Languages of Paradise: Aryans and Semites – A Match Made in Heaven* (New York, Other Press, 1992), 54–57.
46 Said, *Orientalism*, 143.
47 Jung, *Orientalists, Islamists and the Global Public Sphere*, 103.
48 Ernest Renan, *An Essay on the Age and Antiquity of the Book of Nabathæn Agriculture – to Which Is Added an Inaugural Lecture on the Position of the Shemitic Nations in the History of Civilization* (London: Trübner & Co., 1862), 121, 142–143.
49 J.G. Herder, *Reflections on the Philosophy of the History of Mankind* (Chicago, IL: University of Chicago Press, 1968), 78, 116.
50 G.W.F. Hegel, quoted in Albert Hourani, *Islam in European Thought* (Cambridge: Cambridge University Press, 1991), 26.
51 Charles Foster, quoted in Hourani, *Islam in European Thought*, 21–22.
52 Said, *Orientalism*, 133–134.
53 Hannah Arendt, "A Special Supplement: Reflections on Violence," *New York Review of Books*, February 27, 1969, www.nybooks.com/articles/1969/02/27/a-special-supplement-reflections-on-violence/
54 Ernest Renan, quoted in Nikki R. Keddie, *Sayyid Jamal Ad-Din "Al-Afghani": A Political Biography* (Berkeley, CA: University of California Press, 1972), 196.
55 Ernest Renan, quoted in Jung, *Orientalists, Islamists and the Global Public Sphere*, 110.
56 Ibid.

57 Ernest Renan, Sally P. Ragep (trans.), "Islam and Science: A Lecture," www.mcgill.ca/islamicstudies/files/islamicstudies/renan_islamism_cversion.pdf
58 Jamal al-Din al-Afghani, quoted in Keddie, *Sayyid Jamal Ad-Din "Al-Afghani"*, 191.
59 Ibid., 195.
60 Ibid., 179.
61 Jung, *Orientalists, Islamists and the Global Public Sphere*, 115.
62 Keddie, *Sayyid Jamal Ad-Din "Al-Afghani"*, 197.
63 Sam Harris and Maajid Nawaz, *Islam and the Future of Tolerance* (Cambridge, MA: Harvard University Press, 2015), 127.
64 Nawaz, *Radical*.
65 Hannah Arendt, Jerome Kohn (Ed.), Ron H. Feldman (Ed.), *The Jewish Writings* (New York: Schocken Books, 2007), 68–69.
66 Ernest Renan, Albert D. Vandam (trans.), C. B. Pitman (trans.), *The Future of Science: Ideas of 1848* (London: Chapman & Hall, 1891), xx.
67 Khurram Hussain, *Islam as Critique: Sayyid Ahmad Khan and the Challenge of Modernity* (London: Bloomsbury Academic, 2019).
68 Sayyid Ahmad Khan, "Introduction to *Khutubāt-i Ahmadīyah, TFA I & II*, 182–639, *PMaq XI*, 6–16. Quoted in Christian W. Troll, *Sayyid Ahmad Khan: A Re-Interpretation of Muslim Theology* (New Delhi: Vikas Publishing House, 1978), 245–246.
69 Sayyid Jamāl ad-Dīn al-Afghānī, "The Truth about the Neicheri Sect and an Explanation of the Neicheris," in Nikki R. Keddie, Hamid Algar (trans.), *An Islamic Response to Imperialism: Political and Religious Writings of Sayyid Jamāl ad-Dīn "al-Afghānī,"* (Berkeley, CA: University of California Press, 1983), 130–132.

70 Sayyid Ahmad Khan, *Insān ke Khayalat, PMaq V*, 249–256. Quoted in Troll, *Sayyid Ahmad Khan*, 255–256.
71 Frederick Buechner, quoted at the beginning of John Irving, *A Prayer for Owen Meany* (New York: William Morrow & Company, 1989).
72 Sayyid Ahmad Khan, *Tahrīr fī usūl al-tafsīr (TUT) (Agra: Mufīd-i ām Press, 1892)*, 11, *PMaq II*, 207. Quoted in Troll, *Sayyid Ahmad Khan*, 165.

Chapter 5
1 Raymond Williams, *Marxism and Literature* (Oxford: Oxford University Press, 1977), 128–135.
2 David Mitchell, *Cloud Atlas: A Novel* (New York: Random House, 2004), 487–489.
3 As in Cecil B. Rhodes, Arnold Toynbee and Theodore Lothrop Stoddard, the best-selling author of race panic literature such as *The New World of Islam* (1921) and *The Rising Tide of Color against White World-Supremacy* (1925).
4 Pankaj Mishra, "Watch This Man," *London Review of Books*, vol. 33, no. 21, November 3, 2011, pp. 10–12.
5 David C.J. Lee, *Ernest Renan: In the Shadow of Faith* (London: Duckworth, 1996), 52.
6 Mishra, "Watch This Man," ibid.
7 Edward W. Said, *Covering Islam: How the Media and the Experts Determine How We See the Rest of the World* (New York: Vintage Books, 1997), xxix.
8 Jacques Derrida, *Rogues: Two Essays on Reason* (Stanford, CA: Stanford University Press, 2005), 29.
9 Wajahat Ali, Eli Clifton, Matthew Duss, Lee Fang, Scott Keyes and Faiz Shakir, "Fear, Inc.: The Roots of the Islamophobia Network in America," *Center for American*

Progress, August 26, 2011, www.americanprogress.org/issues/religion/reports/2011/08/26/10165/fear-inc/
10 Mahmood Mamdani, *Good Muslim, Bad Muslim: America, the Cold War and the Roots of Terror* (New York: Three Leaves Press Doubleday, 2004), 16–18.
11 Tania Das Gupta, Carl E. James, Roger C.A. Maaka, Grace-Edward Galabuzi and Chris Anderson (Eds.), *Race and Radicalization: Essential Readings* (Toronto: Canadian Scholars' Press, 2007), 85.
12 Mamdani, *Good Muslim, Bad Muslim*, 18.
13 See also Niall Ferguson, *The Pity of War: Explaining World War I* (New York: Basic Books, 1998); *The Cash Nexus: Money and Power in the Modern World, 1700–2000* (New York: Basic Books, 2001); *Empire: The Rise and Demise of the British World Order and the Lessons for Global Power* (New York: Basic Books, 2002); *Colossus: The Rise and Fall of the American Empire* (New York: Penguin Books, 2004); *The War of the World: Twentieth-Century Conflict and the Descent of the West* (New York: Penguin Books, 2006).
14 Ferguson, *Empire*, 304.
15 Mishra, "Watch This Man," ibid.
16 Ferguson, *Empire*, 248.
17 Ibid., 255.
18 Ferguson, *Colossus*, 120.
19 Niall Ferguson, "We Need to Re-Learn the Arts of War and Grand Strategy," *Financial Times*, September 25, 2015, www.ft.com/content/3e1d221a-5e28-11e5-9846-de406ccb37f2
20 Ferguson, *Empire*, 315.
21 Niall Ferguson, quoted in Mishra, "Watch This Man," ibid.
22 Ferguson, *Empire*, 310, 317.
23 Ferguson, *Colossus*, 301.

24 Ferguson, *Empire*, 316.
25 Niall Ferguson, "The Empire Slinks Back," *New York Times Magazine*, April 27, 2003, www.nytimes.com/2003/04/27/magazine/the-empire-slinks-back.html
26 Ibid.
27 Robert D. Kaplan, "In Defense of Empire," *The Atlantic*, April 2014, www.theatlantic.com/magazine/archive/2014/04/in-defense-of-empire/358645/
28 Nur Masalha, *Expulsion of the Palestinians: The Concept of "Transfer" in Zionist Political Thought, 1882–1948* (Washington, DC: Institute of Palestine Studies, 1992).
29 Max Boot, "The Case for American Empire," *Weekly Standard*, vol. 7, no. 5, October 15, 2001, www.weeklystandard.com/the-case-for-american-empire/article/1626
30 Michael Ignatieff, *Empire Lite: Nation-Building in Bosnia, Kosovo and Afghanistan* (London: Vintage, 2003), from the back cover.
31 Charles Pearson, *National Life and Character: A Forecast* (London: Macmillan, 1894), 32, 137.
32 Lothrop Stoddard, *The Rising Tide of Color Against White World-Supremacy* (New York: Charles Scribner's Sons, 1925), 154.
33 Ferguson, *The War of the World*, 641–642.
34 Christopher Caldwell, *Reflections on the Revolutions in Europe: Immigration, Islam and the West* (New York: Anchor Books, 2009), 286.
35 Bruce Bawer, *While Europe Slept: How Radical Islam Is Destroying the West from Within* (New York: Anchor Books, 2006), 32
36 Zareena Grewal, *Islam Is a Foreign Country: American Muslims and the Global Crisis of Authority* (New York: New York University Press, 2014), 18.

37 Samuel M. Behloul, Susanne Leuenberger and Andreas Tunger-Zanetti (Eds.), *Debating Islam: Negotiating Europe, Religion and the Self* (Bielefeld: Transcript, 2013), 40.
38 Ibid., 45.
39 Mamdani, *Good Muslim, Bad Muslim*, 19.
40 Joseph Conrad, *Heart of Darkness and Other Tales* (Oxford: Oxford University Press, 2008), 155.
41 Behloul et al., *Debating Islam*, 349.
42 Niall Ferguson, *Civilization: The West and the Rest* (New York: Penguin Books, 2011), 324.
43 C.A. Bayly, *The Birth of the Modern World, 1780–1914* (Oxford: Blackwell, 2004), 2.
44 Ferguson, *Civilization*, 324.
45 Carl W. Ernst, *Following Muhammad: Rethinking Islam in the Contemporary World* (Chapel Hill, NC: University of North Carolina Press, 2003), 10.
46 Arun Kundnani, *The Muslims Are Coming! Islamophobia, Extremism and the Domestic War on Terror* (New York: Verso, 2015), 148.
47 Ibid., 61.
48 Ibid., 65.
49 Marc Manley, "The Unrecognizable Islam of Reza Aslan," *Marc Manley – Imam at Large: Words, Thoughts, and Insights for the Rest of Us*, February 27, 2017, www.marcmanley.com/the-unrecognizable-islam-of-reza-aslan/
50 Fareed Zakaria, "I Am a Muslim. But Trump's Views Appall Me Because I Am an American," *Washington Post*, December 10, 2015, www.washingtonpost.com/opinions/i-am-a-muslim-but-trumps-views-appall-me-because-i-am-an-american/2015/12/10/
51 Hamid Dabashi, *Can Non-Europeans Think?* (London: Zed Books, 2015).

52 Ferguson, *Civilization*, 325.
53 Mishra, "Watch This Man," ibid.
54 See also Mark Lilla, "The Politics of God," *New York Times Magazine*, August 19, 2007; "France on Fire," *New York Review of Books*, March 5, 2015; "France: Is There a Way Out?" *New York Review of Books*, March 10, 2016; "How the French Face Terror," *New York Review of Books*, March 24, 2016; Michael Walzer, "Islamism and the Left," *Dissent*, Winter 2015, www.dissentmagazine.org/article/islamism-and-the-left
55 Kundnani, *The Muslims Are Coming!*, 113–114.
56 Wendy Brown, "Sovereign Hesitations," in Cheah Pheng and Suzanne Guerlac (Eds.), *Derrida and the Time of the Political* (Durham, NC: Duke University Press, 2009), 130.
57 Nadia Marzouki, *Islam: An American Religion* (New York: Columbia University Press, 2017), 26–27.
58 Ibid., 203, 205.
59 Ibid., 25.
60 Peter O'Brien, *The Muslim Question in Europe: Political Controversies and Public Philosophies* (Philadelphia, PA: Temple University Press, 2016), 64, 236, 247.
61 Edward W. Said, *Culture and Imperialism* (New York: Vintage Books, 1993), xxi–xxv.
62 Seyla Benhabib, *The Claims of Culture: Equality and Diversity in the Global Era* (Princeton, NJ: Princeton University Press, 2002), 184.
63 Said, *Culture and Imperialism*, xxv, xxii.
64 Ibid., xxvi.
65 Ibid., 17.
66 Ibid., 39.
67 Ibid.
68 Ibid., 33.

69 Ibid., 60.
70 Ibid., 51.
71 Ibid., xxv.
72 Ibid., 32.

Conclusion

1 Hannah Arendt, quoted in Elisabeth Young-Bruehl, *Hannah Arendt: For Love of the World* (New Haven, CT: Yale University Press, 2004), xxiv.
2 Hannah Arendt, *The Human Condition* (Chicago, IL: University of Chicago Press, 1998), 7.
3 Hannah Arendt, *Men in Dark Times* (New York: Harvest Books, 1970), 24–25.
4 Hannah Arendt, "The Aftermath of Nazi Rule: Report from Germany," *Commentary*, October 1, 1950, www.commentarymagazine.com/articles/the-aftermath-of-nazi-rulereport-from-germany/
5 Mahmood Mamdani, *Good Muslim, Bad Muslim: America, the Cold War and the Roots of Terror* (New York: Three Leaves Press Doubleday, 2004), 15–16.
6 Andrew March, "Who's Afraid of Tariq Ramadan?" *The American Prospect*, vol. 21, no. 5, 2010, https://prospect.org/culture/afraid-tariq-ramadan/
7 Arnold J. Toynbee, *Civilization on Trial* (Oxford: Oxford University Press, 1948), 90–91.
8 Pavel Kohout, quoted in Hannah Arendt, "A Special Supplement: Reflections on Violence," *New York Review of Books*, February 27, 1969, www.nybooks.com/articles/1969/02/27/a-special-supplement-reflections-on-violence/
9 Frantz Fanon, Richard Philcox (trans.), *Wretched of the Earth* (New York: Grove Press, 2004), 239.
10 Arendt, "A Special Supplement," ibid.

Notes

11 Frantz Fanon, quoted in Arendt, "A Special Supplement," ibid.
12 Arendt, "A Special Supplement," ibid .
13 Jürgen Habermas, *The Postnational Constellation: Political Essays* (Cambridge, MA: MIT Press, 2001), 58.
14 Arendt, *The Human Condition*, 5
15 Marshall Berman, *All That Is Solid Melts into Air: The Experience of Modernity* (New York: Penguin Books, 1982), 5.
16 Hans-Georg Gadamer, J. Weinsheimer and D. Marshall (trans. & rev.), *Truth and Method, 2nd and revised edition* (New York: Continuum, 1975/2004), 305.
17 Hans-Georg Gadamer, *Truth and Method* (New York: Bloomsbury Academic, 2013), 247.
18 Gadamer, *Truth and Method*, 2nd revised edition, 355.
19 Hans-Georg Gadamer, D. Linge (Ed., trans.), *Philosophical Hermeneutics* (Berkeley, CA: University of California Press, 1977), 15.
20 Gadamer, *Truth and Method*, 2nd revised edition, 271.
21 Ibid., 305.
22 Ibid.
23 Scherto Gill, "Holding Oneself Open in a Conversation: Gadamer's Philosophical Hermeneutics and the Ethics of Dialogue," *Journal of Dialogue Studies*, vol. 3, no. 1, p. 17.
24 Ibid., 18.
25 Hans-Georg Gadamer, *The Relevance of the Beautiful and Other Essays* (Cambridge: Cambridge University Press, 1986), 186.
26 See also Seyla Benhabib, *The Reluctant Modernism of Hannah Arendt* (New York: Rowman & Littlefield, 2000).

Bibliography

Deina Ali Abdelkader, *Islamic Activists: The Anti-Enlightenment Democrats* (New York: Pluto Press, 2011).

Kamal Abdel-Malek (Ed.), *America in an Arab Mirror: Images of America in Arabic Travel Literature: An Anthology* (New York: St. Martin's Press, 2000).

Lila Abu-Lughod, *Do Muslim Women Need Saving?* (Cambridge, MA: Harvard University Press, 2013).

Irfan Ahmad, *Religion as Critique: Islamic Critical Thinking from Mecca to the Marketplace* (Chapel Hill, NC: University of North Carolina Press, 2017).

Jalal Al-e Ahmad, John Green and Ahmad Alizadeh (trans.), *Gharabzadegi: Weststruckness* (Costa Mesa, CA: Mazda Publishers, 1992).

Safdar Ahmed, *Reform and Modernity in Islam: The Philosophical, Cultural and Political Discourses among Muslim Reformers* (London: I.B. Tauris, 2013).

Shahab Ahmed, *What Is Islam? The Importance of Being Islamic* (Princeton, NJ: Princeton University Press, 2016).

Muzaffar Alam, *The Languages of Political Islam in India c.1200–1800* (Chicago, IL: University of Chicago Press, 2004).

Seema Alavi, *Muslim Cosmopolitanism in the Age of Empire* (Cambridge, MA: Harvard University Press, 2015).

Bibliography

Ayaan Hirsi Ali, *Heretic: Why Islam Needs a Reformation Now* (New York: Harper, 2015).

Tariq Ali, *The Clash of Fundamentalisms: Crusades, Jihad and Modernity* (London: Verso, 2002).

G. Allana, *Muslim Political Thought through the Ages: 1562–1947* (Karachi: Royal Book Company, 2006).

Evelyn Alsultany, *Arabs and Muslims in the Media: Race and Representation after 9/11* (New York: New York University Press, 2012).

Saied Reza Ameli, *Bibliographical Discourse Analysis: The Western Academic Perspective on Islam, Muslims and Islamic Countries 1949–2009* (London: Islamic Human Rights Commission, 2012).

Tamim Ansary, *Destiny Interrupted: A History of the World through Muslim Eyes* (New York: PublicAffairs, 2009).

Arjun Appadurai, *Modernity at Large: Cultural Dimensions of Globalization* (Minneapolis, MN: University of Minnesota Press, 1996).

Hannah Arendt, *The Human Condition* (Chicago, IL: University of Chicago Press, 1998); *Men in Dark Times* (New York: Harvest Books, 1970); *The Origins of Totalitarianism* (New York: Harcourt, 1968); *The Promise of Politics* (New York: Schocken Books, 2005); *Between Past and Future* (New York: Penguin Books, 2006); *Essays in Understanding 1930–1954: Formation, Exile and Totalitarianism* (New York: Schocken Books, 1994); *The Life of the Mind* (New York: Harcourt, 1978); *Lectures on Kant's Political Philosophy* (Chicago, IL: University of Chicago Press, 1992).

Hannah Arendt, Jerome Kohn (Ed.), Ron H. Feldman (Ed.), *The Jewish Writings* (New York: Schocken Books, 2007)

Sophia Rose Arjana, *Muslims in Western Imagination* (New York: Oxford University Press, 2015).

Bibliography

Talal Asad, *Genealogies of Religion: Discipline and Reasons of Power in Christianity and Islam* (Baltimore, MD: Johns Hopkins University Press, 1993); *Formations of the Secular: Christianity, Islam, Modernity* (Stanford, CA: Stanford University Press, 2003).

Talal Asad, Wendy Brown, Judith Butler and Saba Mahmood, *Is Critique Secular? Blasphemy, Free Speech, and Injury* (New York: Fordham University Press, 2011).

Robert Audi, *Religious Commitment and Secular Reason* (New York: Cambridge University Press, 2000).

Cemil Aydin, *The Idea of the Muslim World: A Global Intellectual History* (Cambridge, MA: Harvard University Press, 2017).

Étienne Balibar, *Secularism and Cosmopolitanism: Critical Hypotheses on Religion and Politics* (New York: Columbia University Press, 2018).

Ian G. Barbour, *Religion and Science: Historical and Contemporary Issues* (New York: HarperOne, 1997).

Ernest Barker, *Ideas and Ideals of the British Empire* (Cambridge: Cambridge University Press, 1941).

Ian Baruma, *Murder in Amsterdam: The Death of Theo van Gogh and the Limits of Tolerance* (New York: Penguin Press, 2006).

Ian Baruma and Avishai Margalit, *Occidentalism: The West in the Eyes of Its Enemies* (New York: Penguin Press, 2004).

Gregory Baum, *The Theology of Tariq Ramadan: A Catholic Perspective* (Montreal: Novalis, 2009).

Bruce Bawer, *While Europe Slept: How Radical Islam Is Destroying the West from Within* (New York: Anchor Books, 2006); *Surrender: Appeasing Islam, Sacrificing Freedom* (New York: Anchor, 2010).

C.A. Bayly, *The Birth of the Modern World: 1780–1914* (Oxford: Blackwell, 2004).

Bibliography

Moustafa Bayoumi, *How Does It Feel to Be a Problem? Being Young and Arab in America* (London: Penguin Books, 2008).

Samuel M. Behloul, Susanne Leuenberger and Andreas Tunger-Zanetti (Eds.), *Debating Islam: Negotiating Europe, Religion and the Self* (Bielefeld: Transcript, 2013).

Christopher de Bellaigue, *The Islamic Enlightenment: The Struggle between Faith and Reason, 1798 to modern Times* (New York: Liveright, 2017).

Cheryl Benard, *Civil Democratic Islam: Partners, Resources and Strategies* (Santa Monica, CA: RAND, 2003).

Seyla Benhabib, *The Reluctant Modernism of Hannah Arendt* (New York: Rowman & Littlefield, 2000); *The Claims of Culture: Equality and Diversity in the Global Era* (Princeton, NJ: Princeton University Press, 2002).

Seyla Benhabib, Robert Post (Ed.), *Another Cosmopolitanism* (New York: Oxford University Press, 2006).

Clinton Bennett, *Muslims and Modernity: An Introduction to the Issues and Debates* (London: Continuum, 2005).

Albert J. Bergesen (Ed.), *The Sayyid Qutb Reader: Selected Writings on Politics, Religion, and Society* (New York: Routledge, 2008).

Marshall Berman, *All That Is Solid Melts into Air: The Experience of Modernity* (New York: Penguin Books, 1982).

Paul Berman, *The Flight of the Intellectuals: The Controversy over Islamism and the Press* (New York: Melville House, 2010).

Homi K. Bhabha, *The Location of Culture* (London: Routledge, 1995).

Leonard Binder, *Islamic Liberalism: A Critique of Development Ideologies* (Chicago, IL: University of Chicago Press, 1988).

Antony Black, *The History of Islamic Political Thought: From the Prophet (PBUH) to the Present* (Karachi: Oxford University Press, 2006).

Bibliography

Paul Blanshard, *American Freedom and Catholic Power* (Boston, MA: Beacon Press, 1952).

Philip Bobbitt, *Terror and Consent: The Wras for the Twenty-First Century* (New York: Anchor Books, 2009).

Alastair Bonnett, *The Idea of the West: Culture, Politics and History* (New York: Palgrave Macmillan, 2004).

Wendy Brown, *Regulating Aversion: Tolerance in the Age of Identity and Empire* (Princeton, NJ: Princeton University Press, 2006).

Matti Bunzil, *Anti-Semitism and Islamophobia: Hatreds Old and New in Europe* (Chicago, IL: Prickly Paradigm Press, 2007).

James M. Byrne, *Religion and the Enlightenment: From Descartes to Kant* (Louisville, KY: Westminster John Knox Press, 1997).

Christopher Caldwell, *Reflections on the Revolutions in Europe: Immigration, Islam and the West* (New York: Anchor Books, 2009).

W.H. Carey, *The Mahomedan Rebellion: Its Premonitory Symptoms, the Outbreak and Suppression* (Lahore: Sang-e-Meel Publications, 2007).

Matthew Carr, *Blood and Faith: The Purging of Muslim Spain* (New York: New Press, 2009).

Jose Casanova, *Public Religions in the Modern World* (Chicago, IL: University of Chicago Press, 1994).

M. Ikram Chaghatai (Ed.), *Jamal al-din al-Afghani: An Apostle of Islamic Resurgence* (Lahore: Sang-e-Meel Publications, 2005); *1857 in the Muslim Historiography* (Lahore: Sang-e-Meel Publications, 2007).

Sylvia Chan-Malik, *Being Muslim: A Cultural History of Women of Color in American Islam* (New York: New York University Press, 2018).

Mustafa Chérif, *Islam and the West: A Conversation with Jacques Derrida* (Chicago, IL: University of Chicago Press, 2008).

Bibliography

Daniel Chernilo, *Debating Humanity: Towards a Philosophical Sociology* (Cambridge: Cambridge University Press, 2017).

Joseph Conrad, *Heart of Darkness and Other Tales* (Oxford: Oxford University Press, 2008).

Michale Cook, *Forbidding Wrong in Islam* (Cambridge: Cambridge University Press, 2003).

Christopher R. Cotter, Philip Andrew Quadrio and Jonathan Tuckett (Eds.), *New Atheism: Critical Perspectives and Contemporary Debates* (London: Springer International Publishing, 2017).

Edward E. Curtis IV (Ed.), *The Bloomsbury Reader on Islam in the West* (London: Bloomsbury Academic, 2015).

Hamid Dabashi, *Can Non-Europeans Think?* (London: Zed Books, 2015); *Brown Skin, White Masks* (New York: Pluto Press, 2011); *Being Muslim in the World* (New York: Palgrave Macmillan, 2013).

Dante Alighieri, C.H. Sisson (trans.), *The Divine Comedy* (New York: Oxford University Press, 1981).

William Dalrymple, *White Mughals: Love and Betrayal in Late 18th Century India* (New York: Penguin Books, 2004).

Charles Darwin, *The Origin of Species* (New York: Signet, 2003).

Richard Dawkins, *The God Delusion* (New York: Mariner Books, 2006).

Nandini Deo (Ed.), *Postsecular Feminism: Religion and Gender in Transnational Context* (London: Bloomsbury Academic, 2018).

Jacques Derrida, *Rogues: Two Essays on Reason* (Stanford, CA: Stanford University Press, 2005).

Faisal Devji, *Muslim Zion: Pakistan as a Political Idea* (Cambridge, MA: Harvard University Press, 2013).

Souleymane Bachir Diagne, *Open to Reason: Muslim Philosophers in Conversation with the Western Tradition* (New York: Columbia University Press, 2018).

Bibliography

John J. Donohue and John L. Esposito (Eds.), *Islam in Transition: Muslim Perspectives* (Oxford: Oxford University Press, 1982).

W.E. Dubois, *The Soul of Black Folk* (New York: Dover Publications, 1903).

Richard S. Dunn, *The Age of Religious Wars, 1559–1715* (New York: W.W. Norton & Company, 1979).

Carl W. Ernst, *Following Muhammad: Rethinking Islam in the Contemporary World* (Chapel Hill, NC: University of North Carolina Press, 2003).

John Esposito, *Who Speaks for Islam?* (New York: Oxford University Press, 2009).

John L. Esposito and John Obert Voll, *Islam and Democracy* (Oxford: Oxford University Press, 1996).

Roxanne L. Euben, *Enemy in the Mirror: Islamic Fundamentalism and the Limits of Modern Rationalism* (Princeton, NJ: Princeton University Press, 1999).

Roxanne L. Euben and Muhammad Qasim Zaman (Eds.), *Princeton Readings in Islamist Thought: Texts and Contexts from al-Banna to Bin Laden* (Princeton, NJ: Princeton University Press, 2009).

Khaled Abou el Fadl, *The Great Theft: Wresting Islam from the Extremists* (New York: HarperCollins, 2007).

Frantz Fanon, Richard Philcox (trans.), *Wretched of the Earth* (New York: Grove Press, 2004); *Black Skin, White Masks* (New York: Grove Press, 2007); *A Dying Colonialism* (New York: Grove Press, 1965).

Niall Ferguson, *The Pity of War: Explaining World War I* (New York: Basic Books, 1998); *The Cash Nexus: Money and Power in the Modern World, 1700–2000* (New York: Basic Books, 2001); *Empire: The Rise and Demise of the British World Order and the Lessons for Global Power* (New York: Basic Books, 2002); *Colossus: The Rise and Fall of the American*

Empire (New York: Penguin Books, 2004); *The War of the World: Twentieth-Century Conflict and the Descent of the West* (New York: Penguin Books, 2006); *Civilization: The West and the Rest* (New York: Penguin Books, 2011).

Gary B. Ferngren (Ed.), *Science and Religion: A Historical Introduction* (Baltimore, MD: Johns Hopkins University Press, 2002).

E.M. Forster, *A Passage to India* (New York: Harvest Books, 1984).

Charles Freeman, *The Closing of the Western Mind: The Rise of Faith and the Fall of Reason* (New York: Vintage Books, 2002).

Betty Friedan, *The Feminine Mystique* (New York: W.W. Norton & Company, 1963).

David Frum and Richard S. Perle, *An End to Evil: How to Win the War on Terror* (New York: Random House, 2003).

Francis Fukuyama, *The End of History and the Last Man* (New York: Free Press, 1992).

Hans-Georg Gadamer, *Truth and Method* (New York: Bloomsbury Academic, 2013); *The Relevance of the Beautiful and Other Essays* (Cambridge: Cambridge University Press, 1986).

Hans-Georg Gadamer, D. Linge (Ed., trans.), *Philosophical Hermeneutics* (Berkeley, CA: University of California Press, 1977).

Hans-Georg Gadamer, J. Weinsheimer and D. Marshall (trans. & rev.), *Truth and Method*, 2nd revised edition (New York: Continuum, 1975/2004).

S. Waqar Ahmad Gardezi, Abdul Waheed Khan (trans.), *West versus Islam* (New Delhi: International Islamic Publishers, 1992).

Mohammad Akram Gill, *Modernity and the Muslim World* (Bloomington, IN: AuthorHouse, 2006).

Paul Gilroy, *The Black Atlantic: Modernity and Double Consciousness* (Cambridge, MA: Harvard University Press, 1993).

Bibliography

Christopher GoGwilt, *The Invention of the West: Joseph Conrad and the Double-Mapping of Europe and Empire* (Stanford, CA: Stanford University Press, 1995).

Nilüfer Göle, *The Daily Lives of Muslims* (London: Zed Books, 2017).

Lewis R. Gordon, *What Fanon Said: A Philosophical Introduction to His Life and Thought* (New York: Fordham University Press, 2015).

Todd H. Green, *The Fear of Islam: An Introduction to Islamophobia in the West* (Minneapolis, MN: Fortress Press, 2015).

Brad S. Gregory, *The Unintended Reformation: How a Religious Reformation Secularized Society* (Cambridge, MA: Belknap Press, 2015).

Zareena Grewal, *Islam Is a Foreign Country: American Muslims and the Global Crisis of Authority* (New York: New York University Press, 2014).

Tania Das Gupta, Carl E. James, Roger C.A. Maaka, Grace-Edward Galabuzi and Chris Anderson (Eds.), *Race and Radicalization: Essential Readings* (Toronto: Canadian Scholars' Press, 2007).

Jürgen Habermas, *The Postnational Constellation: Political Essays* (Cambridge, MA: MIT Press, 2001); *The Inclusion of the Other* (Cambridge, MA: MIT Press, 1998).

Samira Haj, *Reconfiguring Islamic Tradition: Reform, Rationality, and Modernity* (Stanford, CA: Stanford University Press, 2009).

Wael Hallaq, *The Impossible State: Islam, Politics and Modernity's Moral Predicament* (New York: Columbia University Press, 2014).

Mohsin Hamid, *The Reluctant Fundamentalist* (New Delhi: Penguin Books India, 2007).

Shadi Hamid, *Islamic Exceptionalism: How the Struggle over Islam Is Reshaping the World* (New York: St. Martin's Press, 2016).

Bibliography

Sam Harris, *The End of Faith: Religion, Terrorism and the Future of Reason* (New York: W.W. Norton & Company, 2004); *The Moral Landscape: How Science can Determine Human Values* (New York: Free Press, 2010).

Sam Harris and Maajid Nawaz, *Islam and the Future of Tolerance* (Cambridge, MA: Harvard University Press, 2015).

Mona Hassan, *Longing for the Lost Caliphate: A Transregional History* (Princeton, NJ: Princeton University Press, 2016).

Mushirul Hasan, *From Pluralism to Separatism: Qasbas in Colonial Awadh* (New Delhi: Oxford University Press, 2004).

Robert W. Hefner, *Civil Islam: Muslims and Democratization in Indonesia* (Princeton, NJ: Princeton University Press, 2000).

G.W.F. Hegel, *The Philosophy of History* (Amherst, NY: Prometheus Books, 1991).

G.W.F. Hegel, V.A. Miller (trans.), *Phenomenology of Spirit* (New York: Oxford University Press, 1977).

J.G. Herder, *Reflections on the Philosophy of the History of Mankind* (Chicago, IL: University of Chicago Press, 1968).

Christopher Hitchens, *God Is Not Great: How Religion Poisons Everything* (New York: Twelve, 2007).

Eric Hobsbawm, *On Empire: America, War and Global Supremacy* (New York: New Press, 2008); *The Age of Extremes: The Short Twentieth Century, 1914–1991* (New York: Time Warner Books, 2002).

Marshall Hodgson, *The Venture of Islam. Vol. 1–3* (Chicago, IL: University of Chicago Press, 1974).

Axel Honneth, *The Struggle for Recognition: The Moral Grammar of Social Conflicts* (Cambridge, MA: MIT Press, 1995).

Max Horkheimer and Theodor W. Adorno, *Dialectic of Enlightenment: Philosophical Fragments* (Stanford, CA: Stanford University Press, 2002).

Bibliography

Albert Hourani, *Islam in European Thought* (Cambridge: Cambridge University Press, 1991); *Arabic Thought in the Liberal Age 1798–1939* (Cambridge: Cambridge University Press, 1983).

Aaron W. Hughes, *Muslim Identities: An Introduction to Islam* (New York: Columbia University Press, 2013); *Theorizing Islam: Disciplinary Deconstruction and Reconstruction* (London: Acumen, 2014).

Shireen T. Hunter (Ed.), *Reformist Voices of Islam: Mediating Islam and Modernity* (New York: M.E. Sharpe, 2009).

W.W. Hunter, *The Indian Musalmans* (New Delhi: Rupa & Co., 2002).

Samuel P. Huntington, *Who Are We? The Challenges to American National Identity* (New York: Simon & Shuster, 2005); *The Clash of Civilizations and the Remaking of World Order* (New York: Touchstone, 1996).

Khurram Hussain, *Islam as Critique: Sayyid Ahmad Khan and the Challenge of Modernity* (London: Bloomsbury Academic, 2019).

Julian S. Huxley and Alfred C. Haddon, *We Europeans: A Survey of Racial Problems* (London: Jonathan Cape, 1939).

Qurratulain Hyder, Qurratulain Hyder (trans.), *River of Fire* (New York: New Directions Press, 1989).

Michael Ignatieff, *Empire Lite: Nation-Building in Bosnia, Kosovo and Afghanistan* (London: Vintage, 2003); *The Needs of Strangers* (New York: Picador, 2001); *The Lesser Evil: Political Ethics in an Age of Terror* (Princeton, NJ: Princeton University Press, 2004).

Muhammad Iqbal, *The Reconstruction of Religious Thought in Islam* (Stanford, CA: Stanford University Press, 2012).

Muhammad Iqbal, R.A. Nicholson (trans.), *The Secrets of the Self (Asrar-I Khudi)* (New York: Cosimo Classics, 2010).

Bibliography

Muhammad Iqbal, A.J. Arberry (trans.), *The Mysteries of Selflessness (Rumuz-I Bekhudi)* (Lahore: Kazi Publications, 2001); *Javid-Nama* (London: George Allen & Unwin, 1966).

Muhammad Iqbal, Khushwant Singh (trans.), *Shikwa and Jawab-I Shikwa: Iqbal's Dialogue with Allah* (New Delhi: Oxford University Press, 1991).

John Irving, *A Prayer for Owen Meany* (New York: William Morrow & Company, 1989).

Reva Jaffe-Walter, *Coercive Concern: Nationalism, Liberalism, and the Schooling of Muslim Youth* (Stanford, CA: Stanford University Press, 2016).

Ayesha Jalal, *Partisans of Allah: Jihad in South Asia* (Cambridge, MA: Harvard University Press, 2008).

Sylvester Johnson, *African American Religions, 1500–2000: Colonialism, Democracy and Freedom* (Cambridge: Cambridge University Press, 2016).

Mark Juergenmeyer, *The New Cold War: Religious Nationalism Confronts the Secular State* (Berkeley, CA: University of California Press, 1993).

Dietrich Jung, *Orientalists, Islamists and the Global Public Sphere* (Sheffield: Equinox Publishing, 2011).

George Kateb, *Hannah Arendt: Politics, Conscience, Evil* (Totowa, NJ: Rowman & Allanheld, 1983).

Nikki R. Keddie, *Sayyid Jamal Ad-Din "Al-Afghani": A Political Biography* (Berkeley, CA: University of California Press, 1972).

Nikki R. Keddie, Hamid Algar (trans.), *An Islamic Response to Imperialism: Political and Religious Writings of Sayyid Jamāl ad-Dīn "al-Afghānī,"* (Berkeley, CA: University of California Press, 1983).

Ahmed Paul Keeler, *Rethinking Islam and the West* (Cambridge: Equilibria Press, 2019).

Bibliography

Gilles Kepel, *The War for Muslim Minds: Islam and the West* (Cambridge, MA: Belknap Press, 2004); *Jihad: The Trail of Political Islam* (Cambridge, MA: Belknap Press, 2002).

Carool Kersten, *Cosmopolitans and Heretics: New Muslim Intellectuals and the Study of Islam* (London: Hurst & Company, 2011).

Tabish Khair, Renu Kaul Verma (Ed.), *Muslim Modernities: Tabish Khair's Essays on Moderation and Mayhem* (New Delhi: Vitasta Publishing, 2008).

Imran Khan, *All Round View* (London: Mandarin Paperbacks, 1992); *Pakistan: A Personal History* (London: Bantam Books, 2011).

Naveeda Khan, *Muslim Becoming: Aspiration and Skepticism in Pakistan* (Durham, NC: Duke University Press, 2012).

Sir Sayyid Ahmad Khan, *Maqalat-e-Sir Sayyid (Complete Works), 16 Volumes* (Lahore: Majlis-eTariqi-e-Adab, 1996).

Yasmin Khan, *The Great Partition: The Making of India and Pakistan* (New Haven, CT: Yale University Press, 2007).

Benjamin Kidd, *The Principles of Western Civilization: Being the First Volume of a System of Evolutionary Philosophy* (London: Macmillan, 1902).

Richard King, *Orientalism and Religion: Postcolonial Theory, India and "The Mystic East"* (New York: Routledge, 1999).

Deepa Kumar, *Islamophobia and the Politics of Empire* (Chicago, IL: Haymarket Books, 2012).

Arun Kundnani, *The Muslims Are Coming! Islamophobia, Extremism and the Domestic War on Terror* (New York: Verso, 2015).

Charles Kurzman (Ed.), *Modernist Islam: 1840–1940* (New York: Oxford University Press, 2002).

Cécile Laborde, *Liberalism's Religion* (Cambridge, MA: Harvard University Press, 2017).

Bibliography

Ira M. Lapidus, *A History of Islamic Societies* (Cambridge: Cambridge University Press, 2002).

Bruno Latour, Catherine Porter (trans.), *We Have Never Been Modern* (Cambridge, MA: Harvard University Press, 1993).

Bruce Lawrence, *Shattering the Myth: Islam beyond Violence* (Princeton, NJ: Princeton University Press, 1998).

Nathan Lean, *The Islamophobia Industry: How the Right Manufactures Fear of Muslims* (London: Pluto Press, 2012).

David C.J. Lee, *Ernest Renan: In the Shadow of Faith* (London: Duckworth, 1996).

Catherine LeGouis, *Positivism and Imagination: Scientism and Its Limits in Emile Hennequin, Wilhelm Scherer, and Dimitri Pisarev* (Cranbury, NJ: Associated University Press, 1997).

Daniel Lerner, *The Passing of Traditional Society: Modernizing the Middle East* (New York: Free Press, 1958).

Bernard Lewis, *Islam and the West* (Oxford: Oxford University Press, 1993); *The Muslim Discovery of Europe* (New York: W.W. Norton & Company, 2001); *The Political Language of Islam* (Chicago, IL: University of Chicago Press, 1991); *The Crisis of Islam: Holy War and Unholy Terror* (New York: Random House, 2003).

David Levering Lewis, *God's Crucible: Islam and the Making of Europe, 570–1215* (New York: W.W. Norton, 2008).

Martin W. Lewis and Kären E. Wigen, *The Myth of Continents: A Critique of Metageography* (Berkeley, CA: University of California Press, 1997).

Mark Lilla, *The Stillborn God: Religion, Politics and the Modern West* (New York: Vintage Books, 2008).

Douglas Little, *American Orientalism: The United States and the Middle East since 1945* (Chapel Hill, NC: University of North Carolina Press, 2008).

Bibliography

Ania Loomba, *Colonialism/Postcolonialism: The New Critical Idiom* (New York: Routledge, 2005).

Audre Lorde, *Sister Outsider* (Berkeley, CA: Crossing Press, 2007).

Alasdair MacIntyre, *Against the Self-Images of the Age: Essays on Ideology and Philosophy* (Notre Dame, IN: University of Notre Dame Press, 1989).

Saba Mahmood, *Religious Difference in a Secular Age: A Minority Report* (Princeton, NJ: Princeton University Press, 2016).

Fateh Mohammad Malik, *Iqbal's Reconstruction of Political Thought in Islam* (New Delhi: MediaHouse, 2004).

Rashida Malik, *Iqbal: The Spiritual Father of Pakistan* (Lahore: Sang-e-Meel Publications, 2003).

Mahmood Mamdani, *Good Muslim, Bad Muslim: America, the Cold War and the Roots of Terror* (New York: Three Leaves Press Doubleday, 2004).

Irshad Manji, *The Trouble with Islam Today: A Muslim's Call for Reform of Her Faith* (New York: MacMillan, 2003); *Allah, Liberty and Love: The Courage to Reconcile Faith and Freedom* (New York: Free Press, 2011).

Andrew March, *Islam and Liberal Citizenship: The Search for an Overlapping Consensus* (New York: Oxford University Press, 2009).

Timothy Marr, *The Cultural Roots of American Islamicism* (Cambridge: Cambridge University Press, 2006).

Karl Marx, *Surveys from Exile: Political Writings, Volume 2* (London: Penguin Books, 1992); *Capital, Vol. I & II* (London: Pelican Books, 1976); *A Contribution to the Critique of Political Economy* (New York: International Publishers, 1970).

Karl Marx and Frederick Engels, *On Religion* (New York: Dover Publications, 2008).

Nadia Marzouki, *Islam: An American Religion* (New York: Columbia University Press, 2017).

Bibliography

Nur Masalha, *Expulsion of the Palestinians: The Concept of "Transfer" in Zionist Political Thought, 1882–1948* (Washington, DC: Institute of Palestine Studies, 1992).

Ehsan Masood (Ed.), *How Do You Know: Reading Ziauddin Sardar on Islam, Science and Cultural Relations* (London: Pluto Press, 2006).

Joseph A. Massad, *Islam in Liberalism* (Chicago, IL: University of Chicago Press, 2015).

Tomoko Masuzawa, *In Search of Dreamtime: The Quest for the Origin of Religion* (Chicago, IL: University of Chicago Press, 1993).

Luca Mavelli, *Europe's Encounter with Islam: The Secular and the Postsecular* (New York: Routledge, 2012).

Ann Elizabeth Mayer, *Islam and Human Rights: Tradition and Politics* (Boulder, CO: Westview Press, 2013).

Achille Mbembe, Laurent DuBois (trans.), *Critique of Black Reason* (Durham, NC: Duke University Press, 2017).

Russell T. McCutcheon, *Manufacturing Religion: The Discourse on Sui Generis Religion and the Politics of Nostalgia* (New York: Oxford University Press, 2003).

Sheila McDonough, *Muslim Ethics and Modernity: A Comparative Study of the Ethical Thought of Sayyid Ahmad Khan and Mawlana Mawdudi* (Waterloo: Wilfred Laurier University Press, 1984).

Uday Singh Mehta, *Liberalism and Empire: A Study in Nineteenth-Century British Liberal Thought* (Chicago, IL: University of Chicago Press, 1997).

Barbara D. Metcalf, *Islamic Contestations: Essays on Muslims in India and Pakistan* (New Delhi: Oxford University Press, 2006); *Islamic Revival in British India: Deoband, 1860–1900* (Karachi: Royal Book Company, 1989).

Thomas R. Metcalf, *Ideologies of the Raj* (Cambridge: Cambridge University Press, 1997).

Bibliography

Walter Mignolo, *The Darker Side of Western Modernity: Global Futures, Decolonial Options* (Durham, NC: Duke University Press, 2011).

Gertrude Millin, *Rhodes* (London: Harper & Brothers, 1933).

Pankaj Mishra, *Age of Anger: A History of the Present* (New York: Farrar, Strauss & Giroux, 2017); *From the Ruins of Empire: The Revolt against the West and the Remaking of Asia* (New York: Picador, 2012).

David Mitchell, *Cloud Atlas: A Novel* (New York: Random House, 2004).

Mansoor Moaddel and Kamran Talattof (Eds.), *Modernist and Fundamentalist Debates in Islam* (New York: Palgrave Macmillan, 2002).

Anwar Moazzam, *Jamal al-Din al-Afghani: A Muslim Intellectual* (New Delhi: Concept Publishing Company, 1984).

Joel Mokyr, *A Culture of Growth: The Origins of the Modern Economy* (Princeton, NJ: Princeton University Press, 2017).

Sir Leo Chiozza Money, *The Peril of the White* (London: W. Collins Sons & Co., 1925).

Ilyse R. Morgenstein-Fuerst, *Indian Muslim Minoroties and the 1857 Rebellion: Religion, Rebels, and Jihad* (New York: I.B. Tauris, 2017).

David Motadel (Ed.), *Islam and the European Empires* (New York: Oxford University Press, 2016).

Sir William Muir, *The Life of Mahomet* (Whitefish, MT: Kessinger Publishing, 2003).

Douglas Murray, *The Strange Death of Europe: Immigration, Identity, Islam* (London: Bloomsbury Continuum, 2018).

V.S. Naipaul, *A Bend in the River* (New York: Vintage Books, 1979).

Abdullah Omar Naseef (Ed.), *Today's Problems, Tomorrow's Solutions: Future Thoughts on the Structure of Muslim Society* (London: Mansell, 1988).

Bibliography

Seyyed Hossein Nasr, *Islamic Philosophy from its Origins to the Present* (Albany, NY: SUNY Press, 2006).

Qaiser Nazir, *Iqbal and the Western Philosophers* (Lahore: Iqbal Academy, 2001).

Maajid Nawaz, *Radical: My Journey out of Islamic Extremism* (Guilford, CT: Lyons Press, 2013).

Reinhold Niebuhr, *The Essential Reinhold Niebuhr: Selected Essays and Addresses* (New Haven, CT: Yale University Press, 1986); *The Nature and Destiny of Man* (New York: Charles Scribner's Sons, 1964); *Christian Realism and Political Problems* (New York: Charles Scribner's Sons, 1953); *Moral Man and Immoral Society* (New York: Charles Scribner's Sons, 1960); *The Children of Light, and the Children of Darkness* (New York: Charles Scribner's Sons, 1972).

Asra Nomani, *Standing Alone: An American Woman's Struggle for the Soul of Islam* (New York: HarperOne, 2006).

Max Nordau, *Degeneration* (Scotts Valley, CA: CreateSpace, 2016).

Pippa Norris and Ronald Inglehart, *Sacred and Secular: Religion and Politics Worldwide* (Cambridge: Cambridge University Press, 2011).

Michael Novak, *The Universal Hunger for Liberty: Why a Clash of Civilizations Is Not Inevitable* (New York: Basic Books, 2004).

Sari Nusseibeh, *The Story of Reason in Islam* (Stanford, CA: Stanford University Press, 2017).

Peter O'Brien, *The Muslim Question in Europe: Political Controversies and Public Philosophies* (Philadelphia, PA: Temple University Press, 2016).

Maurice Oleander, Arthur Goldhammer (trans.), *The Languages of Paradise: Aryans and Semites – A Match Made in Heaven* (New York: Other Press, 1992).

Bibliography

Richard G. Olson, *Science and Scientism in Nineteenth-Century Europe* (Urbana, IL: University of Illinois Press, 2008).

George Orwell, *Animal Farm* (New York: Brawtley Press, 2012).

Anthony Pagden, *The Enlightenment: Why It Still Matters* (New York: Random House, 2013).

Richard Palmer, *Hermeneutics: Interpretation Theory in Schleiermacher, Dilthey, Heidegger, and Gadamer* (Evanston, IL: Northwestern University Press, 1969).

Muhammad Ismail Pani Pati (Ed.), *Letters to and from Sir Syed Ahmad Khan* (Lahore: Sadat Art Press, 1993).

Charles Pearson, *National Life and Character: A Forecast* (London: Macmillan, 1894).

Cheah Pheng and Suzanne Guerlac (Eds.), *Derrida and the Time of the Political* (Durham, NC: Duke University Press, 2009).

Kenneth Pomeranz and Steven Topik, *The World That Trade Created: Society, Culture and the World Economy, 1400 to the Present* (New York: Routledge, 2012).

Jasbir Puar, *Terrorist Assemblages: Homonationalism in Queer Times* (Durham, NC: Duke University Press, 2007).

Syed Abdul Quddus, *Islamic Polity in Modern Times* (Lahore: Ferozsons, 1987).

Sayyid Qutb, *Milestones* (Chicago, IL: Kazi Publications, 2007).

Tariq Ramadan, *To Be a European Muslim* (Markfield: The Islamic Foundation, 2003); *Islam, the West, and Modernity* (Markfield: The Islamic Foundation, 2009); *Western Muslims and the Future of Islam* (Oxford: Oxford University Press, 2003).

John Rawls, *Political Liberalism* (New York: Columbia University Press, 1995).

Ernest Renan, *The Life of Jesus* (New York: Prometheus Books, 1991); *An Essay on the Age and Antiquity of the Book of Nabathæn Agriculture – to Which is Added an Inaugural*

Bibliography

Lecture on the Position of the Shemitic Nations in the History of Civilization (London: Trübner & Co., 1862); *History of the People of Israel: From the Rule of the Persians to That of the Greeks* (Boston, MA: Roberts Brothers, 1895).

Ernest Renan, Albert D. Vandam (trans.), C.B. Pitman (trans.), *The Future of Science: Ideas of 1848* (London: Chapman & Hall, 1891).

J.M. Roberts, *The Triumph of the West: The Origin, Rise and Legacy of Western Civilization* (New York: Barnes & Noble Books, 1985).

Maxime Rodinson, *Europe and the Mystique of Islam* (New York: I.B. Tauris, 2009).

Amr G.E. Sabet, *Islam and the Political: Theory, Governance and International Relations* (London: Pluto Press, 2008).

Abdulaziz Sachedina, *The Islamic Roots of Democratic Pluralism* (New York: Oxford University Press, 2001).

Edward W. Said, *Culture and Imperialism* (New York: Vintage Books, 1993); *Humanism and Democratic Criticism* (New York: Columbia University Press, 2004); *Orientalism* (New York: Vintage Books, 1979); *Covering Islam: How the Media and the Experts Determine How We See the Rest of the World* (New York: Vintage Books, 1997).

Tayeb Salih, Dennis Johnson-Davies (trans.), *Season of Migration to the North* (New York: New York Review of Books, 1969).

Ziauddin Sardar, *The Future of Muslim Civilizations* (London: Croom Helm, 1979); *Islamic Futures: The Shape of Ideas to Come* (London: Mansell Publishing, 1986); *What Do Muslims Believe? The Roots and Realities of Modern Islam* (New York: Walker & Company, 2007).

Birgit Schaebler and Leif Stenberg (Eds.), *Globalization and the Muslim World: Culture, Religion, and Modernity* (Syracuse, NY: Syracuse University Press, 2004).

Bibliography

Annemarie Schimmel, *Mystical Dimensions of Islam* (Chapel Hill, NC: University of North Carolina Press, 2011).

Carl Schmitt, *The Nomos of the Earth in the International Law of the Jus Publicum Europaeum* (New York: Telos Press 2003); *The Concept of the Political* (Chicago, IL: University of Chicago Press, 1996).

Noan Wallach Scott, *The Politics of the Veil* (Princeton, NJ: Princeton University Press, 2007).

Iqbal Singh Sevea, *The Political Philosophy of Muhammad Iqbal* (Cambridge: Cambridge University Press, 2012).

Mary Shelley, *Frankenstein* (New York: Dover Publications, 1994).

Andrew Shryock (Ed.), *Islamophobia Islamophilia: Beyond the Politics of Enemy and Friend* (Bloomington, IN: Indiana University Press, 2010).

Adam Smith, *The Theory of Moral Sentiments* (Amherst, MA: Prometheus Books, 2000).

Wilfred Cantwell Smith, *Islam in Modern History* (Princeton, NJ: Princeton University Press, 1957).

Herbert Spencer, *The Study of Sociology* (New York: Appleton, 1874); *The Principles of Biology, Vol I & II* (New York: Appleton, 1990).

Oswald Spengler, *The Decline of the West: An Abridged Edition* (New York: Oxford University Press, 1991).

Avi Max Spiegel, *Young Islam: The New Politics of Religion in Morocco and the Arab World* (Princeton, NJ: Princeton University Press, 2015)

Marietta T. Stepanyants, *Comparative Ethics in a Global Age* (Washington, DC: Council for Research in Values and Philosophy, 2007).

Theodore Lothrop Stoddard, *The New World of Islam* (Charleston, SC: BiblioLife, 2009); *The Rising Tide of Color against White World-Supremacy* (New York: Charles Scribner's Sons, 1925).

Jeffrey Stout, *Democracy and Tradition* (Princeton, NJ: Princeton University Press, 2004).

Charles Taylor, *A Secular Age* (Cambridge, MA: Belknap Press, 2007).

Abdulkader Tayob, *Religion in Modern Islamic Discourse* (New York: Columbia University Press, 2009).

Michael J. Thompson, *Islam and the West: Critical Perspectives on Modernity* (New York: Rowman & Littlefield, 2003).

Arnold J. Toynbee, *Civilization on Trial* (Oxford: Oxford University Press, 1948); *The Western Question: In Greece and Turkey, a Study in the Contact of Civilizations* (London: Constable & Company, 1922).

Christian W. Troll, *Sayyid Ahmad Khan: A Re-Interpretation of Muslim Theology* (New Delhi: Vikas Publishing House, 1978).

David Tyrer, *The Politics of Islamophobia: Race, Power and Fantasy* (New York: Pluto Press, 2013).

Bryan W. Van Norden, *Taking Back Philosophy: A Multicultural Manifesto* (New York: Columbia University Press, 2017).

Dana Villa, *Arendt and Heidegger: The Fate of the Political* (Princeton, NJ: Princeton University Press, 1996).

Gauri Viswanathan (Ed.), *Power, Politics, and Culutre: Interviews with Edward Said* (New York: Vintage Books, 2001).

Chibueze C. Udeani, Veerachart Nimanong, Zou Shipeng and Mustafa Malik (Eds.), *Communication across Cultures: The Hermeneutics of Culutre and Religion in a Global Age* (Washington, DC: Council for Research in Values and Philosophy, 2008).

Voltaire, M. Nugent (trans.), *Essay on Universal History, the Manners, and Spirit of the Nations: From the Reign of*

Bibliography

Charlemagne to the Age of Lewis XIV (Farmington Hills, MI: Gale Ecco Print Editions, 2010).

Michael Walzer, *Thick and Thin: Moral Argument at Home and Abroad* (Notre Dame, IN: University of Notre Dame Press, 1994).

Michael Warner, *Publics and Counterpublics* (New York: Zone Books, 2005).

William Montogomery Watt, *The Formative Period of Islamic Thought* (Oxford: Oneworld Publications, 2006).

Putnam Weale, *The Conflict of Colour; Being a Detailed Examination of Racial Problems throughout the World with Special Reference to the English-Speaking Peoples* (Sydney: Wentworth Press, 2016).

Max Weber, *The Protestant Ethic and the Spirit of Capitalism* (New York: Pearson 1 Edition, 1977).

H.G. Wells, *The Island of Dr. Moreau* (Oxford: Oxford University Press, 2017).

Raymond Williams, *Marxism and Literature* (Oxford: Oxford University Press, 1977).

Richard N. Williams and Daniel N. Robinson (Eds.), *Scientism: The New Orthodoxy* (London: Bloomsbury Academic, 2015).

William Appleman Williams, *Empire as a Way of Life: An Essay on the Causes and Character of America's Present Predicament along with a Few Thoughts about an Alternative* (New York: Oxford University Press, 1980).

Mehdi Ha'iri Yazdi, *The Principles of Epistemology in Islamic Philosophy: Knowledge by Presence* (Albany, NY: SUNY Press, 1992).

Elisabeth Young-Bruehl, *Hannah Arendt: For Love of the World* (New Haven, CT: Yale University Press, 2004).

Muhammad Qasim Zaman, *The Ulama in Contemporary Islam* (Princeton, NJ: Princeton University Press, 2002); *Modern*

Islamic Thought in a Radical Age: Religious Authority and Internal Criticism (Cambridge: Cambridge University Press, 2012).

Vazira Fazila-Yacoobali Zamindar, *The Long Partition and the Making of Modern South Asia: Refugees, Boundaries, Histories* (New York: Columbia University Press, 2007).

Index

Abduh, Muhammad, 111, 139, 295
Abdul Hamid II, Sultan, 111
ACT for America, 245
'administrative massacres', 127
'affective norms', 273
Afghanistan, 252–3
Africa, scramble for, 122
'age of anger', 50
Ahmad Khan, Syed, 110
Ahmad, Jalal Al-e, 115
Ahmadinejad, Mahmoud, 139
aid politics, 253
al-Afghani, Sayyid Jamal al-Din, 110–11, 139, 222–4, 229–31, 233, 235, 295; -Renan debate, 226
al-Baghdadi, Abu Bakr, 57, 76
al-Banna, Hasan, 65
Al-e Ahmad, Jalal, 138–9
al-Qaeda, 55–6, 249; diseased limb metaphor, 57
al-Shabab, 53, 55, 249
Alavi, Seema, 111–12
Aleppo, 175
Ambedkar, B.R., 183
Ameli, Saied Reza, 159
American black religion, Islamic aspect, 21
Amor Mundi, 289–91
'angloglobalization', 245
Ansari, Aziz, 267–8
anthropology studies, 17
anti-American sentiment, Tahrir Square, 143

anti-colonial movements: glossing over, 248; twentieth century, 9
anti-Muslim animus: formulaic narratives, 82; simple theories of, 19
anti-Semitism, 16; Europe, 7; rise of, 108
anti-sharia legislations, 261
Arab Spring 2011, 74
archaic ideologies, essentializing theories, 24
Arendt, Hannah, 25, 40, 44, 50–1, 87, 122, 128, 173, 195, 222, 226–7, 279, 283–5, 287, 294; *Amor Mundi/The Human Condition*, 38–9, 86, 283, 296; *The Origins of Totalitarianism*, 108
Aristotle, 20, 39, 51, 71, 212
Asad, Talal, 107, 203–4
Aslan, Reza, 268
Attaturk, Kemal, 138
Augustine, 71
Austen, Jane, 38, 281
authenticity, futile rhetoric of, 107
avant-garde, need for, 44
Averroes, 224
Aydin, Cemil, 176

Bacon, Francis, 131, 192
Balibar, Etienne, 246
Balkans, nationalist movements, 111
Baruma, Ian, 66, 68, 139, 205–6; Ramadan interviews, 67
Bataclan theatre Massacre, Paris, 274

Index

Bawer, Bruce, 257–8
Bayley, C.A., *The Birth of the Modern World*, 263–4
Bazargan, Mehdi, 183
Behloul, Samuel M., 259
bekhudi (selflessness), 179–80
belonging, desire for, 23; collective, 40
Ben-Gurion, David, 253
Benhabib, Seyla, 44, 278
Berger, Peter, 119
Bergson, Henri, 179
Berman, Marshall, 45
Berman, Paul, 66–72, 76, 79, 165, 167, 272, 294; *The Flight of the Intellectuals*, 64
Bernard, Cheryl, 158
Bhabha, Homi, 37, 167
bigotry, anti-Islam, 205
Biko, Steve, 92
bildung, 295
Bin Laden, Osama, 57, 76, 138, 165, 249
binary habits, politics, 184
Binder, Leonard, 155
biology analogical misuse, 114, 146; evolution, 237 (USE)
'black', 2; blackness humanizing viewpoint, 3; earlier generation intellectuals, 14
Blair, Tony, 138; 'British values', 275
blasphemy, 208; Muslim concerns ridiculed, 11; process of repeated, 207–8
Boko Haram, 53, 55
Boot, Max, 253
Brandom, Robert, 90
Britain: Brexit, 82, 290; India colonialism, 84
British Empire, 251; syrupy treatises on, 248
British East India Company, India, 105, 112
Brown, Wendy, 81, 273
Bruno, 131, 192
Buddhism: 'constructed', 255; repurposing of, 15
Buechner, Frederick, 233
Bulgaria, Ottoman incursion, 211

'burkinis', 262
Bush, George W., 29, 47, 52, 58–60, 76, 79, 137–9 144, 158, 162, 182, 254, 275; London speech, 150; post 9/11 speech, 56; rhetoric of, 63

Cabral, Amilcar, 38, 281
Cairo, emigres to, 112
Caldwell, Christopher, 246, 257
Caliphate, 1926 disappearance, 27
Carey, W.H., *The Mahomedan Rebellion*, 105
Carlos, John, 169; black world heroized, 170
Casanova, Jose, 185
Catholic Church: conservatives, 120; unity broken, 119
Centre for American Progress, *Fear, Inc*, 245
Ceuta, defensive bulwark as, 257
Chan-Malik, Sylvia, 21
Chateaubriand, F.-R. de, 213
chauvinism, nationalistic, 37, 238
China, 253
Christendom-Islam understanding idea, 163
Christianity, 8; Catholic Church; 119–20; Christians, 207; history of, 202; power to classify, 192
Civil rights movement, USA, 14, 131, 170
civilization: anti-political abstraction, 285; civilizing mission, 90, 241, 251; civilizational decline theme, 113; development of, 101; differences, 161; ladder of, 9; Western, 15, provincial notions of, 291
Clapper, James, 143–4
'clash of civilizations', 160; internal, 82
CNN, 268
'Coca-Colonization thesis', 161
Cold War, 82, 131, 137, 242, 251, 269–70; end of, 290; Western propaganda, 275
colonialism: India regime of servitude, 32; neo, 42; post-Enlightenment English, 167; psychopathology of, 93

Index

coloniality: architecture of power, 43; concept of, 42
common good, capacity to discuss, 51
community, notions of, 186
Comte, Auguste, 103, 212–14, 217, 228, 234
Concert of Europe, 98, 111
condescension, 125, 132, 152
Confederate monuments, USA, 16
conformists, 149, 158, 162, 168; -exceptionalists back and forth, 148, 173, 232; Islamic tradition excavators, 171; thinking, 157
Conrad, Joseph, 125, 173, 254; *Heart of Darkness*, 261
Constantinople, 119
contamination, fear of, 145
contempt, European, 91
'cosmology of progress', 102
cosmopolitan imperial system, 104
Coulter, Ann, 245
Cowen, Joseph, 121
Critical Islam, 2, 6, 16, 140, 149, 186, 291, 294; archive, 28, 40; archive unopened, 13–14; context of, 4
Crusades, 210
cultural preservation, as absolute right, 16
culture(s): civilizational panic, 288; culturalist arguments, 269–70; Darwinist culturalism, 243; decadent, 219; essentializing theories, 24; Euro-American norms, 35; exceptionalist assumptions, 278; 'immutable', 246; 'of complaint', 277
culture talk, 237–8, 246, 269; asymptotic quality, 37; West vs the rest, 247
cynicism, Indian Muslims colonial period, 35

Dabashi, Hamid, 42
dangerous ideology, Islam as, 6
Dante, 210
Darwin, Charles, 192
Darwininism, consequences, 101; social, 122
David Horowitz Freedom Center, 245
Dawkins, Richard, 194, 196, 199–200
De Bellaigue, Christopher, 41, 98
De Gobineau, Count Arthur, 100
decolonization, 43; 20th century, 74
deficient geographies, essentializing theories, 24
dehumanization, oppressor-victim, 37
democracy, Muslim world, 142
Dennett, Daniel, 197
depoliticization, 4–5, 14–15, 19, 41, 53, 267, 269
Derrida, Jacques, 194–5, 244
Descartes, René, 131
'desert mentalities', 106
dialectics, 90, 93–4
dialogue, 291
discourse, rationing of, 52
discursive strategies, 52
Djait, Hichem, 45
double-consciousness, 7
doubt, 234
drone strikes, 290
Dubois, W.E., 7

'Eastern' as Muslim Question, 100, 106
Egypt: Christian minority, 143; European takeover, 111; modernizing state, 166; Napoleon invasion, 73, 98; reformist elites, 98; 1798 events, 27; 2012 uprising, 142
either/ors, Islam characterisations, 49, 78, 81, 83, 89; futility, 140; Iqbal avoidance of, 177; options, 108; regurgitations, 79
el Fadl, Khaled Abou, 155, 157
elites: Muslim reformist, 98; Muslim westernized, 183; racist European, 101
empire(s): cosmopolitan, 97; historical experience of, 23; lived reality of, 42; 'of human rights', 185; race weaponized, 126
Enlightenment, the, 34, 63, 137; hierarchical humanism, 126; Nietzschian critique of, 12; universality claim, 204

Index

Erasmus, 192
Esposito, John, 156–7
essence, 'prison' of, 51
essentialism, post 9/11 weaponized, 89
ethical choices, Muslims imposed, 64
eugenics, 237
Europe: as World-Subject, 103; Enlightenment trajectory, 34; foreign policy consequences, 274, globalized capital, 73; imperial hegemony, 105, 114; Jewry, 168; Muslim neighbourhoods, 258; Muslim presence in, 260; Muslims internalized, 211; Renaissance notion of, 120; right-wing movements/parties, 256, 261; transcendental idea of, 100; wars of religion, 163
European discourse, 'compartmentalized world', 288
European intervention, Muslim societies, 74
European powers, Muslim admiration, 113
European superiority, Muslim responses, 30
Euro-American imperialism, 8–10, 42, 116; Christianized frontiers, 100; civilizational mission sentiments, 30; power expansion of, 49–50, 73
evolution, biological, 35
ex-Muslim critics, 212, 234; books of, 48; Islam as corrupt death cult, 208
exception, conformity, Islam either/ors of, 168, 201
exceptionalists, 149, 150; Muslim, 164–5; Western, 171; thesis of, 160
exoticism, 254
expansive humanism, 38
'exterminism', 265
extinction, Darwinian fear, 146

Faiz Ahmed Faiz, 84, 86, 183, 295
Fanon, Frantz, 38, 44, 50, 86–7, 91, 93–5, 97, 116–18, 125, 132, 136–7, 153, 281, 285, 287, 294; labelling of, 92
feedback loop, discursive, 109; self-referential, 285

feminism, 2
Ferguson, Niall, 138, 173, 184, 241–3, 245, 247–53, 256–7, 269, 271; *Civilization*, 263, 270; Hegelian fantasies of, 264; imagination lack, 282; magical thinking of, 279; re-Christianized Europe fantasies, 275
First World War, 104, 122
Flynn, Tom, 197
forked tongues, imperialist, 167
France: burqa hysteria, 262; Catholic conservatives, 120; colonialism, 116; French Revolution, 120, 131, 212; Third Republic, 21
Frankenstein figure, 75; Muslims analogy, 76
Frashëri, Şemseddin Sami, 110
free speech, as absolute right, 16; Western weaponized, 11
freedom: critical Muslim voices need, 20; Islamic concepts of, 11; Islamic evaluations of, 12; judgmental rhetoric, 175; political, 33; provincial notions of, 291; valences, 32; Western monopoly claim to, 265
freedom talk, of Islam, 140, 48, 154; adjustments in, 173 either/ors, 180
Freud, Sigmund, 192
Friedan, Betty, 'the problem that has no name', 7
Frum, David, 155
Fukuyama, Francis, 247; *The End of History*, 243
'fusion of horizons', 39

Gadamer, Hans-Georg, 39–40, 44, 291, 293; horizon(s) of expectation, 292
Gaffney Jr, Frank, 245
Galileo, 131, 192, 224
Gandhi, Mohandas, 118, 178
Garvey, Marcus, 118
Geller, Pamela, 245
Germany, post-war, 284
Ghalib, Mirza Asadullah, 110
Gibbon, Edward, 99
global world: agora mainstream center, 25; public sphere, 24; Smith and Carlos heroized, 170

Index

globalization: economic, 8; fragmenting effects, 75
Godwin's law, 7
Goethe, Johan von, 179
good life, notions of, 186
Gordon, Lewis R., 93
Gould, Stephen Jay, 197
governmentality, Western colonialism, 107
grand narratives, suspicion of, 294
Greece, War of Independence, 100
Grewal, Zareena, 94
growth, 9, 129; organizing principle of, 130
Guevara, Che, 92
guilt, by association, 71

Habermas, Jürgen, 293
Haddon, Alfred C., 117
hadith, 112
Haider, Quaratulain, 183
Haim, Sylvia, 164
hakimiyyah, Quranic concept, 166
Hallaq, Wael, 164
Hamid, Moshin, 295
Hamid, Shadi, 164
Harris, Sam, 138, 194, 196, 198, 200–1, 203, 212, 222, 226, 228
Harvard University, 242
Hegel, G.W.F., 11, 71, 90–3, 97, 136, 179, 190, 218, 287
Henri-Levy, Bernard, 138
Herder, John Gottfried, 218
Hinduism, 'constructed', 255; repurposing of, 15
Hirsi Ali, Ayaan, 69, 204–5, 207–8, 212, 217; FGM activism, 206
historical materialism, 103
historicization, comparative, 101
history, arrested, 70; historical analogies, 154
Hitchens, Christopher, 196, 198–200, 205, 271
Hitler, Adolf, rise of, 126
Hizb ut-Tahrir, 226
Hodgson, Marshall, 164; *Islamicate Weltanschauung*, 73
Holocaust, the Polish role whitewashing, 16

homosexuality, Muslim 19th century permissive, 15, 174
Hook, Sidney, 190
'horizons of expectation', 40; contesting, 41, 289
Horrox, Giles, 271
Hourani, Albert, 99
Hughes, Aaron, 41
human condition, biologization of, 287
humanity: contemporary common problems, 186; grading, 193; political beings, 39
Hume, David, 131, 192
humility, ethos of, 292
Hungary, Ottoman incursion, 211
Hunter, W.W., *The Indian Musulmans*, 105
Huntington, Samuel, 160, 161–2, 165, 244–6; *The Clash of Civilizations*, 243
Hussain Hali, Khwaja Altaf, 110
Huxley, Julian S., 117
Hyder, Qurratulain, 295; *River of Fire*, 83

ideas, global marketplace, 24
identitarian politics, progressive intellectuals, 29, 47
identity(ies): formation, 77; global marketplace, 24; intersectional reality, 21; 'politics', 3
Ignatieff, Michael, 138, 173, 184; modernization theory, 253
ijitihad, appropriation of, 153
impractical utopias, Western, 12
inclusion/exclusion: colonial, 116; rhetoric, 160
'incomprehensibility', Muslim, 35
India, 253; British advances, 99; Muslim identity, 181; Muslim population, 30, 35; Muslim power diminished, 90; Partition, 84; Sepoy Mutiny 1857, 27, 98, 105, 111, 126, 176; 20th century Muslim body politic, 177
Indo-Persionate imperium, 112
'influencers', 25
Ingraham, Paula, 245
Inquisition, the, 189

Index

intellectuals: elite Muslim, 113; -institutions of power alignment, 280; 'moderate' Muslim, 142
internationalist utopians, 142
internet, power of, 207
inversions, 190
Iqbal, Muhammad, 12, 33, 44, 177–8, 180, 182–3, 229, 295; freedom conception, 181; *Javid-Nama*, 180; poetic self-reflections, 40
Iran, 183, 244; reformist elites, 98; White Revolution, 175
Iraq, 252, invasion of 152; War, 253–4
ISIS (Islamic State), 53, 55, 57, 249
Islam: a 'certain' 195; 'abominable anachronism', 199; Abrahamic religion, 151; 'adversarial civilization', 162; ahistorical, 107; alternative conception of, 27; American black religion, 21; animating essence, 114; appropriations of, 81; Arab birth of, 161; assimilation modes, 6; babble of talk about, 53, 286; binaries imposed, 68; 'common sense' view, 17, 294; concept evolution, 273; condemnations of, 193, 204; conformist thinking, 150, 160; 'contemporary threat', 201; critical edge, 52; crude depictions of, 194; *culture talk*, 36, 266, 275; debates about repetition, 48, 147; 'de-essentialisation', 204; 'deficient', 33, 103; developmental lag, 32, 225; discursive straitjacket, 11, 49; early founding texts, 246; Enlightenment treatments, 99; essentialized, 148, 218; exception conceptions, 196; fear of, 232; European attacks on, 110; *freedom talk* about, 31, 141; fundamentalist form, 114; golden age, 113–14; identitarian politics rejecting, 47; ideology of life, 181; independent category, 188; Indian, 230; 'interpretative strategy', 41; 'Jeffersonian project' for 210; judging of, 142, 158; marginalization of, 296; medieval Christian imaginary, 211; marginalization of, 296 ; 'moderate', 64; modern constructions of, 78; *modernity resistant*, 260; 'moral contagion', 261; 'moral vocabularies', 146; nativist disdain for, 271; othering discourses of, 80; political boundary term, 264; political ideology, 8, 205, 262; post 9/11 opinions deluge, 77; prior rejection, 197; 'problem' of, 290; providential purpose, 219; public debates, 26; reconstruction of, 179; 'reason resistant', 203, 263; regressive culture label, 267; rejuvenation desire, 108; religion of peace, 63, 110; semitic spirit, 217; special case, 198; *speciest*, 145; totalizing authority, 10; tradition, 109; *true*, 55, 58, 111; uniformity of faith as threat, 105; visible presence, 260; vocabulary emptied, 76; West's evaluations, 15, 18, 29, 80

Islamic lifeworlds, 13; 'DNA', 114; societies different types of, 74
Islamicate Weltanschauung, 279
Islamicate world, disaggregated, 75
Islamicists, French, 82
Islamism, 71; Islamists, 31, 54, 141
Islamophilia: depoliticizing, 19; Euro-American, 115
Islamophobia, 26, 266; growing literature, 17
Island of Doctor Moreau, 146
Israel, 244
Istanbul, emigrés to, 112

Jamat-e-Islami, 178
Jaspers, Karl, 283
Jasser, Zuhdi, 209–10
Jefferson, Thomas, 61
'Jeffersonian compromise', 61–3, 73
Jewish people, 207; European, 168; medieval stubborn trope, 211; racial other, 220
Jinnah, Muhammad Ali, 177

Index

Kant, Immanuel, 91
Kaplan, Robert, 252
Keddie, Nikki R., 224
Kedouri, Eli, 164
Khamenie, Ayatollah Ali, 183
Khan, Imran, 182–3, 295,
Khan, Sayyid Ahmad, 44, 139, 229–35; naturalism, 233; reason account, 35; theological rationalism, 40
Khomeini, Ayatollah, 138, 200
khudi, (selfness)concept of, 12, 33, 178–80
Kidd, Benjamin, 134, 167, 243; triumphalist militarism, 138
Kipling, Rudyard, 125, 173, 251, 254, 281; 'The White Man's Burden', 116
Kohout, Pavel, 285
Kristol, Irving, 151
Kulturkampf, 274
Kundani, Arun, 266–7, 272

laïcité, 16
language, as 'mold', 215; linguistic racialization, 216
Latin America: as immigrant contagion, 165; Catholic conservatives, 120
lay messianism 19th century, 211
Le Bon, Gustave, 101
Le Pen, Marine, 82
Le Point, 67
legibility, 5
Lerner, David, 154
Lewis, Bernard, 162–4, 245–6
LGBTQ movement, successes of, 171
liberal humanitarianism, 253; righteousness rhetoric, 171
liberal philosophers, 142
Lilla, Mark, 271
Ling Qichao, 118
literalism, Quranic, 114
Locke, John, 209
Lorde, Audre, 22
lordship and bondage, pathology of, 91
Ludwig Maximilian University, Munich, 179
Lustrodo, Domenico, 272
Luther, Martin, 137, 209, 224

Mahdi rebellion, Sudan, 249
Malcolm X, 92
Mamdani, Mahmood, 18, 52, 87, 259; *Good Muslim, Bad Muslim*, 246
Mamluk kingdom, reform need recognition, 73
Manji, Irshad, 138–9, 152–3, 158, 209
March, Andrew, 64–5, 68–9, 71, 78–9, 87
Marx, Karl, 71, 103, 120, 188–91, 193, 228, 235, 257; 'Asiatic mode of production', 121
Marzouki, Nadia, 273
mass migration, 20
Massad, Joseph, *Islam in Liberalism*, 157
master race, 125; colonial, 123
master-slave dialectic, 90
Maududi, Sayyid Abul A'la, 114, 138–9, 166, 178
Mecca, emigres to, 112
Medina, Prophet's community, 113
messianism, European, 102
Middle Ages, 97; Church zealotry of, 194
Middle East: Forum, 245; military interventions, 209; Muslim control, 30; Muslim power diminished, 90; oil in, 244
Mignolo, Walter, 42
Mishra, Pankaj, 50, 77, 242, 248, 269–70
missionaries, Christian, 105
Mitchell David, *Cloud Atlas*, 239–41
modern anti-modernism, Muslim, 115
modern Islam, archive of, 13
modern world: debates, 1; Europe created, 95
'modernism', Islamic, 235
modernity(ies): alternative, 50; amorphous concept, 8; connective tissue, 44; 'contraptual' approach, 281; general category analysis, 41; hierarchy ideas, 9; horizons of, 291; hydra of, 10; Islam critical engagement of, with, 11; major axes of, 18; Muslim experience of, 2, 27, 177, 182; postcolonial, 83; shifting evaluative standards, 37; universal orbit, 45; Western, 185

Index

modernization theorists, 142, 147
Mokyr, Joel, 129
Money, Sir Leo Chiozza, 127
Montesquieu, Charles-Louis de, 121
moral relativists, 147
Morgan, Lewis H., 101
Mosque construction, arguments against, 260
Mubarak, Hosni, ouster of, 142
Mughal India: British encroachments, 73; political order unraveling, 111
Muhammad, the Prophet, 218; caricatures of, 273; Dante version, 210; favourable view of, 99
Muhammad Anglo-Oriental College, 229
Murray, Douglas, 246, 257
Muslim(s): alternative cartographies, 40; alternative views of the world, 289; American women of colour, 21; 'antithesis', 259; apologists, 110, 225ascriptive identity, 266; bans on, 290; complex views of, 176; critical ex, 34; cultural symbols, 36, 238; cynicism, 234; 'demographic threat', 257; depoliticization of, 4–5, 14, 19, 41, 53, 267, 269; developmental lag implied, 160, 168; discursive binaries, 84; essentialist treatments of, 30; European, 65–6, 88, 244, 258; fear of, 48; futility, 72, 78, 80–1, 83 'good-bad', 34, 196; Hobbesian rendering of, 140; humanity of questioned, 20; infantilized, 153; inferior civilization label, 102, 106; internal critics dismissed, 69; intellectual mobilization, 4; lifeworlds, 295; liminal humanity imposed, 79; 'moderate' intellectuals, 32; natives, 219; neo-conservative, 152; news media personnel, 268; objects of observation, 6–7, 53, 272; 'peril', 105, 249; political beings, 10, 144, 208; pre-19th century writers, 97; racial profiling call, 209; 'real', 60; re-politicizing need, 8, 27; recent global impact, 55; recognition need, 72; reform movements, 109; religion of peace appropriation, 77; religious enthusiasm surfeit accusation, 188; semitized, 211; subjectivity, 24; useful ciphers, 18; Western imagination binary, 6; women, 261, 265

Muslim Brotherhood, 143; 'largely secular', 144; Egypt, 65; specter of, 14
Muslim League, 177
Muslim Question, 27, 52, 139, 196, 202, 229, 276, 285–6, 295, 296; cyclical, 145; political question, 31, 297
Muslim world: abstract democratization, 155; circular debates about, 196; colonial control, 157 common sense reality, 87; democracy and secularism, 32; 'despotism' Ottoman identified, 104; ethnographic accounts, 17; freedom in, 174; 'golden age', 233 imperial fantasies stage, 254; judgment rhetoric, 175; modern world created, 15; novel concept, 90; political power loss, 73; provincial backwater, 104; 'reform' talk, 64; 'religion-building', 158; re-make attempts, 242; violence, 269–70; West's relations with, 94; Western interventions, 20, 54, 165; world system interrupted, 74, 95
Muslimness: public signs of, 80; racialized, 104
mutinies, Muslim soldiers Iraq, 249

naming, power of, 50–1
Nanjani, Kumail, 268; *The Big Sick*, 267
Napoleon, 99; Egypt 1798 invasion, 98
Nasser, Gamal Abdul, 165
nation-state, 8, 13
national security: as absolute right, 16; identitarian politics of, 272

362

Index

national self-determination, 9
nativism, resurgent, 262
natural history, notion of universal, 103
Nawaz, Maajid, 138–9, 209, 222, 226
Nazi Germany, 125; Anglo-American war against, 131; racist politics, 117
negative solidarity, 50, 53; forces of, 86
neo-conservatives, 147, 151; condescension, 152; interventionist, 153; religion utility, 151; thinkers, 32, 142
neo-imperialism, 184, 242–3, 257, 262
Netflix, 267
New Atheists, 34, 188, 194–8, 200, 202–5, 210, 212, 221, 228, 234
'new man', 91
New World, European discovery of, 62
Newton, Isaac, 103
Niebuhr, Reinhold, 188–91, 221, 235
Nietzsche Friedrich, 179, 192, 287
9/11, events of, 54 60, 204; iconic, 20, 49; interpretations of, 57; Muslim futility icon, 72; post- 97, 242, 250; post-Islam mainstream consciousness, 30; post-Muslim rhetoric, 29, 47; post-punitive tropes, 33; sense of farce, 37
noblesse oblige, 127, 147, 191, 243, 288; colonial, 123; Islamic, 167; Western, 153
Nomani, Asra, 139, 209
non-European thinkers, provincializing, 93
Nordeau, Max, *Degeneration*, 127
Novak, Michael, 152, 158

O'Brien, Peter, 273–4
Oeuvres de Saint-Simon, 103
Olympic Games: 1968 protest, 169; Sochi 2010, 169–70
Orient, the: colonial concept of, 95; European imaginary, 106; 'Oriental despotism', 121; Orientalism, 108, 148
Ottoman Empire, 249; Europe incursions, 211; pan-Islamic Caliphate, 111; reform need recognition, 73; *Tanzimat* reform, 98; universalism intent, 104
Oxbridge, 242; imperialists of, 252

Pakistan, 183; Muslim homeland, 177; Muslim identity, 84, 181
particularity, 'prison' of, 51
patriarchy: feminist critiques of, 5; Muslim milieu, 206; political paternalism, 238; problematic, 4
peace, 63; vocabulary of, 61
'Peak Islam', 48
Pearson, Charles, *National Life and Character*, 127
Perle, Richard S., 155
Pew Research, 143, 156
philology, 215
piety, Muslim level of, 104
Pink Floyd, 117
Pipes, Daniel, 245
plurality, condition of, 279; political love of, 39
polis, 286–7
political Islam, as secular, 152
politics: deliberation, 87; humans as political beings, 10, 20, 31; institutions bureaucratized, 8; laicization of, 217; of difference, 50; public speech acts, 39; Schmittian concept, 184; 'settled consensus', 7
positivism, 102, 212–13; Comtian, 35, 237; 19th century, 194
postcolonial studies, 38; theory, 42
private spheres, Muslim re-engineering, 238
'progress', 130; anti-political abstraction, 285; narrative of, 94; teleological narratives, 35
Protestant Reformation, 119
punitive tropes, revival of, 33

Quran, 111–12, 228; regime of rights, 113
Qutb, Sayyid, 65, 138–9, 165, 167; fundamentalist label, 12; vanguard advocated, 115, 166

Index

race: biologized politics, 126; competition, 147; consciousness, 90, 117, 254; degeneration notions, 101; panics, 127, 241; talk, 243; 'pollution' fear, 125, 127; world architecture of, 3
racism, 118, 219; imperial, 122; modern, 93; moral danger recognition, 170; 'post-racial', 259
'radicalization', 265
rage, postcolonial, 291
Rahman, Fazlur, 183
Ramadan, Tariq, 12, 41, 66–7, 69, 71–2, 139, 167, 272, 294; attacks on, 65; Berman rejection, 76; caricatured, 295; derision of, 47; rejections of, 68
RAND, 158
rational powers (*quwat-i 'aqli*), 231
reason, 35; as objective arbiter, 191; as trap, 222; capacity constrained, 35; concept of, 11; critical Muslim voices need, 20; European monopoly claim, 203; notion of, 34; origin myths, 198; provincial notions of, 291; realm of admission price, 207; specific history of, 201; uncertainty, 233; various renderings of, 189
'reason talk', about Muslims, 33, 187–8, 194, 202, 209, 211, 229; either ors, 227; grooved histories of, 235; provincial universalisms of, 288; race-religion, 220; rules of engagement, 224; spectacle of debate, 221
recognition: assymetric relationship, 94, 97; failures, 136; need for, 75; provincial universalisms corrective, 278
reconquista, 220
'reform', panoramic term, 31, 141
Reformation, the, 62, 192
refugees, Western produced, 20
regression, Islamic norms, 36
religion: contempt for, 191; Enlightenment critique, 100; objectification, 193; 'of Humanity', 213, 235; of peace talk, 60; private sphere of, 62; privatized demand, 210; public manifestations regulated, 62; religion association, 61; science of, 193; Studies, 17; violence association, 61; wars of, 62
Renaissance, the, 192
Renan, Ernest, 33, 102, 107, 187, 211–2, 215–19, 223–4, 228–30, 242; -al-Afghani debate, 226; 'Islam and Science', 34, 222; philology conception, 220; *The Future of Science*, 214
'rhetoric of blame', 38
Rhodes, Cecil, 130, 241
rights discourse, internationalization of, 8
Rome, 119
Rorty, Richard, 61
Roy, Oliver, 82
Rushdie, Salman, 69; fatwa against, 200
Russia, 253; LGBT accusation, 169; Stalinist regime, 190

Said, Edward W., 23, 39, 44, 106–8, 121, 147, 162, 212, 220, 243, 276–8, 280–2; 'contrapuntal approach', 38; cosmopolitan New Yorker, 279; grand humanism, 40
Salih, Tayeb, 83, 295; *Season of Migration to the North*, 82
Sarsour, Linda, 272
Schilze, Richard, 261
Schimmel, Annemarie, 180, 183
Schlegel, Friedrich, 213
Schmitt, Carl, 62
science: elevation of, 217; Scientific Revolution, 34; scientism, 214
scientific racism, European elites, 101
Second World War, 81, 118
secularism, 16, 73; Christian emerging, 163, 164
self, the, 13, 178–80, 186; accounts of, 12; -consciousness, 93; 'underground', 106
self-determination, 32; concepts of, 178; Muslim exposition, 181; parameters of collective, 180

Index

'semitic, the', 215
Sepoy Mutiny 1857, 98, 105, 126, 176; aftermath, 111
Shahwaliulla, Delhi Naqshbandi Sufi 111
Shariati, Ali, 92, 183
Shelly, Mary, 75
slaves, 10; retribution reversal, 287; slavery, 9
slavophiles, Russian, 119
Smith, Tommie, 169; black world heroized, 170
Sochi Winter Olympics 2010, 169–70
Social Darwinism, 35, 237
Soroush, Abdulkarim, 183
South Africa, apartheid regime, 171
Southern Poverty Law Centre, 206
Soviet communism, 188; communism, collapse of, 184
'space of appearance', 25
Spain: Catholic conservatives, 120; *conversos*, 220
Spencer, Herbert, 101, 126
Spencer Robert, 245
Spinoza, Baruch, 192
Sputnik, launch of, 296–7
'Stand by Your Man', 5
Stanford University, 241–2
state, the nation: modern infrastructure, 63; use of force monopoly, 61
Stoddard, Lothrop, 127, 241, 255
Strauss, Leo, 138
'structures of feeling', 36, 237
Sudan, postcolonial modernity, 83
'superiority': Muslim responses to European, 90; Western claims rejected, 115
'survival of the fittest', 111

Tagore, Rabindranath, 118, 178
Tahrir Square 2011, 176; protesters, 143
taklif, 35
Taliban, Afghanistan, 57; recent negotiations, 55
talking and listening, 26
tauhid, 233

Taylor, Charles, 293
The West, modern world created, 15
think-tanks, anti-Muslim, 245
Toynbee, Arnold, 135, 138, 167, 241, 243, 285; 'Christology', 133–4, 145
trade: European colonial encroachment, 97; networks shared Muslim consciousness, 112; 'tragic performative contradiction', 273
'traitors to their own faith' rhetoric, 58
Trinity College, Cambridge, 179
Trump, Donald, 82, 209, 290; literal wall aspiration, 276
Tryer, David Llewelyn, 259
Tunisia, European takeover, 111; reformist elites, 98

ulama, 229
umma, 13; nostalgia for unified, 109
uncertainty, 234
Uncle Tom's Cabin, 5
universal reason: inverted God, 191; messianic mission, 220
universalism, totalitarian, 146
USA, 256; black people's experience, 258; Muslim civil society advocacy, 209; Muslim Student Associations, 261; political right, 271; security, 155
'useful knowledge', 129
USSR (Union of Soviet Socialist Republics), 117, 296; end of, 244
utopianism: internationalist, 32; practical, 12

veiling, furious debates on, 261
Victorian imperialists, 248
violence: as cathartic, 93; resorts to, 288
vocabulary, Muslim political, 176
Voltaire, 101, 192, 209

Walzer, Michael, 271
'War on Terror', 29, 51–2, 89, 272
wars: Islamic world, 250; of religion, 189
Weale, Putnam, *The Conflict of Colour*, 127

Index

'West', the, 4, 22, 118, 129, 132; 'and the rest' feedback loops, 43; 'bastion of freedom', 275; Christian cultural unity, 261; conceptual history of, 23, 90, 121; duality projected, 24; eschatological yearnings, 136; exceptionalism, 19; exclusive history making, 135; global domination rationalised, 241; haters of, 26; human values, 149; 'international community' possession, 13; lamentations of decline, 256; mainstream view of, 285; mirror of, 6; moral consensus historical nature, 120, 169; 1990s, 184; naming power, 51; normative values evolved, 70, 150, 187; provincial moral lexicon, 146, 186 ;rhetorical invention, 131; right-wing politics, 175; superiority claims, 138, 277

Western identity(ies), bifurcated form, 18; Islam as internal aspect, 28

Western media, Muslim representation, 17

Western modernity, Islam appropriations, 81

'white Crisis'/panic, literature of, 127, 254, 256

white men's burden, version of, 5

'White Mughals', Euro-Indian, 99

white supremacy, 4–5; social movements against, 3; world, 255

whiteness, 91, 93–4, 116, 118, 128, 132; imperial version, 123

William of Ockham, 192

Williams, William Apple, 122

Wilson, Woodrow, 138

Wolf, Gary, 196

women: diversity of, 2; earlier generation intellectuals, 14

Wordsworth, William, 213

World-Subject(s), 289; 'properly constituted', 269; West as, 248

Zakaria, Fareed, 268

Zaman, Muhammad Qasim, 75

zero-sum competition, global context, 135

www.ingramcontent.com/pod-product-compliance
Lightning Source LLC
Chambersburg PA
CBHW051626230426
43669CB00013B/2196